# Current Research Trends in Commerce and Management

# Current Research Trends in Commerce and Management:
## A Survey
(A: Commerce)

**Dr K. L. Narasimha Murty**
Chief Editor Ph.D (Andhra)

GYAN

ISBN: 978-81-212-2045-3

Published, 2021

*Published by*

Gyan Publishing House
5, Ansari Road
Daryaganj, New Delhi-110002
Phone: 011-47034999, 9811692060
www.gyanbooks.com
E-mail: books@gyanbooks.com

*Printed at:* Gyan Press, Delhi.

## Dedicated to My Teachers

**Sri Nanduri Subbarayudu Garu**, M. Com.
Seniormost Lecturer in Commerce,
D.N.R. College, Bhimavaram.

**Sri Vangapandu Upendra Rao Garu,**
"Sahitya Ratna" M. Com. F.C.A., F.I. C.W.A. B.G.L.
"V. R. Upendra & Co."
Senior Lecturer in Commerce
D.N.R. College, Bhimavaram.

# Contents

## E. Analysis (A)



## F. Research Project Proposal

# Preface

The good contributions of the authors are to a tune of 17 chapters in the field of Commerce and Management Research: A survey 2021 and it is a systematic and scientific study that have been thematically spread over and blended into five major themes. They are:

(A) Business Environment (B.E.); (b) Business Organisation (BO) ; (C) Industry and Trade (IT); (D) Organisation and Management of Social Environment (O&MSE); (E) Quantitative Techniques and Research Methodology (QT&RM) thesis; (F) Analysis; (G) Innovative areas of Research; (H) Project Proposal; and (I) Conclusions.

A deviation from normal traditional outlook and structure, an attempt has also been made to include new methods of banking such as e-banking, digitalization in banking and also the analysis of core chapters have been carried out and presented. The editor also intends to present the innovative areas of research exclusively, summative analysis and study relating to research funding in the form of (1) ICSSR project proposals for the award of minor/major research project – a model study. Special efforts have been made to design the volume in order to cater to the needs of the present and future researchers. The entire researched work is related to current research trends of the scholars and projects in which the author's have made commendable contributions through excelled academic excellence. The present work represents through Business Environment (BE), Business Organisation (BO), industry and trade (IT): Organisation and Management of social environment (O & MSC) Quantitative techniques, and research methodology (QT & RM) thesis, Analysis and finally innovative areas of research in Commerce and Management i.e. current trends of Research in Commerce & Management and Conclusions.

The following are the contribution's of the contributors to this volume. First chapter deals with introduction, authored by Dr. K. L. Narasimha Murthy, wherein, certain gaps have been identified and the same were projected and answered in the form of research contributions of the authors.

The second chapter, Covid-19 has been presented by professor G. Tulasirao, intensively over an extensive area such as changing the total business environment. Third chapter, deals with trade environment relating to corporation finance of Life Insurance Corporation of India; Fourth Chapter deals with Indian Banking as a service industry (S.I.), with its Historical perspective including current performance of Indian Banking with a five years period (i.e.) from 2015 to 2020 and the Fifth chapter deals with the non-life Insurance Corporation and its performance over a period of time geared up by the New India Assurance Company Limited, Mumbai; 3rd, 4th and 5th chapters were presented by Dr K.L. Narasimha Murthy, Editor-in-Chief of this volume.

Dr Karuna and Dr Hanumantha Rao have contributed to the new trends of Commerce i.e. E-commerce in India and it is a new dimension and an addition to the traditional theme of commerce and banking (6th chapter).

In chapter 7, the patterns of International trade has been presented with a view to understand the changing patterns of demand and supply besides balance of payments. The goods have such a demand by the borrowing countries to a large extent (volume and value) in the total trade scenario by Dr A. Venkata Rayadu.

In chapter 8, Professor S. Ramakrishna and et al have presented the MSME in Telangana State, India and stressed the need to develop MSME, keeping in view of its activity. In Chapter 9, Smt. Y. Padmini and et al have presented the solid waste management (SWM) in GVMC, A.P. to facilitate the reader to understand the Hydrogeomorphic mapping and need of GHR in the current research in Chapter 9.

In the areas of Social Engineering (SE), Prof. T. Kama Raju and et al have presented an excellent paper represents the 10th chapter of this volume, entitled "Human Resource Development in the knowledge economy: A Global perspective" and has highlighted the preliminary function and helps to understand the process behind it. HR should be managed substantially to achieve substainability on scientific lines over a period of time.

Sri. G. Ernest Leslie has presented an elaborative account relating to "Self Help Groups – The Mechanism for social and Women Empowerment and it is possible through SHGS. The social aggregation is the weapon to achieve women empowerment in any society and there is no exception to any unit/state/nation/nations in a given human environment in Chapter 11.

The last part of this volume have been dealt with analysis. It consists of six chapters relating to analysis, summative analysis, new areas of research

(NAR), ICSSR major project proposal. These in turn may help the future researchers which facilitates and guides their activity both intensively and extensively.

Finally, the justification of the title of the volume, could be seen in the 12th Chapter, Ph.D. Thesis are in Commerce has been presented in order to understand the total process in the whole process of research and development of thought in this regard. The editor-in-chief feels that this volume may be helpful for the beginner researchers and also the seasoned personnel not only at the National level but also at the International level as a connective link indeed. The contributors to this volume have made commendable contributions in the shape of current knowledge in commerce and Management studies 2021. Dr. Murthy has detailed interaction with Dr. K.R.C. Murthy; (NIA) Mr K.S.D. Murthy (L.I.C.) and Mr A.N. Murthy (Indian Bank) for evaluating the work.

Dr. Murty expresses his gratitude to all the contributors of this volume and to his beloved teachers, Sri. N. Subbarayudu garu, Seniormost lecturer and Head Department of Commerce and Sri V. Upender Rao Garu popularly known as "V.R. Upendra" Senior Lecturer in Commerce, DNR College, Bhimavaram, West Godavary District, Andhra Pradesh, India. Dr K. Ravi Kumar, Osmania University, Hyderabad, Asst. Professor of Commerce, has provided the 71st All India Commerce Conference of ICA, 20-22 December, 2018 Souvenir, Dr. Murty is highly thankful to them for the academic help in this endeavour.

03rd January, 2021

**K.L. Narasimha Murty**
305, Manikanta Saisudha Appts,
Meena Cafe Lane,
Warasiguda,
Hyderabad-500 061,
Telangana State, India.
Cell No. 7207337962

# Acknowledgements

**Dr K. L. Narasimha Murthy** is highly indebted to Professor P.V. Sarma M.A., M.Sc. Ph.D., Department of Economics, Andhra University, Visakhapatnam (R) for the encouragement of research activity and also to my teachers specially, Sri Nanduri Subbarayudu Garu, seniormost lecturer in commerce, who taught the Elements of Book Keeping in DNR college, Bhimavaram during 1966-67 besides Sri (late) K. Siva Rama Raju, Senior Lecturer in Commerce.

Dr Murthy has a special flavour and favour in General Commercial Knowledge (G.C.K.) and the same was taught by Sri V. Upendra Rao Garu M. Com, Sahityaratna, F.C.A., F.I.C.W.A. (India), B. G. L., Senior lecturer in commerce, DNR college, Bhimavaram, Andhra Pradesh and he's a leading practitioner of Chartered Accountancy in Bhimavaram town at present. Sri (late) S. P. Butcheswara Rao, Lecturer in commerce, who laid the foundation and created taste for me in General Commercial Knowledge.

**Dr (Late) A. V. Ramanujam** senior lecturer in economics and Sri M.V.S.S.L Rao, senior lecturer in Economics, taught the Principles of Economics and Banking respectively during 1966-67 later Prof. G. Hanumantha Rao Garu, Head of the department of Economics, who taught Money, Banking, International Trade and Public Finance in Final year degree and Sri V. Narashima Rao popularly known as Sri VNR taught Indian Economics (Agricultural & Industrial Economics) besides Dr. (late) A.V. Ramanujam, who lectured on, "Principles of Economics" during 1968-69. Dr. Murty is very much indebted to them always.

**Professor R. B. Singh**, Ph.D., President, International Geographical Union (IGU), Department of Geography, Delhi School of Economics, University of Delhi, Delhi-110007, and Professor C.R. Pathak, IRS, Kolkata (W.B.) for the encouragement received by Dr. Murty from them.

**Professor P. S. Tiwari** (R), University of Madras, Chennai, Tamil Nadu, is highly active, reactive and interactive source and resource of encouragement for this academic activity till today. Dr. Murthy, whole heartedly congratulate all the members for their contributions to this valuable volume, "Current Research Trends' in Commerce and Management: A survey (2021)".

**Professor G. Tulasi Rao**, Department of Commerce and Management Studies, Dr. B. R. Ambedkar University has presented Covid-19, Etcherla, Srikakulam A.P. Professor T. Kama Raju has presented the Human Resource Development in the Knowledge, Economy respectively, to this volume and Smt. Y. Padmini, Department of Geo-Sciences, Dr. B. R. Ambedkar University, Etchela, Srikakulam, has contributed good paper on Solid Waste Management (SWM), in the field of SWM to this volume. Once again, Dr. Murty expresses his sincere gratitude to all the contributors and authors of the leading papers of National and International repute and had academic interaction in the form of discussions and no words can fully reflect the heartfelt gratitude to numerous persons and institutions, without whose help, this work would not have been successfully completed in this form of a valuable volume.

# List of Contributors to the Present Volume

1. **Professor G. Tulasi Rao**, Department of Commerce & Management, Dr. B. R. Ambedkar University, Etcherla, Srikakulam, Andhra Pradesh (Chapter two).
2. **Dr Karuna**, Department of Commerce, M.R.P.G. Centre, Vizianagaram, Andhra Pradesh (Chapter 6).
3. **Smt. Y. Padmini**, Assistant Professor, Department of Geo-sciences, Dr. B.R. Ambedkar University, Etcherla, Srikakulam, Andhra Pradesh (Chapter 9).
4. **Professor S. Ramakrishna (R)**, Department of Geography, Osmania University, Hyderabad, Telangana State, India, (Chapter 8).
5. **Dr A Venkata Rayudu**, Joint Director (R), A.P. Tribal Welfare, Hyderabad, Telangana (Chapter 7).
6. **Professor T. Kama Raju**, Department of Commerce & Management, Dr. B. R. Ambedkar University, Etcherla, Srikakulam, Andhra Pradesh (Chapter 10).
7. **Sri G.E. Leslie,** Research Officer, Regional Centre for Urban & Environmental Studies, Osmania University, Hyderabad, Telengana State, India (Chapter 11).
8. **Dr K. L. Narasimha Murty**, Principal (R), Government UG and PG College (Men), Srikakulam and Former Research Consultant, Center for Economics & Social Studies, Begumpet, Hyderabad, and Regional Centre for Urban & Environmental Studies, Osmania University, Hyderabad, Telengana (Chapter 1, 3, 4, 5, 14, 15, 16 & 18).
9. **Dr S. Tarakeswara Rao**, Assistant Professor, Department of Commerce & Management, Dr. B. R. Ambedkar University, Etcherla, Srikakulam, Andhra Pradesh, (Chapter 12).

# A. Business Environment (B.E.)

# 1

# Introduction

This volume of work deals with the identification of commerce as a social science by Indian Council of Social Science Research, New Delhi. A pertinent question has been answered keeping in view of the track of performance of commerce, Economics and Geography. Broadly, the literature of commerce terms and terminology have been stated, to enable the reader particularly the non-commerce people to aquaint and accomodate themselves to carryout their research in the areas multidisciplinary and interdisciplinary areas to meet the challenges at the international level. The review work has been described in the following paragraphs. They are: Part – A deals with Accountancy, Cost Accountacy, Business Organisation, Business Management and Business Statistics are important subjects besides Financial Management (environment) and practical auditing. Economic and commercial geography would help to identify and understand the sources and resources based industries in India has been reviewed as model study. Banking theory, law and practice by Maheswari and R. B. Paul has been reviewed in order to understand the concept of Banking and its influence of law and its relation. (Text book based reviews).

Part – 'B' deals with the aspects of the following themes:

1. Impact of Environment on Agriculture.
2. Business Environment/Industrial Environment.
3. Health Management.
4. Human Development.
5. Social Engineering/Social groups for acquiring the required financial resources and

Part – 'C' deals with commerce particularly Management (review of articles based on journals and also deals with current scenario as well as the design of the volume, its need has been stated and finally conclusions have been presented in this volume to enable the researcher to conduct the interdisciplinary and multi-disciplinary approach to a research topic (current) of them.

Indian Council of Social Science Research (ICSSR), New Delhi has recognized and identified commerce and Management as two important subjects as social sciences (As per communication). 'Commerce' is a branch of "Economics" and "Management" is a branch of commerce. Business Economics, Business Organisation and Business Management are important subjects of commerce faculty.

A pertinent question that arises to a general reader is about the definition of Commerce, Economics and Geography. There is every need to state the definitions of the above in the following paragraphs that are useful to the researchers other than the commerce community. People who are interested to conduct inter-disciplinary and multi-disciplinary research using commerce and management and these methods may be useful to utilise in their research. This is the principal aim and design of this volume.

According to Chamber's Twentieth Century Dictionary of English (1972) "commerce is defined as, to interchange of merchandise on a large scale between the nations or individuals; extended trade or traffic, particularly the term 'commerce' is the activity relating to trade, to have communication with". The term commerce has been defined as "buying and selling, a craft, to exchange commercially to barter".

Economics is defined as the science relating to behaviour of man to make/act precisely and wisely in a quoted price to purchase/to a quoted price to sell goods besides the use of internal and external resources for human welfare, for example-land, labour, capital and organisation are quite important to identify and recognise the utility of land, labour, capital and organisation and the derivatives are rent, wages, interest and profit to an optimum level with least cost factor.

'Geography' is defined as the study relating to human activity in a given environment with special marked and spatial variations.

For example Commercial geography is referred to as a resource and resource base, using it to the optimum level with least cost factor in a given environment, physical as well as economic environment.

Important definitions and concepts have been presented at the end of this chapter as 'Notes' to enable the reader/community (non-commerce personnel) to acquaint with the terms of commerce terminology in vogue.

The entire introduction have been divided into three parts. They are as follows:

Part- 'A' Deals with Accounting/Financial Accounting/Management Accounting and Cost Accounting and these are given in the following paragraphs.

Part-'B' Deals with the literature relating to journal based one.

Part-'C' Deals with Current scenario, the identiful gap in research and chapterisation of the proposed volume at the end.

**Part - A**

Accounting/Financial Accounting/Management Accounting and Cost Accounting are presented in the following paragraphs:

According to S.P. Jain and K. L. Narang that, the modern system of accounting based on the principles of Double Entry system owes its origin to Luco Pacidi, who first published the principles of Double Entry System in 1494 at Venice in Italy. Thus, the art of accounting has been practised for centuries but it is only in the late thirties that the study of the subject, 'Accounting' has been taken up seriously. Further, it has been identified thus, "Accounting is a discipline which records, classifies, summerises and interprets financial information about the activities to a concern so that intelligent decisions can be made about the concern".

## Classification of Accounting

(1) Financial Accounting consists of financial operations and its analysis.

(2) Cost Accounting: cost accounting relates to the collection of classification, ascertainment of cost and its accounting and cost control of the various elements of cost.

(3) Management Accounting: It relates to the use of accounting data collected with the help of financial accounting and cost accounting for the purpose of policy formulation, planning, control and decision making by the Management.

Finally, 'to make a study into the financial operation of a particular firm, the research scholar needs detailed accounting informatoin relating to purchases, sales, expenses, cost of materials used, current assets, current liabilities, fixed assets, long-term liabilities and shareholder's funds which is available in the accounting records maintained by the firm".[2]

'Cost accounting is a major specialisation at the under-graduate and post-graduate level in commerce faculty cost accounting relates to materials, labour, overhead-costs, unit or output costing, contract Accounts, process accounts reconciliation of cost and financial accounts, marginal costing and P/V ratio are important aspects of cost accounting.

According to R. P. Trivedi, 'financial accounting consists of classification, recording and analysis of the transactions in a systematic manner according to the nature of expenditure so as to enable the presentation at periodic intervals, of statement of profit or loss of the business and on a specified date of its financial state of affairs the day-to-day transaction are journalised, and posted in the ledger and at the end of the year a profit and loss account and a balance sheet are prepared without financial accounting, it would have been difficult for any enterprise to know the profit or loss made by it and its position as on a particular date".[3]

It is opined that financial accounting is a major method in a business, a firm or an industry which reveals the financial structure and status of a company with some limitations. It is further identified that the other records relating to finance should have to be examined in order to identify and recognize the state, status and structure.

'Final accounts' are prepared to achieve the objectives of accountancy. In order to know the profit or the loss earned by a firm, income statement or trading and profit and loss account is prepared. Balance sheet may present the financial environment of the firm and good fitness on a particular date. These two statements (1) Trading and profit and loss account and Balance sheet are prepared to give the final results of the business, that is why both these are collectively called as final accounts. Thus, final accounts include the preparation of :

(1) Trading and profit and loss account and

(2) Balance Sheet

It is finally opined that final accounts summarise all the accounting information recorded in the subsidiary books and the ledger running into hundred or thousands of pages".[4]

K. V. Jagadamba,[5] has presented in a document relating to financial analysis involving study of finance using various approaches and methods. It depends on efficiency and effective utilisation of resources and division of maker's attitude. Financial analysis helps to analyse the strengths and bottlenecks of the organisation. Financial function relates to planning, directing and controlling.

According to Hampton, "a financial statement is an organised collection of data according to logical and consistent according to procedures. Its purpose is to convey an understanding of some financial aspects and realities of a business firm. It may show a position at a moment of time as in the case of balance sheet or may reveal a series of activities over a specified period of time, as in the case of an income statement.

Following tools of finanacial analysis are described:

1. Ratio Analysis 2. Funds flow analysis and 3. Trend analysis.
   She has covered the aspects, such as –

1. Ratios are composite of many figures
2. Liquidity ratios, current ratio, and quick ratio
3. Liquidity Analysis - overview
4. Turn over ratio
5. Debtor's turn over
6. Inventory turnover
7. Fixed assets turnover
8. Activity Analysis - An overview
9. Leverage Ratios - Debit Equity Ratios
10. Total Debit Equity Ratio
11. Debt Total capital Ratio
12. Total Debt - Total capital Ratio
13. Coverage Ratio
14. Leverage Analysis - overview
15 Profitability Ratio - Net profit - Sales Ratio
16 Return on capital employed
17. Return on total Assets and operating Ratio and finally profitability Analysis has been attempted.

What is practical Auditing and what is Economic & Commercial Geography?

"Practical Auditing" the Indian Edition by S.V. Ghatalio, has been published by Allied Publishers, New Delhi (1968) useful both to the practioners and students have to depend on English edition for the principles and practice of auditing. This work has been dealt with the statutory provisions affecting accounts and brought the audit procedure in conformity with Indian practices and conditions. The impact of companies Act, on auditing practice has a telling effect. The problems of company audit have assumed new dimensions and acquired greater complexity.

1. Banking and insurance companies sets out briefly the relevant positions affecting their accounts and audit. The author has dealt with the following items specially banking companies.

(a) Restriction on Business
(b) Capital and Reserves
(c) Cash Reserves
(d) Dividends
(e) Managing Agents, Managing Director etc.
(f) Annual Accounts
(g) Form of Accounts
(h) Authentication of Annual Accounts etc.
(i) Audit
(j) Auditors Certificate
(k) Powers and liabilities of the Auditor
(l) Auditor's duty
(1) Auditor's duty

2. Life Insurance Corporation.
3. General Insurance Business.

(a) Registration
(b) Deposits
(c) Assets of Insurer
(d) Provisions relating to manager's etc.
(e) Agents
(f) Register of Policies
(g) Register of claims
(h) Commission and Rebates.
(i) Prohibition of loans.
(j) Limitaton of expenses of Management.
(k) Separation of Accounts and Funds
(l) Accounts and Balance Sheet
(m) Audit
(n) Insurers outside India
(o) Auditors Duty"

"Economic and Commercial Geography",[7] with a detailed treatment of Indian Republic and Pakistan has been authored by A. Das Gupta, Professor of Business Administration, Delhi School of Economics, University of Delhi formerly Head of the Department of Commerce and Business Administration, Government of India, Delhi Polytechnic, Delhi,

Professor of Economic Geography and Commerce, Vidyasagar College, Kolkata (Twenty first Edition, 1964).

This volume contains a comprehensive enrolment of the economic development of the different countries of the world from the point of view of production and utilisation of resources and stated that this volume is meant primarily for the students of commerce. Economic Geography to a commerce student is a study of regional economy and its growth. The author has shown his interest in analyzing stable and variable factors about resources for interpretation of the process of economic development in a region. He has mainly taken into consideration the syllabus of economic and commercial Geography as recommended by the Indian Universities for commerce courses and a few professional bodies like the Indian Institute of Bankers.

This volume is quite useful to the students of both Commerce and Geography Post-graduate students to cater to the needs of M.A. (Previous) paper 2, "Economic Geography". But the commerce faculty has drastically cut down its existence in the present syllabus of undergraduate courses of commerce. It has its terrible impact on faculty as well as student community. But, there is every need to revise it by introducing the same paper at the under-graduate commerce courses as a course of study. It's a dire need, and it is a felt need of the community to have this in the undergraduate curriculum for a detailed study.

"Banking theory and law and practice" by S. N. Maheswari and R.R. Paul[8] is an important volume and it gives a comprehensive coverage to the course requirements of the under-graduate students of commerce. It provides a conceptual and legal framework, the book also contains practical hints which are useful to the borrower and the banker.

Section I deals with an introduction, which contains a full picture of the overall banking scenario. The law relating to negotiable instruments-an enactment of vital importance to bankers (Section II).

Section III, explains matters relating to banker customer relationships and Section IV explains how a banker employs his funds.

Section V, deals with financing specific sectors of economy particularly the primary sector, Section VI deals with specific problems relating with credit management. The recommendations of Tandan committee and core committee have been explainded with complete clarity.

Section VII incorporates the various financial tools which a banker has to use in performance of his job of financial appraisal and performance.

Finally, section VIII contains formats in which the required information is to be given on account of some recent developments in commercial banking besides uptodate interest rates structures both for deposits and advances".

Varshney, R.L., "Managerial Economics" (1999)[8.1] K. Aswathappa, "Essentials of Business Environment"[8.2] (1998), M. Gangadhara Rao "Organizational Behaviour"[8.3] (1999); and K. Aswathappa, "Human Resource and Personnel Management"[8.4] (1999) are important referral works (Basic Works) for understanding the core concepts in this direction.

In the field of Accountancy, Cost Accountancy, and financial accounting the following are the most important and essential referral volumes to carryout research work. Maheswari, S.N. "Cost and Management Accounting"[8.5] (1999), Gupta, R.L. "Advanced Accountency."[8.6] (1999); and B.L. Bajoria, "Cost Accounting Methods and Problems"[8.7] (2000); are quite important additions derive additional knowledge.

L.M. Prasad, "Principles and Practice of Management"[8.8] (1999); M.Y. Khan, "Financial Management"[8.9] 4Ed, Mary Nisbet, "Financial Accounting" (1995)[8.10]; C.B. Mamora, "Personnel Management" (1988)[8.11], M.Y. Khan, "Management Accounting"[8.12] and V.K. Saxena, "Cost Audit and Management Audit"[8.13] (1999) are important voluminous volumes to the existing literature relating to Commerce and Management survey. This is considered as an ever useful material to each student, scholar and a seasoned practitioner of Accountancy as well as Manager of any field of similar needs.

**Part – B**

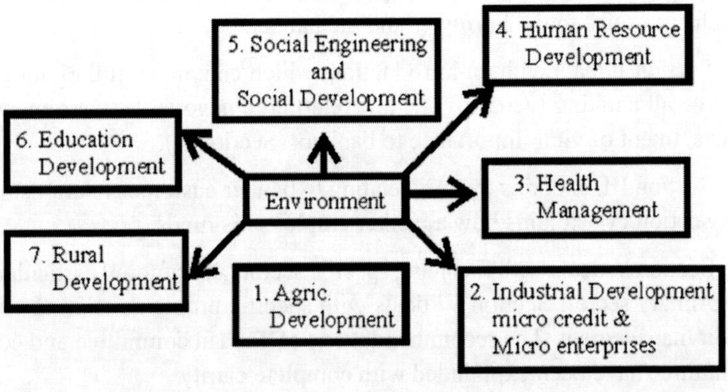


The aggregation of agricultural development, industrial development, Health Management & Development, infrastructural development,

Educational development, Social development and rural development are important aspects which are covered intensively have been included in the review of literature. (Fig. 1) Backdrop of Research).

The important aspects that have been covered in literature are as follows:

1. Impact of environment on agriculture.
2. Business Environment/ Industrial Development.
3. Health Management.
4. Human Development and Human Resource Management.
5. Social engineering, and Social Development.
6. Education Development, Commerce & Management (By Research).

Scarch & Research : Gap

(OR)

Current Research Trends in Commerce & Management:

A Survey (2021).

"Development Research" (title) is the tentative title of the proposed volume of work for current publication in the 21$^{st}$ Century.

## 2.1 Impact of Environment on Agriculture

Impact of Environment upon various fields such as agriculture and health. An attempt is made to assess its impact in the following paragraphs. "Impact of Physical and infrastructural factors on agricultural scenario of Ghazipur District" has been presented by Jagdev and Santosh Kumar Ram[8] Agriculture is an important source of livelihood even today over the years inspite of growing industrialisation and urbanisation in the world and nearly fifty percent working population is still engaged in agriculture and agricultural sector has been a principal source of employment and largest source of income. It contributes 50 percent to national income and provides direct employment to about 68 percent of total population and gives about 35 percent countries exports besides supplying wage goods required the non-agricultural section in industry. Agriculture is perhaps the most complex phenomenon. This is because of the large number of geohydrological, environmental, biological and socio-economic variables influencing the agricultural production. As a result, diversities abound, not only in the cropping system but also in farming system as well. Environmental factors exert direct and indirect influence on the agriculture land – use and yield of crops besides cost benefit ratios in agriculture environment influences the yield directly by effecting the structural characteristics of the crops such as density of plants, no. of tillers, vegetative growth, and weight of grains etc. It is known that environmental factors like relief, slopes, accessibility of distance from frost, precipitation, temperature, sun-shine etc. have a profound influence on agriculture and agriculture land-use".

### Major Findings

(1) It is necessary to develop cost affective measures to achieve agricultural development. Agricultural activities fail even in this and wherever due to cost of input exceed output.

(2) Poor drainage of soil and deficiency of micronutrients in soil components. Hence, it is difficult for them to cope up technological gap, reasons for non-adoption, land, of availability, lack of knowledge and lack of resources, lack of availability of newer hybridised seeds, lack of government support towards drought and flood etc".

### 2.2 Industrial Development

"It is noted that some of the problems leading to poor performance of the industrial sector in India include technical issues, resource constraints, business environment as well as socio-economic problems and organised constraints. It is highly needed that sector specific industrial policies and planning are made to improve the backward and forward linkage of comprehensive developments. It will enhance the potential of industrial marketing and cut down production cost and enhance the competitiveness of product prices, it will automatically improve industrial development environment".

Study of cost benefit Analysis in agriculture is a dire need to understand input and output ratios.

The authors have put in the main objectives such as –

(1) To study the nature and role of industrial development in order to recognize the comprehensive development of the study area.

(2) To identify the nature and potential of industrial development.

(3) To identify the different factors and variables that affect the industrial development of the study area.

(4) Further to identify the new areas of industrial development that will improve employment generation and economic upliftment of the study area.

Finally, identified the contributions of agriculture and its allied sector in the economic growth and development. They have suggested the SNOW Model of industrial setup in the study area.

- S - Strength
- N - Need
- O - Opportunity
- W – Weakness

At the end, they have presented in a table format, i.e. number of registered factories, small industries and khadi gramodyog units consisting of 14 blocks, where in number of factories and number of workmen".

### 2.3 Micro Credit and Micro Enterprises

U.P. Raghav[11] has presented thematically the 'Micro Credit'- A Study of Kukumbashree projects in Kerala, India and identified and recognised that, "poverty alleviation schemes" based on micro-credit system have been implemented in many of the developing countries in recent years. The Government of Kerala state in India has introduced a novel scheme of poverty alleviation based on micro-credit and self-help groups. Kudumbashree (prosperity of the family), the scheme aims of improving the living levels of the poor women in rural and urban areas. It helps to bring the poor women folk together to form the gross root organisation to help enhance their economic security. The principal aim is to remove poverty among rural women households through setting up of micro credit and productive enterprises. The activities such as micro-credit and micro-enterprise, under the scheme were undertaken by the locally formed community development societies comprising poor women.

It has been proved without doubt that 'Women empowerment' is the best strategy for poverty eradication. It opens new vistas in development history. A new paradigm of participatory "economics has been found emerging in, "God's own country" Kudumbashree presents an unique model of participatory development, which can very well, be emulated by other developing countries".[11]

## 3. Environmental and Health Management: Synoptic View

Health play an important role in human life term of living. Aich, M et als 12/2014 "A study on socio-economic condition and Nutritional profile of Women workers in shrimp and agriculture sectors in selected two districts of Bangladesh, Int. Res. J. Social Sec. 3(3), pp. 15-21.[12]

12.1 Barly R. Acharya and et al (2010), "In-equalities in Access to Health services in India: Caste, Class and Region, Economic and Political Weekly 65 (38);

12.2 Choubey, K (2008) "Healthcare delivery in Madhya Pradesh, India, Healthcare patterns and planning, et al. by Akhitar, R, ABH Publishing Corporation, New Dellhi.

12.3 Dadbhavi, R. V. and Bagalkoti, S. T. 2000, "Reforms and Regional Inequalities in India: An Analysis, The Indian Economic Journal, 54(2), pp. 21-23.

12.4 Debapriya, A. and Mohanty M. K. 2006, " Inter-District Variation in the level of Human Development of Odisha, Utkal Economic paper, 12, pp. 50-53.

12.5 Dreze, J and Sen, A. 2005. India Development and participation, Oxford University Press, New Delhi.

12.6 Joseph, A.E. and Phillips, D.R. 1984. Accessibility and Utilization: Geographical perspectives on healthcare delivery Herper & Row Ltd., London.

12.7 Pradad, B.A. 2013. Occupational Health Problems of Women Migrant Workers in Thogamabi, Karur District, Tamil Nadu, Int. Res. J. Social Sci. 2 (4), pp. 7-15.

12.8 Ghabnam, S. 2012. Spatial Inequality in Healthcare Infrastructure in West Bengal, Indian J. of Regional Sciences 34(2), pp. 26-34.

12.9 Sunik K. Kamalapur, M and Reddy S. 2013. Women Health in India: An Analysis, Int. Res. J. Social Sci. 2 (10) pp. 11-15.

12.10 Trivedi, R and et. al. 2014, Prevalence of practices of preventive Healthcare Measure and its causes among Medical professionals of Shyam Shah Medical College, Rewa India, Not. Res. J. Social Sec, 3 (6), pp. 11-12 and

12.11 WHO 1978 Alma-Ata 1978, Primary Healthcare: Health for All, Sr. No. 1, World Health Organisation, Geneva are the most Important works belonging to this branch.


"Spatial Inequality in Healthcare Infrastructure in Allahabad District: A geographical study by Amit Kumar Singh and V. K. Kumara[12] wherein, analysed the block level disparities in healthcare infrastructures would help to identify specific deficiencies and suggested connective measures to improve the healthcare system in the district for achieving the goal of 'Health for all'. The State government needs to adopt viable policies and programmes and take some immediate actions to improve the healthcare infrastructure in Allahabad district".

**Various steps**

1. Evaluated the existing infrastructure for healthcare services in Allahabad District;
2. Assessed the inter-block variations in healthcare facilities in the study area, and
3. Found out the regional pattern in the distribution of healthcare infrastructure of Allahabad District".

## 4. Human Development

"Genesis of human development in North-East India: A Diagnostic Analysis" has been presented by D. Bidari[13] and it has long been a victim of not only related to economic development but poor performance in terms of the indicators of quality of life as well. This study has been centred and based on (1) Per capita income, (2) Net State Domestic product of N.E. Region (3) Financial assistance for N.E. Status (4) Expenditure on social sector for human development, keeping in view of the expenditure and budgetary allocation such as (1) Education (2) Sports & Culture (3) Medical and public health and family welfare (4) Water supply and sanitation (5) Housing (6) Urban development (7) Welfare of SC/ST and other backward classes (8) Labour and Labour welfare (9) Social sector welfare (10) Nutrition and (11) Relief on account of National calamities were studied.

Education and literacy which is an important indicator of human development. Health is a crucial factor of social infrastructure, which no policy maker can afford to ignore. In fact, a significant part of the success of economic reform in South-East Asian nation is attributed to health sector, health along with education as one of the basic objectives of the development.

The analysis with typical general level of living, low level of living is manifested in low level of income, poor housing and poor health condition, low level of literacy, high infant mortality, low life expectancy, along with high degree of illness and diseases. These have hampered the long term development of the region. Various aspects of human well-being such as food, shelter, education, health and various other amenities of life all of which combine to contribute towards quality of life. The author has studied the aspects such as (1) Economic status and human development (2) Physical infrastructure and human development (3) Level of consumption and quality of life (4) Housing facilities and quality of life and (5) Consumption of electricity and quality of life.

Finally, the author aimed that "the involvement of voluntary organisations and local institutions may expedite monitory and proper implementation of policies in social sector, which will surely go long way in raising the indicators of human development and ensure improving the quality of life almost different socio-economic and ethnic groups spread across a wide range of area of the states of north-eastern Region".

"Development of scheduled castes in India: A review" by Darshan Singh[14] is considered as the most important work in the subdiscipline of human development.

"India has realised the significance of the development of weaker sections specially the Scheduled Castes since independence. Consequently, planned efforts have been made further upliftment by the government. In this paper, it is examined that the progress made with regard to their social (health, housing, workforce participation, availability of basic amenities and wage employment under income generation schemes), educational and occupational status. Based on secondary data, it has been found that no doubt, a positive change on various socio-economic parameters has been recorded but, that change has touched merely less than half of their population. Further, the gap between the mainstream and scheduled caste population still persists significantly in Indian traditional society.

Keeping in view of this point, there is an urgent need to reorient and focus the strategy in order to support the lesser privileged by providing qualitative education and infusing among them the individualistic and moralistic values of self-denial, temperance, fore thought, thrifts, soberity and self-reliance are essential to bring these down-trodden into the national mainstream.

### 5. Social Environment/Social Engineering/Skill and Management Banking Among the Social Groups

"Development of Rural poor through Self-help Groups". By Shanker Chattarjee[15] (2003) @ centre for monitoring and evaluation, NIRD, Hyderabad.

C.R. Pathak has identified and recognised that, "this book is the outcome of two studies – one is Jaunpur District, U.P. and other on Ahmednagar District of Maharashtra conducted in the year, 2002. The main aim of these studies are to assess the formation of Self-help Groups (SHGs) and implementation of Swarnajayanthi Gram Swarozgar Yojana (SGSY) in the district. Some of the author's similar studies previously completed have been documented and put-in inset boxes".

First chapter deals with introduction, second chapter throws light on the nature and extent of poverty in the districts of Jaunpur and Ahmednagar and in the chapter, the author describes the salient features of SGSY as an integrated programme of self-employment of the rural poor launched on the 1st April, 1999, by restructing IRDP programme including five other programmes viz. DWCRA, TRYSEM, SITRA, MWS and GKY. The basic objective of measuring all these programmes into SGSY was to eradicate the rural poverty by assisting the poor families to alleviate above poverty line through SHG, with training, capacity building, creating income generating assets through bank credit link schemes, with subsidy being an enabling component. The salient features of the SGSY have been reproduced here from the Annual Report 2001-2002; Divn. of Rural Development, Govt. of India. The fourth chapter contains the findings of the study and in the fifth chapter, the author has put forward his suggestions for better functioning of the programme through improvement of literacy, development of fisheries, vegetable production and marketing, formation of SHG's and proper implementation of the progress through NGO as govt. officials do not always come forward to accelerate the pace of development.

The self-help group (SHG) approach to reveal development has not only replaced the IRDP and other community approaches, will address the poor families which could with this joint effort eradicate their own problems at their own initiative, and it is an innovative approach. The strategy is to hit the problem at the source" (C.R. Pathak).

**Social Aggregation Process through Education**

### 6. Education Development Index

Education Development Indix-Rajasthan: Spatio-temporal Appraisal at Panchayati Samithi Block level (1991-2000) has been presented by Hemalatha Joshi, Institute of Development Studies, Jaipur.

"Since the formulation of the Human Development Index (HDI) in the early 1990's construction and use of various types of index-so as to capture the nature of qualitative groups undergoing in different sectors of economy and society, have became rather fashionable among the social scientists. These indices not only help one to compare performance of different economic sectors etc. across space and time but also they are often sought to be used as allocative criteria say, the more backward a region in terms of HDI, the larger should be its share in plan allocation. The study primarily focuses on (a) changing relative status of P.S. in Educational Development Index (EDI) and Gender-related Educational Development Index (GEDI) in Rajasthan, (b) changing spotial distributional pattern of EDI and GEDI and (c) Growth trends.

This study has been conducted at the microlevel of PSS. The methodology of constructing these indices is based on UNDP-HDR framework, though in a modified form. The EDI is a composite index comprising of two parameters: Total literacy rate (TLR) and Female literacy rate (FLR). It is calculated as EDI=1-Compound Index of deprivation (COOD) COID as been been defined, is the weighted average index of deprivation of TLR and FLR. Between 1981 and 2001, as the TLR and FLR increased, CIOD reduced consequently from 0.80 to 0.45 in Rajasthan, though it is still much higher than the national average of 0.39.

The correlation co-efficient between TLR and FLR and between TLI and FLR is high. The forms curve shows high dispersion in the distribution of TLI among the PSS. In 1991, although the male literacy rate (MLR) in rural Rajasthan was more than double of Female literacy rate (FLR), still it is much below in comparison to other states. It is also unfortunate to note that female literacy and, more particularly, the female literary among the rural SC/ST population in Rajasthan is extremely low and the worst in India."

(Santanu Ghosh, Lecturer in Economics, Presidency College, Kolkata).

**Social Disaggregation Process through Natural Disasters.**

**Social Break up/Cyclones/Natural Disasters and Disaster Management Urban/Rural areas – A review.**

Cyclones are considered as Natural disasters and administrator's administration is needed to mitigate the disaster. (Hence, disaster management has grown as a good subject to augment in the field of administration besides management to help by the administrator and the Manager and head

**Cyclones as Natural Disasters**

Reports indicate that between 1891 and 2020 nearly 450 cyclones who born in Bay of Bengal and about 90 cyclones in the Arabian Sea. A study of cyclone of 1977 by P. Cohen, C.V. Raghavulu (1979), gives the causes and physical and social impact of cyclones. According to Aqueil Ahmed,[17]" to identify disaster preparedness and response as a separate but independent analytical and empirical categories, to distinguish structural preparedness from behavioural readiness and systematic response from individual action and to delineate independent primary and secondary systems of preparedness and response; and to introduce economic infrastructure as an important variable in disaster management are some of the novel features of the framework with far reaching policy implications for disaster management and mitigation. Natural disasters cause hindrance in implementation of economic plans.

United Nations declared 1990's as the International decade for natural disaster Reduction.[18] It has altered all the National Governments to detect warn and help people of the areas to take minimum preparations for safety and to mitigate all the ill-effects caused by disasters. According to their recommendations, flood management is more appropriate than flood control. According to Clark (1989) density of population has a direct relationship to the magnitude of disaster.[19] Depending on the physical and human characteristics, every natural disaster has a particular way to be dealt with.

The involving interaction by the people and the environment effects the opportunities and the costs that the floods of nature may reap. This provides the scope for the study of disasters, their characteristics, mitigation and management.[20]

In a study of tropical cyclones, Anjaneyulu[21] (1973) observed that it was possible to avoid loss of life and minimise damages by taking precautionary measures well in advance[21]. Kayastha[22] (1996) states that natural disasters compel interest because of their dramatic violence and human suffering.

## Part-C

In this part, the author has presented the current scenario of research in Commerce and Management Science in the following paragraphs in the areas of Banking – Digitalization and Banking.

K. Anjaneyulu[23] has identified and made a distinction from leadership and management. "Leadership entails working with people, which management entails as well. Leadership is concerned with effective goal accomplishment and so is management. Leadership is also different from Management. The study of leadership can be traced back to Aristole, management emerged around the turn of twentieth century with advent of our identified society. Management was created as a way to reduced chaos in organisations, to make them run more effectively and efficiently the primary function of management, as first identified by Fayol (1916), were planning, organising and controlling. These functions are still representative of the field of management is about seeking order and stability, leadership is about seeking adaptive and constructive changes.

Bennis and Nanus made the distinction very clear in their frequently quoted sentence, "managers are people who do things right and leaders are people who do the right things."

"Performance of SBI in the Era of Digitalisation" by K. Anjaneyulu[24] has stated that SBI became one of the 50 largest banking in the world. It has 198 offices in 37 countries and 301 correspondents in 72 countries. Besides this, Ranoth Safeena, Hema Date, Abdullah Kammadi and Nisar Hundewale (2012), technology is considered as the key driver for the changes taking place around the world. Mobile banking is the latest and most innovative service offered by the Banks.

Shari Mohammed (2013)[25], this study aims at identifying the factors affecting the customers demand for E-Banking services, by analyzing a sample of 450 consumers" responses who have been interviewed personally through structured questionnaire in three districts of Uttar Pradesh, India; Lucknow, Kanpur and Varanasi. The factor analysis using principal component extraction method with varian rotation has extracted four factors which explained the 62.84 percent of the variance. All the four factors ambiance and infrastructures, technology and innovation, services and security, and consumer support and timmings represent different banking attributes important to customers. This provides a basis for the banks in order to modify and offer demanding services to the banks".

The following are important references to be referred.

They are:

1. Banking frontiers – July 2017
2. Business today – 7th May, 2017.
3. The Management accountant – January, 2017
4. Trends and progress of Banking in India – September, 2018.
5. The Equity Master – Year book, 2018.

"Corporate Social responsibility initiatives by IOCL : A case study of Guwahati Refinery Noonmati" authorised by Chandan Kashyap and Dr. Amrit Pal Singh, 25C Professor, Department of Commerce, Guwahati University, Guwahati – 781 014, Assam has presented good paper in 71st All India Commerce Conference of ICA, 20-22, December, 2018 (pp.120), conference Theme: Innovations, Entrepreneurship & Sustainable Development, organised by: Department of Commerce, Osmania University, Hyderabad, Telangana State, India, in collaboration with Telangana State Council of Higher Education and Institute of Public Enterprise, Osmania University.

**Part –C**

**Active Research**

## Current Research

Keeping in view of the gaps in research, the present volume has been designed to cater to the needs of the beginner researcher as well as seasoned/ professional research personnel. It is opined that this voluminious volume may be a good addition as research reference book and the present chapterisation of the volume is as follows:

**Proposal Contents**

A. Business Environment (B. E. )

01. Introduction – Dr. K. L. Narasimha Murty

02. Covid-19 – Prof. G. Tulasi Rao

B. Business Organisation (BO)

03. Trade (LIC) – Dr. K. L. Narasimha Murty

04. Banking (Indian Bank) – Dr. K. L. Narasimha Murty

05. Commerce (The New India Assurance Co) :
—Dr. K. L. Narasimha Murty

06. E-Commerce – Dr. Karuna and Dr. Hanumantha Rao

C. Trade & Industry (T&C)

07. International Trade –Dr. A. Vcnkatarayudu

08. M.S.M.E. in Telangana State – Prof. S. Ramakrishna
– Dr. P. Anjaneyulu

09. Solid Waste Management (SWM) : Smt. Y. Padmini and
– Dr. Bendalam Srinivas.

D. Social Engineering (S. E. )

10. Human Resource Management in the Knowledge Economy – Prof. T. Kama Raju
11. Self Help Groups (SHGS) – Sri G. Ernest Leslie
12. Ph.D thesis – Dr. S. Tarakeswara Rao
13. Analysis – Dr. K.L. Narasimha Murty
14. Summative Analysis – Dr. K. L. Narasimha Murty
15. New Area of Research (NAR) – Dr. K. L. Narasimha Murty
16. I.C.S.S.R. Major Research Project Proposal – Dr. K. L. Narasimha Murty
17. Conclusions – Dr. K. L. Narasimha Murty

*Annexure* - 1

*Annexure* - 2.

## Conclusion:

It is concluded that this knowledge through this volume may bring sweeping changes in the areas of research and development particularly commerce and management studies at the National level. There is every need to publish it as a reference work (book) to meet the ever growing needs in order to identify and recognise the standard trends for the future researchers in particular 2021. Primarily it would be an important principal and precise document to many such as i.e. commerce, management and administrator. The concepts are presented in the form of "Notes". An attempt has been made to present the Business Environment, particularly " Impact of Covid-19 on Indian Economy – A Study on new business opportunities with Corona virus in India", in the second chapter.

### Notes – Trade

1. **Trade:** The activity relating to goods for selling and purchasing (Trade: internal trade/external trade/individual/group/groups/ national/international level).
2. **Board of Trade:** A department of government for matters of industry and commerce
3. **Trade Cycle:**The recurring series of conditions in trade from prosperity to depression and back to property.
4. **Trade Mark:** Any name or distinctive devise warranting goods for sale as the production any individual or firm

### Commerce

5. **Commerce:** The term commerce has been defined as, "buying and selling, a craft, to exchange commercially to barter".

### Industry

6. **Industry:** Industry has been defined as, "systematic economic activity, any branch of trade or manufacture heavy industry relating to such basic industries as coal mining, steel making, ship building etc. involving heavy equipment, light industry to smaller factory processed goods.
7. **Industrial relations:** "Relations between management and workers or labour in general".
8. **Organisation:** "Act of organising, the state of being organised, the manner in which anything is organised, an organised system, body or society, to co-ordinate and prepare for activity".
9. **Chain Management:** "Act or activity of managing, manner of directing or of using anything, administration, skilful treatment, a body of managers/manager-one who manages, a person who controls a business or other concern, one who organises other people's doing".
10. **Management consultant:** "One who advises a firm on the most efficient procedures applicable to particular business or industries".
11. **Business:** "Dealings, commercial activity, a commercial/industrial concern".
12. **Resource Economics:** "Resources are used on scientific lines which gives optimum utilisation for human welfare processing of resources for economic welfare".
13. **Management (Chain):** "A series of links on passing through one another, a number of things connected in series, a linked series".

## References

1. S. P. Jain & K. L. Narang, Accountancy, Part - I. Published by Kalyani Publishers, Hyderabad. 1995, ISBN, 81-7096-694-9, pp. 1-6.
2. *Ibid.*
3. B. M. Trivedi, " Problems in cost accounting", Pankaj Publications, 1999, Shivashakti Apartments, Barakatpura, Hyderabad-27.

4. S.P. Jain & K. L. Narang, "Accountancy, Part-I, published by Kalyani Publishers, Hyderabad, 1995, ISBN. 81-7096-694-9, pp. 189.

5. K.V. Jagadamba, "Financial Environment: A Case study", Pub. in "Applied Environmental studies" pp. 137-149, by Mangal Deep Publications, Jaipur (2008).

6. S.V. Ghatalia, "Practical Auditing" by Allied Publishers Private Limited, 1968, New Delhi.

7. A Das Gupta, "Economic and Commercial Geography with a detailed treatment of Indian Republic".

8. S.N. Maheswari & R.N. Paul, "Banking Theory and Law & Practice" pp. 244, Published by Kalyani Publishers, Ludhiana, Second Edition, 1996.

8A. National Geographer, Vol. 51, Number H2 (Jan, June, July, Dec. 2016. pp. 85-907.

9. Manoj Kumar Pandey and Sarveh Tripathe, " Comprehensive Industrial Development: A case study of Basti District, (U.P.), Published in National Geographer, Vol. L1, Nos. 1+2 (Jan-June, July-Dec. 2016) pages 133-140.

10. District Statistical Magazine.

11. Journal of Rural Development, Vol. 28, No. (4), pp. 469-484 NIRD, Hyderabad.

12. Referred NGJI (National Geographical Journal of India): International Referred Journal Since 1955 Vol. 62, No. 3, September, 2016.

13. Published in Journal of Rural Development, Vol. 28, No. 4, October-December, 2009, pp. 545-547, National Institute of Rural Development, Rajendranagar, Hyderabad, Telangana, India.

14. Journal of Rural Development, Vol. 28. No. 4, pp. 529-542, NIRD, Hyderabad.

15. Published in Indian Journal of Regional Science, Vol. XXX, Number 2, 2003 (pp. 144-145).

16. Indian Journal of Regional Science, Vol. XXXV, No. 2, 2003.

17. Aqueil Ahmed, Ed. (1981). Disaster Management preparedness and response, Washing proceedings, pb, ASC 17 ARTIC.

18. R. B. Singh (1996), Disaster Environment and Development, Oxford & IBH, Publishing Co.

19. Clark, John, T.P., Curson, Kayasthe S. L. and Nag, P. (1989). Population and Disaster, Bansil Bachwell Oxford, pp. 173.

20. Kayastha, S. L., Disaster Environment and Development, Ed. R. B. Singh (1996), Oxford & IBH Pub. p. 63.

21. Anjaneyulu, J.S.S. (1973). Cyclones – The navoe caused by them and the planning required, Vayumandal, pp. 71-78.

22. Kayasta, S. L. Op. Cit. p. 70.

23. K. Anjaneyulu (2020). "Innovations in leadership and Management" published in International Research in Social Sciences, Pub.by R. K. Books, New Delhi (2020) pp. 225-226.

24. K. Anjaneyulu, (2020). "Performance of SBI in the Era. of Digitalisation" Pub. International Research in Social Sciences by R.K. Books, New Delhi, pp. 260-277.

25. *Ibid.* : pp. 260.

25C. 7/All India Commerce Conference of ICA, 20-22 Dec, 2018 Souvenir. (Ref. : Annexure – 1).

# 2

# Impact of Covid-19 on Indian Economy — a Study on New Business Opportunities with Corona Virus in India

***Prof. G. Tulasi Rao, Dr S. Tarakeswara Rao, Dr M.P. Suri Ganesh***

**Abstract**

*The Indian economy was already going through a rough patch before the arrival of the pandemic. With nationwide lockdown, the economy has taken a very bad hit and inflicted untold miseries especially to the poor people of the country. There has been significant reduction in orders and cash flow across the sector, deep hit in the supply chain, and a significant downslide effect on businesses. The travel and hospitality sector has suffered one of the harshest blows, and airline companies are on the verge of facing bankruptcy, with global and domestic travel networks being shut. In this regard this article is a roadmap on defining technology impetus required to push India, post COVID-19 towards self reliance and being a global major manufacturing hub.*

***Keywords:*** *Covid-19, Indian Economy, New business opportunities, Pandemic.*

## Introduction

A crisis refers to "a sudden and unexpected event that threatens to disrupt an organisation's operations and poses both a financial and reputational threat" (Coombs, 2007:163). The Covid-19 crisis manifested in China in December 2019 and soon after became a global pandemic. As of May 26, 2020, 213 countries were affected, a total of 5,591,677 people infected, 347,944 deaths, and 2,368,016 patients recovered (Worldometers, 2020). Compared with previous crisis, the Covid-19 is more complex. It created immense social and economic problems at all levels, including social phobia, unemployment, supply chain disruption, stock market crashes, economic lockdown, and de-globalisation Due to the uniqueness of the Covid-19 crisis, previous research may not be sufficient to understand it.

The Covid-19 pandemic has hit the entire world like a tsunami, unaware and unprepared, and jeopardised the global growth including that of developed economics the US, UK, Germany etc. And India as well Originating from Wuhan city in Hubei province, China sometime in December 2019, this pandemic has shaken almost the entire globe, with death tolls approaching over a lakh, and looming to a further rise, in coming days. With no proven vaccine or drug as yet, most countries have resorted to lock-down in a desperate attempt to contain the spread of COVID-19 and all economic activities are put to a big halt. It has unleashed death, destruction, misery, loss and panic of a scale never seen before. The United States has more than four times as many confirmed cases as any other country. India, with prompt actions, has so far done exceedingly well in containing the pandemic with around one lakh infections and more than 3000 associated deaths by third week of May, 2020.

As a result of lockdown in varying degrees, virtually the entire world has enforced travel ban and social distancing. This has brought the wheels of the global economy to virtual grinding halt. The situation is such that saving lives is paramount while saving economy has become a secondary consideration. Hon'ble Prime Minister on 24th March 2020 had called for a complete lockdown of the country which has now been extended with relaxations till 31st May 2020.

The Indian economy was already going through a rough patch before the arrival of the pandemic. With nationwide lockdown, the economy has taken a very bad hit and inflicted untold miseries especially to the poor people of the country. There has been significant reduction in orders and cash flow across the sector, deep hit in the supply chain, and a significant downslide effect on businesses. The travel and hospitality sector has suffered one of the harshest blows, and airline companies are on the verge of facing bankruptcy, with global and domestic travel networks being shut.

However, human race is very resilient. We have bounced back from every crisis shall overcome this too. In a matter of months, COVID-19 would be behind us. But, COVID-19 will leave behind a profound effect and impact. Post pandemic, there would be a paradigm shift in our social structure, global cooperation and economic cooperation as well. The global supply chains are crumbling and so is the world order. In such a scenario, it is critical how fast we internalise the lessons, look ahead and prepare ourselves for the World beyond. To bounce back from such a situation, India needs to strengthen building blocks of the economy as well as that of society. The Hon'ble Prime Minister of India has also made a clarion call to utilise this challenging time not as a national crisis, but as an opportunity for economic revival, to promote 'Make in India' initiatives and become self reliant.

As per an IMF estimate, the pandemic, even if swiftly controlled, could shrink per capita GDP across 170 nations by at least three percent. It could result in drastic drop in industrial production, uncertainty over the supply chain, large scale unemployment and even drop agricultural production etc. The scenario looks very grey with global lockdown in force and resultant impact on the demand and supply scenario.

In India, COVID-19 infection is yet to reach the peak. With preemptive, proactive and graded control, India would be able to flatten the growth curve. Even if plateau is reached, prolonged control measures have to be ensured. IMF has also projected the reduction of GDP growth for India from 5.8 percent to 1.9 percent. Current estimates are even lower in case of prolonged lockdown. As such recoveries would take many months but in case of a repetition of outbreak next year, recovery could take several years. IMF also forecasted growth in Asian countries to fall to zero percent. If so, it would be the worst performances since last 60 years. China's growth could decelerate to 1.2 percent. However, India and China are the only two countries in the world predicted to have positive GDP growth this fiscal year.

## Scale of Impact on Economy Sectors

Based on a detailed analysis of various sectors in reference to employment and GDP contribution as defined under National Industrial Classification System, the impact of COVID-19 has been highlighted in Table 1. The following factors were taken as input parameters for each sector and its category:

- Normal labour availability
- Critical labour availability
- Regular inward stock
- Critical inward stock
- Inward logistics

- Working capital availability
- Outward logistics
- Distribution efficiency

**Table 1: Impact of Covid-19 on different sectors**

| *Sectors* | *GDP as %* | *Employment (2018-19)* | *Covid-19 Impact In 2020-21* |
|---|---|---|---|
| Textiles | 2 | 45 Million | Med-High |
| Auto | 7-8 | 40 Million | High |
| Aviation and Tourism | 11.4 | 43 Million | High |
| Building and Construction | -10 | -- | High |
| Retail | 10 | 10% of total Workforce | Med-High |
| Education and Skilling | 3 | -- | Medium |
| Financial sector (including Insurance) | 9 | -- | Medium |
| Food and Agriculture | 15 | 43% of total Workforce | Medium |
| MSME | 30 | 11.4 crore (99% micro) | High |

## Impact of Covid-19 on Indian Economic Sectors

COVID-19 with global shutdown and quarantine has severely affected the supply of economy without collateral damage to the demand side. However, mankind history is replete with several instances of not only recovering but also coming back strongly from several pandemics including two world wars. We shall overcome COVID-19 also. In order to calculate impact on demand, correlations between demand, lockdown and spread were taken into account. Impact of COVID-19 on supply and demand in various subsector of economy also has been analyzed and presented in the table as annexed.

It is inferred from the table that supply side in the sectors of Mining, Manufacturing, construction, food, entertainment and recreation have been badly impacted whereas in sectors like agriculture, textile, electrical equipment, education and healthcare services, the demand is not so affected. Some sectors which are crucial to the national economy like: Healthcare, Agriculture and Food Processing, Manufacturing & Machinery, ICT and Electronics etc. have been studied in greater details in next section. However, the broad approach in each sector is mentioned below :

1. **Agriculture and allied sectors:** The production is not as impacted as most other sectors, while the demand exists. This is a sector that can help India in covering losses posed by other sectors, if the right kind of technology support is provided. Technology adoption is also required to strengthen Public Distribution System, to reduced post harvest losses and mechanisation for agriculture operations.
2. **Manufacturing:** Some categories of this sector are severely impacted, while not so much in other categories. The difference in impact across categories within the sector poses an interesting challenge where there may be need of shift of roles for a number of stakeholders in the sector.
3. **ICT and electronics:** Some of the categories within the sector are showing a boost for the economy, thus, creating a need of technological interventions in this sector for helping other sectors.
4. **Healthcare:** This sector has components that show increase in demand while limitations are projected on supply side. This calls for technology boosts using ICT and new-age technologies to make this sector a positive earner for India.

**Factors Causing hindrance in post Covid-19 recovery**

- Cuts in spending on durable goods (e.g. cars, appliances)
- Extent of behaviour shift (e.g. restaurant spend, gym activity)
- Extent of travel reduction (percent flight cancellations, travel bans)
- Late payments/credit defaults
- Stock market & volatility indices
- Purchasing managers index
- Initial claims for unemployment
- Bounce-back in economic activity in countries that were exposed early in pandemic
- Early private and public sector actions during the pandemic to ensure economic restart

Recovery of Indian economy will depend upon adoption of appropriate measures e.g. Policy support to unconventional strategies, depth and breadth of foreign partnerships, leveraging international partnerships in important sectors like: agriculture (viz. Partnership with Israeli companies), MSMEs (with German companies) and large manufacturing tie ups with US and Japan under Start up India etc. Planning ahead would warrant a detailed understanding of sector-wise business imperatives, demand supply position, technology status in India, existing capacity, its further strengthening and initiatives (long term and short term).

## New Business Opportunities with Covid-19

The corona that rocked the world and shattered the economy now offers new opportunities for innovators. Many businesses have been damaged with Corona. Almost all industries except the pharmacy industry have suffered losses due to the corona and thousands of employees have lost their jobs. However, this pandemic situation creates new business opportunities for innovators and job / employment opportunities to jobless and migrants. There are many opportunities in the manufacture and sale of things like sanitizers, masks, immunosuppressant and healthy food items.

Within weeks of the COVID-19 outbreak, many companies and individuals are turning the corona into a business perspective and making a profit. Companies that produce FMCG in particular are transforming them into new objects by adding corona binding elements to their products in the corona background. For example, Dabur strengthend its portfolio of immune-boosting products, including health juices such as Amla, Giloi, Giloi-Neem-Tulsi and Aloe Vera, as well as products such as Tulsi Drops, Haldi, and AYUSH Quat Kathi. And also introduced many other products in the market. Mayur Suiting's, a clothing company has added a virus-secure fabric coating to their garments. It comes with an anti-viral protective coating on the fabric to provide protection from SARS-CoV-2. This fabric is used to make uniforms for frontline healthcare workers, school children, security and police personnel as well as casual wear.

Visakha Dairy, a leading dairy company in Andhra Pradesh state has launched Haldi Milks as a new immune boosting product. CalvinKare has developed a new product called SaaFoo which helps to remove germs, chemicals and pesticides from vegetables, fruits and meats. Leading Ayurvedic Company Patanjali has launched Divya Corona Kit for protection against corona. Corona is also an integral part of corporate advertising. Advertisements from Domex claim that their floor cleaner can kill the corona virus in as little as 60 seconds.

Insurers are also introducing health insurance with a focus on the corona virus. Some insurance companies offer their services through policies such as Corona Kavach Policy. Overall the corona has hit some businesses and employment opportunities while offering new opportunities to some. Everyone from footpath traders to multinational corporations are turning the corona into a business venture.

## Drone Delivery

The Covid-19 outbreak has sent shivers down the spine of the global economy. The virus has hit hard the global supply chain network, and extensively hits automobile and manufacturing sectors around the globe. In such a scenario, not all businesses have been disrupted; some other business opportunities are making its way along it, such as Drone Delivery. As the outbreak of coronavirus COVID-19 began from China and to spread all over the world now, tech companies especially MedTech companies are rolling out drones and robots to fight off the virus and deliver services and care to those isolated or following social distancing.

Drones are not just using for delivery purposes but also for maintaining rules and regulations. In India, the Karimnagar Commissionerate of Police in Telangana used drones to ensure effective implementation of lockdown in the town. In the times of a social distancing environment, authorities have found drones as an effective technology. Drones are scalable, work 24/7, everywhere. So, this tech can be used to deliver goods, along with other purposes across locations and can be controlled remotely.

## Virtual Exhibitions

These are events where people visit virtually rather than physically. As technology advances rapidly, conferences and exhibitions will no longer require a physical presence and will enable people to come together under a single roof, regardless of their location. In the corona virus time as the entire world is under lockdown, this concept is emerging exponentially limiting the spread of the virus by enabling social distancing. For example, last year, Art Basel's March Hong Kong edition of the world-famous art fair drew in a record crowd of 88,000 visitors. But this year due to the pandemic it had no choice but to go fully virtual for the first time, with Online Viewing Rooms, which hosted galleries' collections for buyers and collectors to peruse and purchase. So, there will be tremendous opportunities in the area of virtual exhibitions where corporate can come together, network, watch live events, and much more.

## Masks

As the world is facing a severe pandemic, the Masks market is on the rise. Since they cover half of the face the demand for creativity in designs is increasing. Several companies are rushing to increase their production amidst Covid-19. On the other hand, if the market demand augments, most of the apparel brands might start manufacturing masks especially luxury or designer brands.

## Vending Machine

It is an automated machine that provides items like snacks, beverages, lottery tickets, and others to consumers after money, a credit card, or a specially designed card is inserted into the machine. In Europe, the European Vending & Coffee Service Association (EVA) has emphasised that vending machines across the continent remain safe and open amid corona virus fears. According to the association, operators and technicians of vending machines have employed measures which ensure that vending machines remain hygienic, including heightened cleaning and disinfection of surfaces such as buttons. As these machines are available 24/7, they don't require human intervention or contact and can be deployed anywhere within limited space.

## Hand Sanitizers

It is observed that the high demand of Hand Sanitizers because of Covid-19 outbreak, the market sees a massive rise of new players in this field. As the coronavirus has led to a huge uptick in the demand for hand sanitizers across the globe, the major CPG companies are also ramping up their production and optimising their supply chains to cater to the sudden spike. It has largely being grown because of people are started panic-buying hand sanitizers as a preventive measure. As per reports, the global marketplace is witnessing high demand of health and wellness products, including sanitizers, floor cleaning products and other cleaning products that reduce the impact of infectious diseases like Covid-19. This has resulted in substantial growth in the global hand sanitizer market due to the shift in consumer preference towards convenient hygiene products.

So, the Covid-19 outbreak has not just impacted businesses globally but also fuelled new business opportunities and innovations. Since airline profitability, tourism and others are getting disrupted globally, remote working, on the other side, is being encouraged by tech and non-tech companies. Thus, we believe that some of these changes are direct, short-term responses to the crisis and will revert to regular levels once Covid-19 passes. However, some of these shifts will continue, creating a long-term digital disruption that will form businesses in the future.

## Covid-19: how Businesses are Innovating with 'Corona Products'

The covid-19 pandemic is forcing businesses staring at a bleak future to enter the field of what they term "corona products". In the US, eager travellers are opting for vehicles that are now being labelled "covid campers". These are nothing but traditional RVs, also known as motor homes or travel trailers. According to a recent report by *Bloomberg*, some people are spending upwards of $100,000 (around ₹85 lakh) so they can travel while staying away from everyone else. "Social distancing is apparently a lot easier when you can bring along your own kitchen, bathroom and bedroom," the report adds.

In India, too, businesses that have suffered losses are trying to think innovatively, either looking at new product or modifying their existing ones. Be it customised face masks and face shields or digital infrared thermometers and sanitizing tunnels.

Take the face masks category. A recent report published in *The Lancet* medical journal says wearing a face mask can actually bring down the chance of infection to just three percent. According to the report, face shields and goggles could "add" substantial protection. The comprehensive report is based on 172 observational studies across 16 countries and six continents. Given what's happening because of covid-19, luxury is out of the question right now for many people. Everyone's looking to procure the basic requirements and face masks are an absolute must. Who wouldn't want them? I wouldn't leave the house without one," says Dalvir Singh, director, The Flag Company, a Mumbai-based firm. The company, which has been manufacturing flags, banners and backlit fabric light boxes, has of late turned to making face masks.

It has come out with customizable two-ply fabric face masks that are breathable, UV protected and washable. They are made from 100 percent woven polyester and can be personalised for a particular brand or company—there are customised masks for children and masks that can have half of your face printed on them too. "It's a great way of advertising and creating awareness about the importance of face masks at the moment. So far, everyone from small to large enterprises has shown interest in the product. We are also expecting to start exporting them soon," adds Singh. For now, the company has fixed the minimum order at 12 pieces. But at ₹125 each, the affordability factor is also taken care of. "Till the time there is no vaccine or medicinal intervention, people will be using all the means possible for proper sanitization: one is the hand sanitizer, and the other, face masks," adds Singh.

The Strutt Store, a bootstrapped startup based in Noida, Uttar Pradesh, had been designing travel bags and essentials but has now diversified into handcrafted face masks. “When the pandemic struck, the travel business went down. But we decided to make these masks because travel itself will never stop. People might not be travelling from one city to another but they are still travelling over short distances and the idea was to design these masks to keep them safe,” says Vishesh Khosla, part of the founding team at The Strutt Store. The team went through a detailed market research process before settling on handcrafted four-layered masks that use denim, linen and Khadi cotton. For protection, two filtration layers, including an antibacterial one, are used in every mask. “These are the same layers used in surgical masks,” says Khosla, adding that after a quiet period of business they are now receiving orders of up to 150-200 masks daily. They cost as little as ₹269 for a set of three.

To effectively, mitigate the economic impact of pandemic, and catapult India in the global manufacturing league, new trade effective policy, with technology stimulus, need to be structured for further action by policy-makers and business leaders. Some stringent policy measures may be defined on the basis of:

1. Demand and Supply Shocks (Reduction in supply chain capacity through lost productivity)
2. Second and Third order impacts (Loss in Tourism, foreign exchange volatility, Oil prices crash)
3. 4D Risks (Financial, business and operating models)

The analysis in this paper lists out some focus areas that would be critical for India’s economic growth:

1. **MSME Sector:** needs special stimulus as they are heavily impacted but have the right potential and flexibility to transform leveraging new technologies.
2. **Public Health Systems:** Additional pressure on this system shall make it more dependent on financial and technology stimuli.
3. **Workforce Management:** The significant decrease in growth signals a major impact on India’s workforce, and the right utilisation of the same with intervention through government policies, can help drive the economy.
4. **Global Relations:** Global supply chain shall undergo a complete overhaul, thus, opening new areas of relations globally.

5. **Under-privileged Areas of the Society:** This would have highest impacts of the current situation of people living in such areas.
6. **New Age Technologies:** Special focus on these would help benefit all other areas that need focus.

Based on the understanding of Indian economy, evaluation of the focus areas, suggested policy measures, and insights drawn from opportunities and recommendations in each sector, following policy shifts are recommended:

1. MSME sector needs to be supported on issues of liquidity crunch, credit support and fiscal compliances.
2. Substantial support is needed for the public health systems to ensure regular supply of PPE, medicines, equipment, etc.
3. Policies around tele-medicine and other technologies that enable digital transformation in the domain should be strengthened, to provide better infrastructure.
4. Re-calibrated trade alignments.
5. Re-imagined global institutions.
6. Constant communication at district level for response planning.
7. Increased co-ordination between all levels of government would be needed. Digital Transformation may help drive this.
8. Relax factory compliances to enable the industry to continue operation with a much lesser workforce over longer work/ shift hours but in a healthier environment (Enabling Social distancing).
9. BPL Families to be supported through DBT and use of ICT for transparency.

## Conclusion

Many entrepreneurs have seized this moment as an opportunity to launch a social enterprise businesses that have a dual mission of social impact and financial growth. But how can these entrepreneurs ensure that their short-term innovations can last as viable, long-term businesses?

## References

1. Gupta, Surojit; 'Make in India' push for ventilators, PPEs; The Times of India; April 5, 2020; https:/timesofindia.indiatimes.com/india/COVID-19-make-in-india-push-forventilators-ppes/articleshow/74988501.cms

2. Globe Newswire; Face mask market to surpass $21.2 billion by 2026; March 31, 2020;

https://www.globenewswire.com/news-release/2020/03/31/2008963/0/en/Facemask-market-to-surpass-21-2-billion-by-2026.htmi

3. Fortune Business Insights. Impact of COVID-19 on the medical devices market size, share, industry analysis and regional forecast, 2020-2027. April 2020, Report ID: FBI102629;

4. Lueth, Knud Lesse (04/2020); " Impact of COVID-19 on the Internet of Things Now and beyond the great lockdown", loT Analytics; April 16, 2020.

# B. Business Organisation (B.O.)

# Business Environment, Trade, Business Organisation and Development

An attempt has been made to present the concepts such as (1) Meaning of Environment, (2) Characteristics, (3) International Business Environment, (4) Components of Global environment and (5) Economic environment.

1. 'Environment' has been defined as, "The surroundings external objects influences or circumstances under which solve are or something exists. The environment of any organisation is, the aggregate of all kinds, events and influences that surround and affect it".

   The environment could be classified in terms of domestic, foreign and international spheres of impact. The domestic environment consists of those uncontrollable external forces that affect the business firm in its home markets. The foreign environment could be taken as those factors which operate in those other countries within which MNC operates. Generally, the factors are the same, but they can have widely differing impacts from the home country situation. International environment has been identified as "the interaction between domestic and foreign factors and indeed they cover a wide spectrum of forces".
2. Characteristics of environment may be classified into three. They are: 1. Environment is complex. 2. Environment is dynamic and 3. Environment is multifaceted.
3. **International Business Environment:** It is also known as Global environment. The environment of international business is regarded as the sum of total of all the external forces working upon the firm as it goes about its affairs in foreign and domestic markets. According to Prof. Francis Cherunilam, global environment refers to those global factors which are relevant to business, such as WTO principles, and agreements, other international conventions,

treaties, agreements, declarations, protocols, etc. economic and business conditions in other countries.

A firm in international business encounters three different sets of external environment. They are :

1. Domestic Environment
2. Foreign environment and
3. Global environment.

Business environment differs from place to place, from time to time and country to country. Business environment in developing countries like India, substantially differs from what it is in the developed economies or countries of the world. Companies which operate in the global environment must take care of such environmental differences before they formulate their policies and strategies. This is the reason, why managers who operate in a global environment must have a global approach with local strategy.

## E-Commerce

The phenomenal growth of internet and the associate world wide web has made E-commerce possible. E-commerce is contributing to a growing percentage of cross-border transactions. The web is emerging as the great equaliser. It rolls back some of the constraints of location, distance, scale and time zones. The web allows, both small and large, to expand their global presence at a lower cost that ever before. The web makes it much easier for buyers and sellers to find each other, wherever they may be located and whatever their size".[1]

Keeping in view of the above business environmental conditions, in particular, location, distance, scale and time zones, how the business/trade takes place functions to a large extent over a period of time and space are important. The case studies relating to Life Insurance Corporation of India (LIC) has been presented in the following paragraphs. Origin/growth and development and its associated phenomenal growth and its progress has been presented in detail to understand the business environment, and likely contribution to development not only restricted to internal environment and its demand but also external demand for LIC, its supply (Sale) of policies through structured and innovative strategies.

## Trade: Insurance

An attempt has been made in this chapter to present the indepth and critical analysis of the Life Insurance Corporation of India and the details have been related to various development over a period of time. It is needless to say/identify and recognized as a financial booster in India through the norm or logo, "Yogakshema".

This chapter deals with the following aspects such as :

1. The LIC's Machinery.
2. Administrative organs in India.
3. Overseas offices – Spatial distribution.
4. Different services.
5. Other organisations.
6. Life Insurance Corporation of India: An Assurance for life risks through insurance for millions to get billions.
7. Objectives of LIC.
8. Tax benefits from life insurance.
9. People's money for people's welfare (Table 3.2)
10. Investments in Govt. & Social sectors (Rs. in crores) An Appraisal.
11. LIC's Investments during five years plan periods.
12. LIC's International operations (IOPC).
13. Performance Highlights (1-4-2005 to 31-3-2006).
14. Golden Jubilee Foundation (GJF).
15. Community Development through LIC i.e. Scholarship Scheme and other projects.
16. LIC Mutual Funds.
17. Conclusions.

## Reference

1. B. Polisu, "Business Environment: A Survey (A bridged form) Paper Published in 'Applied Geo-environmental studies" Edl. KLN Murty. Mangal Deep Publications, Jaipur (pp. 114-132) (2008).

# 3

# Trade: Insurance Business: An Adequate Financial Cover

*Dr K. L. Narasimha Murty*

## 1. LIC Machinery

Life Insurance Corporation of India (LIC), was established in the year 1956, and the control office namely "Yogakshema" headed @ Jeevan Bima Marg, Mumbai. Members of the Corporation as on 01-10-2018 with 11(Eleven) members, one chairman and three Managing Directors, and 24 (twenty four) Executive Directors, heading various banches i.e. Engineering, IT/SD, Corporate planning New Project), Marketing/PD, CRM, Direct Marketings, personnel, Investment – RMR, (Board Sectt/GJF), P&GS, IT/BPR, MKTG-B&AC) (Investment-M&A), Micro Insurance, Internal Audit, Legal, Investment Operations, Corporate Communications, MKTg-CLIA, NB&RI, HRD/OD, Personnel, E&OS and Inspection.

## 2. Administrative Organs

Administratively the entire Corporation have been divided into different organs. They are as follows:

1. Central Office, Mumbai.
2. Co-liaison Department, New Delhi.
3. Management Development Centre, Mumbai.
4. Health Insurance, Abids, Hyderabad.
    2. Central zone, Bhopal
    3. Eastern Zone, Kolkata
    4. East Central Zone, Patna
    5. Northern Zone, New Delhi

6. North Central Zone, Kanpur
7. Southern Zone, Chennai
8. South Central Zone, Hyderabad.
9. Bengaluru Zone, Bengaluru.
10. Western Zone, Mumbai.
11. Bancassurance (Gujarat Region), Ahmedabad.

**3. Overseas Offices: Spatial Distribution**

(1) SBU International Corporations, Mumbai

(a) Branch Offices,
Fiji, LIC House, Suva, Fiji.

(2) Mauritius,
5, LIC Centre, Mauritius.

(3) United Kingdom
Middlesex, HA9-OPX, U.K.

(b) Wholly owned Subsidiary

(1) Singapore
LIC Insurance Corporation (Singapore) PTE Ltd. Singapore-Pin 048617.

(c) Joint Venture Companies.

(1) Bahrain
LIC (International) B.S.C., Manerna, Kingdom of Bahrain.

(2) Kenya – Bairobe – 00100 Kenya.

(3) Sri Lanka
Life Insurance Corporation (Lanka) Ltd., Colombo, Sri Lanka.

(4) Nepal
Life Insurance Corporation (NEPAL) Ltd. Kathmandu.

(5) Saudi Arabia
Riyadh-11333, Kingdom of Saudi-Arabia (KSA).

(6) Bangladesh: Life Insurance Corporation (LIC) of Bangladesh, Limited, Dhaka 1212, Bangladesh.

**4. Different Services (D.S.)**

(1) LIC Cards Services Ltd., Connaught Place, New Delhi.
(2) LIC Housing Finance Ltd., Cuffe Parade, Mumbai – 400 005.
(3) LIC Care Homes Ltd., Cuffe Parade, Mumbai.

(4) LIC HFL Financial Services Ltd., Cuffe Parade, Mumbai

(5) LIC HFL Asset Management Company Ltd., Bandra (E), Mumbai-51

(6) LIC Mutual Fund Asset Management Limited, Corporate Office, Churchgate, Mumbai.

(7) LIC Pension Fund Ltd., Corporate Office, Church Gate, Mumbai.

**5. Other Organisations**

(1) Insurance Regulations Development Authority of India, Financial District, Hyderabad – 500 032.

(2) Insurance Institute of India, Bandra East, Mumbai – 400 051.

(3) National Insurance Academy NIA PO, Pune-411 045.

(4) General Insurance Corporation of India, Suraksha, 170, J. Tata Marg, Churhgate, Mumbai.

(5) Office of the Executive Council of Insurance Santacruz (E), Mumbai – 400 054

(6) Omendsman's Offices in India are located in Ahmedabad, Bengaluru, Bhopal, Bhubaneswar, Chandigarh, Chennai, Delhi, Guwahati, Hyderabad, Jaipur, Kochi, Kolkata, Lucknow, Mumbai, Moida, Patna and Pune

## 3.2 Life Insurance Corporation of India

"An Assurance for Life Risks through Insurance for Millions."

In this chapter an attempt has been made to present the profile of the LIC of India in National Building specially in the economic front besides its vision, mission, values culture, objectives of LIC, Insurance plans, term of Assurance plans, children plans, pension plans, Micro Insurance plans, Health insurance plan, Unit-linked plan, other plans, special plans, social security schemes, people's money for people's welfare investments in Govt. and social sector and LIC Mutual Fund. The above aspects are presented in the following paragraphs.

(1) Vision: "A trans-nationally competitive financial conglomerate of significance to societies and pride of India".

(2) Mission: "Ensure and enhance the quality of life of people through financial security by providing products and services of aspirated attributes with competitive returns and by rendering resources for economic development".

(3) Values

- Caring and courtesy
- Initiative and innovation
- Integrity and transparency
- Quality and returns
- Participation and relationship; and
- Trustworthiness and reliability

Culture

- Agility
- Adaptability
- Collaboration
- Commitment
- Discipline
- Empowerment
- Sensitivity; and
- Excellence

(4) Objectives of LIC:

1. Spread life Insurance widely and in particular to the rural areas and to the socially and economically backward classes with a view to reaching all infavourable persons in the country and providing them adequate financial cover against death at a reasonable cost.
2. Maximize Mobilisation of people's savings by making insurance linked savings adequately attractive.
3. Bear in mind, in the investment of funds, the primary obligation to its policy holders, whose money it holds in trust, without losing right of the interest of the community as a whole, the funds to be deployed to the best advantage of the investors as well as the community as a whole, keeping in view national priorities and obligations of the attractive return.
4. Conduct business with utmost economy and with the full realisation that the money's belong to the policy holders.
5. Act as trustees of the insured public in their individual and collective capacities.

6. Meet the various life insurance needs of the community that would arise in the changing social and economic environment.
7. Involve all the people working in the corporation to the best of their capabilities in furthering the interests of the insured public by providing efficient service with courtesy.
8. Promote amongst all agents and employees of the corporation a sense of participation, pride and jobs satisfaction through discharge of their duties with dedication towards achievement of corporate objectivities.

(5). Tax benefits from Life Insurance:

Income-Tax rates for Assessment Year 2019-20 (Financial Year 2018-19) has been presented in Table 3.1.

**Table 3.1**

| | ***Income slabs*** | | ***Tax Rates*** |
|---|---|---|---|
| Individual of age below 60 years and HBF | Individual of age 60 years and more but less than 80 years | Individual of age 80 years and more | |
| Income upto ₹ 2,50,000 | Income upto ₹ 3,00,000 | Income upto ₹ 5,00,000 | Nil |
| ₹ 2,50,000 to ₹ 5,00,000 | ₹ 3,00,000 to ₹ 5,00,000 | | 5% |
| ₹ 2,50,000 to ₹ 10,00,000 | ₹ 5,00,001 to ₹ 10,00,000 | ₹ 5,00,001 to ₹ 10,00,000 | 20% |
| Above ₹ 20,00,000 | Above ₹ 10,00,000 | Above ₹ 10,00,000 | 30% |

**Note:** *The aggregate amount of deduction under U/s. 80C, 80CCC & 80CCD (1) shall not in any case exceed one lakh fifty thousand rupees.*

From Table, the important aspect relating to income tax benefits and they are as follows:

(1) Deduction allowable from income for payment of life insurance premium (Section 80C).

(2) Jeevan Nidhi Plan & Jeevan Suraksha plans (Section 80CCC).

(3) LIC's Jeeven Arogya and LIC's cancer cover plan (Section 80D).

(4) Jeevan Adhar Plan (Section 80DD).

(5) Exemption in respect of commutation of pension under Jeevan Suraksha and Jeevan Nidhi plans (Section 10 (104).

(6) Income Tax exemption on maturity/Death claims proceeds (Section 10 (10D).

## 9. People's Money for People's Welfare

The Life Insurance Corporation of India has been a Nation builder since its formation in 1956. True to the objectives of Nationalisation of the corporation has mobilised the funds invested by the people in the life insurance for the benefit of the community at large.

It has deployed the funds to the best advantage of the policyholders as well as the community as a whole, true to the spirit of nationalisation. National priorities and obligation of the reasonable returns to the policyholders are the main criteria of the reinvestments.

The total funds, so invested for the benefit of the community at large are 27,36,762 crore as on 31st March, 2018. The investment of the corporation's funds is governed by section 27A of the insurance Act, 1938 subsequent guidelines/instructions issued from time to time by the Government of India and the IRDAI by way of regulations.

**Table 3.2: Investment in Govt. & Social Sector**

| *S.No* | *Type of Investment* | *31-3-2016* | *31-3-2017* | *31-03-2018* |
|---|---|---|---|---|
| 1. | Central Govt. Securities | 721000 | 822821 | 912251 |
| 2. | State Govt. & Other Govt. Guarantees/Marketable Securities | 521632 | 655603 | 784701 |
| | Sub Total (A) | 1242632 | 1478423 | 1696952 |
| 3. Housing & Infrastructure table investment. | | | | |
| a. | Housing | 70302 | 65693 | 52405 |
| b. | Power | 120558 | 117398 | 116015 |
| c. | Irrigation/water supply & sewerage | 2319 | 2031 | 1768 |
| d. | Road, Port & Bridges, Railways | 13244 | 35210 | 56004 |
| e. | Others (inet. Telecom) | 36846 | 33824 | 32130 |
| | Sub-total (B) | 243269 | 254156 | 258322 |
| | Total A + B | 1485901 | 1732579 | 1955274 |

**Table 3.3: Investments in Govt. & Social Sector (₹ In Crores) –An Appraisal**

| | | | *As on* | | |
|---|---|---|---|---|---|
| ***Type of Investment*** | ***31-3-62*** | ***31-3-63*** | ***31-3-04*** | ***31-3-05*** | ***31-3-06*** |
| 1. Central Govt. Sec. | 109938 | 137276 | 166939 | 199785 | 236959 |
| 2. State Govt. & Other Govt. guaranted Marketable Sec. | 21463 | 28988 | 37402 | 51283 | 58928 |
| 3. Electricity (SEBS) | 13447 | 14508 | 14805 | 15761 | 15944 |
| 4. Housing | 19054 | 19944 | 20694 | 21436 | 21963 |
| 5. Water supply & Sewerage (Mun+Z.P.) | 4000 | 4420 | 7111 | 10346 | 10374 |
| 6.State Road Transport Corp. | 893 | 1358 | 1373 | 1387 | 1501 |
| 7.Loans to Individual estates | 45 | 45 | 45 | 45 | 45 |
| 8.Loan to sugar Co-op. | 37 | 37 | 37 | 37 | 37 |
| 9.Development Authority | 1 | 1 | 1 | 1 | 1 |
| 10.Roadways, port and Railways | 681 | 781 | 1272 | 2463 | 2477 |
| 11.Power Generation (Private Sector) | 3797 | 6105 | 6412 | 9966 | 18984 |
| 12.Municipality | 14 | 14 | 14 | 14 | 14 |
| Total | 173370 | 213477 | 256105 | 312524 | 367237 |

*Source: LIC, Dairy 2007.*

## Observations:

Changes over a period of time: It seen from take 3.1, 3.2 and 3.3, there has been a spectacular and special features in the utilisation and deployment of funds (funds transfer) are quite vivid and varied which benefits both the policy holders as well as LIC of India, Mumbai. The funds investment patterns are quite attractive.

**Table 3.4: LIC's Investments during five years plan periods**

| *Plan* | *Year* | *Gross Investment in ₹ Crores* | *Plan Year* | | *Gross Investment (₹ in Crores)* |
|---|---|---|---|---|---|
| 2 | 1956-1961 | 184 | 8 | 1992-97 | 56,097 |
| 3 | 1961-1966 | 285 | 9 | 1997-2002 | 1,70,929 |
| 4 | 1969-1974 | 1530 | 10 | 2002-2007 | 3,94,779 |
| 5 | 1974-1979 | 2942 | 11 | 2007-2012 | 7,04,720 |
| 6 | 1980-1985 | 7140 | 12 | 2012-2017 | 14,23,055 |
| 7 | 1985-1990 | 12969 | 13 | 2017-2022 | 3,82,479 |

## Observation

1. It is seen from Table 3.4, that LIC of India has been functioning since 1956. Five years plan period, has been marked as "development block". They are:
2. 1956-61
3. 1961-1966
4. 1969-1974
5. 1974-1979
6. 1980-1985 and
7. 1985-1990
8. 1992-97
9. 1997-2002
10 2002-2007
11. 2007-2012
12. 2012-2017 and
13. 2017-2022.
    (2) Gross investments are on an increasing scale, from ₹ 184 crores to 12,969 crores from 1956 to ₹ 12,969.
    (3) From plan 1992-97 to 13th plan (2017-2022) the gross investments are on an increasing scale, and almost 20 times have been increased upon 1956-1961 gross investments (In ₹ Crores).

## 12. LIC's International Operations

LIC is present in 14 countries globally through branch offices/joint venture companies and wholly owned subsidiary. The details are as follows:

## Branch Offices

1. Fiji, 2. Mauritius, 3. United Kingdom (Wembly).

## Joint Venture Companies

1. LIC (International) B. Sc. (C) Balivaine: A Joint Venture Company promoted by Life Insurance Corporation of India, Commenced operations in July, 1989, with the objective of Offencing U.S. & Demominated policies to cater to the insurance needs of expatriate indian's A company operates in 5 GCC countries of Balvain, VAE (Dubai and Abu Dhabi), Oaman, Kuwait, and Qater.
2. LIC (Nepal I Ltd.): A joint Venture Company promoted jointly in 2001 by LIC of India and Vishal Group of Industries, Nepal which is listed on the stock exchange (Nepal stock exchange Ltd) Operates from 34 branches in Nepal.
3. LIC (Lanka) Ltd. : A Joint Venture company promoted jointly in 2003 by LIC of India and M/s. Bartlect Transcapital Pvt. Ltd., operates from 28 branches in Sri Lanka.
4. Ken India Assurance Co. Ltd., Kenya: A Composite Insurance company formed in 1978 by LIC of India; New India Assurance Co. Ltd., Oriental Insurance Co. Ltd., United India Insurance Co. Ltd., and National Insurance.

## 13. Performance Highlights: (1.4.2005 to 31.3.2006).

- Individual Business – No. of Policies 315.75 lakhs.
- First Premium Income – ₹ 18085.49 crores.
- Sum Assured ₹ 287530.24 crores.
- Pension & Group Business and social security schemes.
- Pension & Group Business

  No. of New Schemes – 11,845

  No. of lives – 51.27 lakhs

  Premium Income – ₹ 3919.00 crores.
- Social Security schemes

  Number of New Schemes – 6315

  Number of lives – 63.41 lakhs

  Premium Income – ₹ 22.78 crores.

  Business in Force as on 31-3-06.
- Individual Assurances:

  Policies – 18.64 crore

Sum Assured ₹ 16,00,683 crores

Group Insurance

Lives 3.15 crore

Sum Assured ₹ 2,01,616 crore.

**Table 3.5**

| Our strength Total Income (FY 2005-06 ₹ 1,32,146 crocre | Total Assets ₹ 5,52,447 Crores | Total As on 31-3-2006 Life Fund Investment (Book Value) ₹ 5,24,017 Crore. |
|---|---|---|

Co. Ltd. and local (Kenyan share holders. Operates from 13 branches in Kenya.

5. Life Insurance Corporation (LIC) of Bangladesh Ltd, Life Insurance Corporation (LIC) of Bangladesh Limited is a joint venture Company between Life Insurance Corporation of India, strategic equity management Ltd. and Mutual Trust Bank Ltd., incorporated in Bangladesh on 14th December, 2015.

Wholly owned subsidiary

Life Insurance Corporation (Singapore) Pvt. Ltd., was incorporated on 30th April, 2012 in Singapore as wholly owned subsidiary in Singapore.

## 14. Golden Jubilee Foundation

LIC Golden Jubilee Foundation was established in the year 2006 as a party of LIC's community service initiative, the objectives of the foundation are relief of poverty or distress, advancement of education, medical relief and advancement of any other object of general public utility. Since inception, the foundation has supported NGO's dedicated to the above areas through 456 projects as on 30-6-2018, which are located across the country. It has reached out to many deprived sections of the society through the infrastructural support provided in the above areas.

The foundation has supported cost of treatment for children afflicted with cancer and undergoing treatment at TATA Memorial Hospital, Mumbai from the year 2013-14 to 2017-18, 110 beneficiaries have benefitted from the scheme across the country. It has funded the purchase of bus for transporting cancer patients from TATA Memorial Hospital, Mumbai to Tata Research Centre at Navi Mumbai.

## 15. Community Development through LIC

LIC GJF has adopted Govindpur Village under Sonabhadra District of Uttar Pradesh for Community Development activities related to literacy campaign and medical relief.

LIC Golden Jubilee scholarship scheme provides scholarships at the rate of ₹ 10,000 P.A. to children from economically weaker sections of the society to pursue higher education till they complete their graduation/ professional course. Approximately 15,196 students have benefitted from the scheme so far.

The other projects are as follows:

1. LIC Cards Services Limited
2. LIC Pension Fund Limited
3. LIC Housing Finance Ltd.
4. LIC HFL Care Homes Ltd.
5. LIC HFL Financial Services Ltd.

   and
6. LIC HFL Asset Management Company Limited.

## 16. LIC Mutual Funds

Finally, LIC Mutual fund is an important, an innovative scheme and the details are as follows:

LIC Mutual Fund (The "Mutual Fund") was constituted as a trust on 2014/1989 in accordance with the provisions of the Indian Trusts Act with LIC of India as the sponsor, the LIC Mutual Fund Trustee Private Ltd., as the trustee and the LIC Mutual Fund Asset Management Ltd. as the investment Manager to LIC Mutual Fund. The shareholders of LIC Mutual Fund Asset Management are LIC of India, LIC Housing Finance Ltd., GIE Housing Finance Ltd. and Corporation Bank.

As of 31st March, 2018, LIC Mutual Fund was managing 25 schemes. During the year 2017-18, AMC has mobilised gross sales of ₹ 4,43,680 crores from all live schemes. The total number of investors as on 31-3-2018 touched at 3,30,901. Average Assets under Management (AAUM) was ₹ 20,118 crore for the last quarter of 2017-18 and within terms of AAVM.

With a network of 212 investor service centres, 23 area offices and 132 sales team. LIC MF is present in more than 200 locations spread over length and breadth of India. LIC MF has one of the widest distribution networks comprising IFAS, National Distributors, wealth management teams, Banks and Key Business partners.

LIC MF has an innovative product feature called "APPS" (Auto premium payment system) whereby the customers can invest their money in liquid or short term schemes and their LIC premium is paid from the mutual fund account. This is a unique feature offered only by LIC MF in the industry similarly, LIC mutual fund is among the 1st Mutual Fund to offer ETF in debt space with LIC MF GSEC long term ETC. The product allows retail investors to invest in GSEC with a very small ticket size at a very competitive cost.

## 17. Conclusion

It is concluded that Life Insurance Corporation of India has been rendering services through its organs (wings) for the integrated and over all development throughout the globe and it helps many millions (through service) of people to gain millions of rupees by the insured population.

2. In a nutshell, LIC of India has been rendering services both for internal and external population and there are no barriers to its trade through corporate machinery.
3. It has been further identified that LIC is one of the corporations to gain of profits both for LIC as well as for people since its inception.
4. There are many competitors are entering the world market to attract many individuals and covers the uncovered aspects of growing life risks. But, the one and only one gain is to its people to a large extent.

Finally it is considered as good booster to development throughout world.

# 4

# Service Industry Indian Banking Industry, Business Organisation and Business Environment

*Dr K. L. Narasimha Murty*

### *Abstract*

*An attempt has been made in this chapter to present the structural components of this bank in particular the aspects such as the machinery relating to Board of Directors, Executives at Corporate Office, General Managers, Deputy General Managers, Assistant General Managers, Executives at Zonal Offices, Inspection centres, Executives Heading Branches - India, Executives at Foreign Branches, Training College, Training centres, Executives in Regional Rural Banks sponsored by the bank, subsidiaries, public relations officers and Nodal Officer for customer service and principal code compliances offices at corporate office.*

## The Important Aspects are Dealt with the Following Heads

They are: 1. Historical Development, 2. Administratives: Executive Machinery of Indian Bank, 3. Executives @ Zonal Offices, 4. Various Deposit schemes, 5. Corporate Banking, 6. Merchant Banking and 7. Performance Highlights and conclusions.

## Indian Bank-Its Origin, Growth, Trend • Development in Economic Sector

An attempt has been made in this chapter to present the structural components of this bank in particular the aspects such as the machinery relating to Board of Directors, Executives at Corporate Office, General Managers, Deputy General Managers, Assistant General Managers, Executives at Zonal Offices, Inspection centres, Executives Heading Branches - India, Executives at Foreign Branches, Training College, Training centres, Executives in Regional Rural Banks sponsored by the bank, subsidiaries, public relations officers and Nodal Officer for customer service and principal code compliance offices at corporate office.

According to Chamber's twentieth century dictionary, 1972, Bank has been defined as, "institution for the keeping lending and exchanging, etc. of money or a stock of money fund or capital, the money the proprietor or other". It is clearly evident that what's bank? and what functions it does? these pertinent questions are answered sequentially and serially.

Further identified that the function of an industry clearly stated that it relates to systematic economic activity and branch of trade or manufacture (P. 668). In this context, the editor felt that and considered the metamorphosized form of bank as well as industry and coined it is as a major thematic function as Banking Industry or Industry-banking. Under its new form, the entire material has been presented systematically in the form of a case study: Indian Bank. Its Origin, Growth, trend and Developments in economic and financial segment/ sector (Sectoral Development) over a period of time. (Space-time).

## About the Bank

### Historical Development

The Indian Bank Limited, the predecessor to Indian Bank, had its genesis in the keen need felt for an Indian Bank, managed by Indians, on western lines in the wake of the widespread misery caused to the depositors by the failure of the house of Arbuternot & Co. in the year 1906. The late Hon'ble Shri V. Krishna Swamy Iyer conceived the idea of starting a bank in Chennai and called a meeting of prominent citizens, on November 3, 1906. Following his further efforts, the Indian Bank Limited was incorporated on March 5, 1907, with an authorised capital of ₹ 2000 lac. The bank commenced business on August 15, 1907.

The Bank began functioning in a portion of the Parry & Co. building in Chennai and a branch was opened in Madurai in December 1908, followed by branches in Mylapore, Triplicane and Esplanade, all in Chennai, in November 1911, June 1914 and July 1916 respectively.

The Bank celebrated its Silver Jubilee in 1932, when it had 10 branches and 5 sub-offices. Total deposits at the end of 1931 were ₹ 1.73 crore. The bank celebrated its Golden Jubilee on December, 27, 1957, under the presidentship of Dr. SWCP Rama Swamy Aiyar. The bank then had deposited of ₹ 32.56 Crore at its 120 branches, including branches in Singapore, Kaulalumpur and Penang, opened in September, November and December, 1941 respectively. A branch of Colombo was restarted in November, 1947 and a branch was offered in Malacca in 1951.

Along with 8 other banks, Indian Bank was nationalised on July 19, 1969. On the eve of Nationalisation, its paid up capital touched at ₹ 88.67 lac; resources at 1.18 crore; deposits at ₹ 89.66 crore; and advances at ₹ 64.94 crore.

The Bank celebrated its platinum Jubilee from August 15, 1981 to August 14, 1982. The celebrations were marked by release of a book on the genesis and growth of the Bank. The posts and telegraphs Department issued a special cover on August 14, 1982 and provided as special cancellation at a Post office in Chennai to work the platinum jubilee of the Bank.

The centenary year celebrations of the Bank was inaugurated by His Excellency, the President of India Shri APJ Abdul Kalam on 4th September, 2006. The conclusion function was celebrated on August 19, 2007 participated by Hon'ble Chief Minister of Tamil Nadu and Hon'ble Finance Minister, Government of India.

The Bank's deposits which amounted to ₹ 89.66 crore at the time of nationalisation have grown to ₹ 116,218 crore as on 30th September, 2011. During this period the Bank's advances have risen from ₹ 64.94 crore to ₹ 86,372 crore.

Now the Bank is a listed entity. The Bank unveiled a mission for the Bank during the centenary celebrations in September, 2006 as under :

To be a common Man's Bank.

To provide all Financial products and services to all customers under one roof, at affordable cost and in a fair and transparent manner.

The Bank lays thrust on "**financial inclusion**" and and has been evolving different "**delivery channels**" to achieve the same.

The Bank has a wide circle of patrons, both deposit and borrowal customers. There has been a progressive improvement in the number of accounts maintained by clients. The Bank continues to render quality service to its customers and enjoy good brand equity in the market.

In time with the national objective of expanding coverage of Bank network in rural areas, the Bank, after Nationalisation, has been improving its branch network in rural areas. The number of branches of the Bank in India has gone up from 219 at the time of Nationalisation to 1924 domestic as on September 30, 2011 of which 1043 are in rural and semi-urban areas.

The total number of employees in the Bank has recorded a manifold increases since nationalisation, from 3,500 to 19,230 as on September 30, 2011.

All branches have been brought under core banking solutions (CBS).

Besides, the full-fledged International Division at Head office, the Bank has three foreign branches, one in Singapore, and in Colombo and Jaffna in Sri Lanka. It also operates a Foreign currency banking unit in Colombo.

The Bank's logo consists of three arrows arranged around a central point. The three arrows represent respectively savings, investment and surplus and that savings lead to investment, investment to income and income in turn to surplus or savings, in a circular chain.

### 1. Administrative & Executive Machinery of Indian Bank

The executive body consists of one chairman and Managing Director, two Executive Directors, eight Directors and Executives at Corporate office headed by chairman & Managing Director besides two Executive Directors.

Seven General Managers heading various offices/departments such as: 1. Priority sector, 2. Credit, 3. Human Resource Management, 4. Accounts, Insurance, Expenditure, domestic operations, investor service cell, O & M and security control, 5. TMD/RMD, 6. Recovery and Legal, credit monitoring cell and 7. International Banking and Treasury.

Eleven Deputy General Managers have been heading various office/ departments. They are heading the departments such as:

1. New Initiative Dept. and credit monitoring cell
2. Inspection and control
3. Credit
4. Premises and Expenditure
5. Accounts
6. Compliance cell
7. RBDFI
8. Rural Banking
9. Recovery, Revival and Rehabilitation
10. Legal services; and

11. Investment and Treasury

21, Assistance General Managers have been heading various/different office/departments. They are :

1. MSME
2. O & M
3. MIS
4. Vigilance
5. Credit
6. RMD
7. Treasury
8. Human Resource Management
9. TMP
10 BOD
11. Inspection
12. Legal Services
13. Premises and Expenditure
14. Credit
15. International Division
16. ES to CMD/Board
17. Credit
18. Accounts
19. Rural Banking (F1)
20. TMD ; and
21. Security

**Executives at Zonal Offices**

There are 33 executives working as Executives at zonal offices across the India and Inspection centres are to a tune of seven @ Chennai, Coimbatore, Hyderabad, Kolkata, Mumbai, New Delhi and Thanjavur.

Executives heading branches in India are to a tune of 54 and two persons at Singapore, and one person at Colombo as DGM/CEO AGM and AGMCEO. One training college has been located at Indian Bank Management Academy for Growth and Excellence, MRC Nagar, Annamalaipuram, Chennai-28, Tamil Nadu and training centres are located in Bengaluru, Chandigarh, Chennai, Kolkata, Mumbai, New Delhi, Thanjavur, Thiruvanthapuram and Vijayawada.

Three executives are working in Regional Rural Banks sponsored by the Bank. Subsidiaries are to a tune of three to leed the Indbank Merchant Banking Services Ltd., Chennai, Indfund Management Ltd. Mumbai and Indbank Housing Ltd., Chennai. The top executive position has been occupied are such as GM/President and non-co-operation wholetime Director, Executive VP/AGM; GM/MD, AGM and GM/MD.

Three Public Relations Officers are working C.O., Chennai, ZO Mumbai and ZO: New Delhi.

Nodal Officers for customer service and principal code compliance officer, at Corporate Office, headed by General Manager (TMD/RMD) Avai Shanmugam Salai, Royapettah, Chennai.

## Steps for Know Your Customer (KYC)

1. Customer Acceptance.
2. Customer Identification.
3. Identification Documents to be submitted by customers for opening an accounts.
4. Towards name proof-photo identification and address proof.
5. Types of customers/accounts additional information/documents.
6. Quoting of PAN.
7. Furnishing of photographs.
8. Introduction of accounts to the Bank.
9. Relaxed KYC procedure.
10. KYC norms for Remittances within India. and;
11. Closure of accounts on account of non-co-operation from the customer.

## Various Deposit Schemes

1. Savings Bank.
2. Power Account for achievers (PAFA) Saving Bank scheme.
3. Saving Bank Platinum with sweep facility.
4. Vikas Savings Khata.
5. Current account.
6. Premium current A/C. with Sweep facility.
7. Supreme current Account.
8. Fixed Deposit.

9. Re-investment plan.
10. Special scheme for senior citizens.
11. IB Tax saver scheme.
12. Capital gains.
13. Facility deposit
14. Recurring Deposit
15. Variable RD
16. IB smart kid SR Account for children of age 1 day to less than 18 years.
17. IB Swarna Nidhi RD/IB Swarna Nidhi VRD; and
18. Tiny Deposit.

## CORPORATE BANKING

The Indian Banks Powerful Corporate banking deploy multiple channels to deliver integrated solutions for all financial challenges field by the corporates.

IB offers an exhaustive range of financial products and services that answers any business or market circumstances. Customer centric products are offered to suit the business sensitivities of each client and each business.

Branches are segmented as corporate, credit intensive, commercial and personal in order to cater to the needs of the varied customers.

Corporate Banking: IB is a one shop providing financial products/ services to wide range for large and medium customers, both domestic and exports.

Working capital financing: Assistance extended both as fund based and non-fund based facilities to corporates, partnership firms, proprietors concerns and all segments of industries and service sector-manufacturing infrastructure, healthcare, educational institutions, and exports etc.

Term Loan: To support capital expenditure for setting and new ventures as also for expansion, renovation, modernisation, brand building etc.

### Trade Finance

Trade finance is extended to retail/wholesale traders.

- To meet the working capital needs for trading activity.
- To meet the term loan requirement for purchase/setting up infrastructure like show cases, basic office amenities, purchase of delivery van etc.

Export Credit: Indian Bank extends the following facilities to eligible exporters.

- Pre-shipment credit
- Post-shipment credit.

## Other Overseas Transactions

- Buyer's credit and suppliers credit
- Booking of forward contracts
- Aquisition financing
- Project export finance.

Technological Upgradation Fund Scheme (TUFS): The Govt. of India, Ministry of Textiles introduced TWFS for textile and jute industries on April 1, 1999 for a period of five years subsequently extended by three years, in the budget for 2007-08, the same was extended for a further period of five years from 31-3-2007.

The scheme is intended to facilitate induction of state-of-the art or near state-of-the art technology in the existing and new units. Indian Bank is designated as one of the nodal agency for operation of the scheme.

***Non-Fund limits:***

*Guarantees:* IB offer to issue various types of guarantees, performance, financial, bidbond, tenders, customs etc.

Letter of credits: For exporters/importers the Bank offers letter of credit service like opening, negotiating or discounting, advising, confirming, standby LC, advising of export letter of credit etc.

Trade related inland letter of credits (fight) Usance are issued by the bank based on the trade requirements of the customer.

## Merchant Banking

Loan Syndication: The syndication desk in the business of assisting companies to raise resources from the institutional market. The products offered and syndicated by the desk include:

- Project finance and term loans.
- Short-term loans-working capital and medium term loans.

Bankers to the Issue: Indian Bank is also one of the leading merchant Bankers, offering specialised services to PSW's, state owned corporations, local statutory bodies and corporate sector. They hold SEBI registration certificate to act as;

"Bankers to an Issue" with network of branches to handle Capital Market" related assignments.

The other services offered are:

- Refund bankers
- Debenture trusteeship

ASBA: Application supportal by Blocked Amount.

ASBA is an application for subscribing to an issue containing an authorisation to block the application money in a bank account Indian Bank in its quest to offer investor friendly services to the customers has become a self certified syndicate bank (SCSB) with SEBI and had launched the ASBA services initially in 12 branches.

## Wealth Management Services

Yet another initiative from Indian Bank to help you realise your dreams.

Managing wealth is a challenge even for the informed, in the complex world of financial markets. Indian Bank can help in managing wealth towards fulfillment of life goals. The experienced team would assist (Person's). In preparing the ideal financial plan matching with (Person's) cash flows, risk, profile, time horizon and financial goals. IB services are available in all major centres across India.

IB would be happy to demystify the intricacies of investment planning, retirement planning, taxation planning and insurance planning for (you), at your doorstep. Get in touch with the nearest branch of Indian Bank to arrange a visit by IB wealth Managers.

**7. Performance Highlights**

**Table 4.1**

| *Particulars* | *31-03-16* | *31-03-17* | *31-03-18* | *31-03-19* | *31-03-20* |
|---|---|---|---|---|---|
| Total Business | 310918 | 314654 | 371020 | 429972 | 466116 |
| Deposits (Global) | 178286 | 182509 | 208294 | 242076 | 260226 |
| Advances (Global) | 132632 | 132145 | 162726 | 187896 | 205890 |
| Investments (Gross) | 53418 | 67956 | 71232 | 68117 | 82622 |
| Interest Income | 16244 | 16040 | 17113 | 19185 | 21405 |
| Non Interest Income | 1781 | 2211 | 2406 | 1883 | 3312 |
| Total Income | 18025 | 18251 | 19519 | 21068 | 24717 |
| Interest Expenses | 11798 | 10894 | 10850 | 12167 | 13798 |

*Contd...*

| | | | | | |
|---|---|---|---|---|---|
| Operating Expenses | 3195 | 3356 | 3668 | 4020 | 4421 |
| Total Expenditure | 14993 | 14250 | 14518 | 16187 | 18219 |
| Operating Profit | 3032 | 4001 | 5001 | 4881 | 6498 |
| Net Profit | 711 | 1406 | 1259 | 322 | 753 |
| Cost of Deposits (%) | 6.76 | 6.03 | 5.40 | 5.28 | 5.34 |
| Yield on Advances (%) | 9.83 | 9.17 | 8.50 | 8.45 | 8.46 |
| Net Interest Margin (%) | 2.33 | 2.59 | 2.90 | 2.96 | 2.87 |
| Return on Assets (%) | 0.36 | 0.67 | 0.53 | 0.12 | 0.26 |
| Equity Share Capital | 480 | 480 | 480 | 480 | 609 |
| Reserves & Surplus (Excluding Revaluation Reserve) | 12998 | 13981 | 15347 | 15813 | 18493 |
| Net Worth | 13478 | 14461 | 15827 | 15785 | 18357 |
| Gross NPA (%) | 6.66 | 7.47 | 4.37 | 7.11 | 6.87 |
| Net NPA (%) | 4.20 | 4.39 | 3.81 | 3.75 | 3.13 |
| Capital Adequacy Ratio: | | | | | |
| -Basel –II | 13.67 | | | | |
| -Basel – III | 13.20 | 13.64 | 12.55 | 1321 | 14.12 |
| Earning Per Share ₹ | 14.81 | 29.27 | 26.21 | 6.70 | 14.33 |
| Book Value per Share ₹ | 290.63 | 301.10 | 329.53 | 328.64 | 301.53 |
| Dividend Per Equity share | 1.50 | 6.00 | -- | -- | -- |
| No. of branches | 2565 | 2682 | 2823 | 2875 | 2890 |
| No. of employees | 20140 | 20924 | 19843 | 19604 | 18758 |
| Business per employee (₹In lakhs) | 1531 | 1486 | 1856 | 2174 | 2462 |

7.Performance Highlights could be seen from Table 4.1 Gross Observations are stated in the following paragraphs.

1. It is seen from Table 4.1, that the total business rose from ₹ 3,10,918 crores to ₹ 4,6,116 crores.
2. The global deposits from ₹ 1,78,286 to ₹ 2,60,226 crores.
3. Global advances from ₹ 1,32,632 to ₹ 2,05,890.
4. The gross investments from ₹ 53,418 to ₹ 82,622 crores.
5. The interest income from ₹ 16,244 to ₹ 21,405 crores
6. The non-interest income from ₹ 1781 to ₹ 3,312
7. The total income from ₹ 18,025 to ₹ 24,717 crores.
8. Interest expenses from ₹ 11,798 to ₹ 13,798 crores.
9. Operating expenses from ₹ 3195 to 4,421 crores.
10. The net profit from ₹ 711 crores to 753. During the 2017, it has been registered as 1406 where in 2018, it has been decreased to a tune of ₹ 153 crores and suddenly, it has been further reduced by ₹ 322 and a slight increase of ₹ 753 crores further.
11. The cost of deposits percentage has been slowly decreased from 6.76 to 5.34 percent.

12. The yield on advances has been registered from 9.63 percent to 8.46 percent with slight undulations.
13. Net interest margin from 2.33 percent to 2.87 percent. It is observed that only 0.54 percent.
14. Return assets from 0.36 percent to 0.26, over a period of time particularly during the year 2019, it has been reduced to 0.12 percent.
15. Equity share capital was constant for years, there is no change in its volumes but during the year 2020, it has been registered at 603 Crores. This is perhaps, due to the bank policies as well it has it effect on share holders share capital or contribution of share.
16. Reserves & Surplus ( excluding Revaluation Resource) has been registered as 12,998 non during 2016, where as it has been further increased amount of ₹ 6,000 crores.
17. Net water has been registered as ₹ 13,478, crores and there is an increase by ₹ 5,000 crores.
18. Gross NPA percent leads from 6.66 percent to 6.87 percent during 17, 18 and 19, it has been registered as 7.47, 7.37 and 7.1, respectively.
19. Net NPA percent has been on an increase by 0.19 percent from time, it has been reduced 0.58 percent and further decreased to a tune of 3.75 percent and 3.13 percent.
20. Capital adequacy Ratio at Base 11 was 13.67 and at base 111 by 13.20 during 2016 and an increase by 0.44 percent. During 2018, it was 12.55 and it has been shown an increase by 0.74 percent and almost 2.00 percent.
21. No. of branches from 2565 to 2890 and it is on the increasing scale, perhaps, it is due to the demand as well as efficient services rendered sufficiently to the public.
22. The number of employees were from 20,140 to 20,924 where as, it was reduced and has been reducing day by day from 19,843 to 19,604. From 19,604 to 18758. The number of employees have been reducing due to the bank policies as well as allowing them to retire voluntarily from their active service. The Major reason for this trend may be interpreted as the interception of banks policies on employees. This is to say that employer and employees relations may be strained slightly.
23. Finally, business per employee (₹ in lakhs) from 1531 to 1488 (2017), from 1856 to 2174, there is a slight increase in its contribution and the further area of progress from 2174 to 2462.

## 8. Conclusion

It is concluded that the Indian Bank has been increasing services both vertically and horizontally with slight changes. The performance is always worth while and praiseworthy in banking sector for providing services to their customers. Latest technological methods have been adopted in the banking to reach its progress to the highest level in various fields from time to time covering the uncovered areas with innovative methods for achieving good performance in the Banking sector.

# 5

# Commercial Activity and Profile of the New India Assurance Co. Ltd.

***Dr K. L. Narasimha Murty***

### Abstract

*An attempt has been made in this chapter to present the commercial activity and profile of the New India Assurance Company Limited which is an India's premier General Insurance Company in trade, commerce and Industry. The entire work is related to the following aspects.*

### They Are

1. New India Network, Global and India
2. New India Assurances' 20 point Action plan
3. Our Vision and Mission and
4. Indian Insurance Detailed account is related to
    1. Policies are available at present from local to global public
    2. New India network, Global and India (List has been enlisted)
    3. Achievements
    4. Office protection shield policy and
    5. Conclusions.

### 4. Commerce

Assurance: The profile of the New India Assurance Co. Ltd. India is premier General Insurance Company in Trade, Commerce and Industry.

In this chapter an attempt has been made to present the profile of the New India Assurance Company Limited which is the India's premier

General Insurance Company in trade, commerce and Industry. The entire work is related to: 1. New India Network Global and India. 2. New India Assurance's 20 point Action plan. 3. Our Vision and our Mission and 4. Indian Insurance.

Policies available at present from local to global public:

1. Griha Suvidha policy – at home at Ease.
2. Long term Motor two wheeler package policy.
3. Corporate social responsibility.
4. Project Insurance policy.
5. Providing social security.
6. Aviation Insurance.
7. Marine Cargo Insurance Policy.
8. Business Credit shield.
9. Fix Insurance Policy.
10. Motor policy.
11. Mediclaim policy.
12. Achievements.
13. Shopkeepers policy
14. Floater mediclaim
15. Personal Accident Policy.
16. Director's and Officer's Liability Policy.
17. Office Protection Shield Policy.

The profile of the above aspects are presented in the following paragraphs:

The New India Assurance Co. Ltd., India's premier General Insurance Company has been registered and headed at New India Assurance Building, 87, M.G. Road, Fort, Mumbai – 400 001 with www.newindia.co.in. The Board of Directors and Corporate Management headed by one chairman-cum-Managing Director, three Directors, 10 General Managers, one Chief Vigilance Officer, Appointed Actuary, 13 Deputy General Managers and one company secretary.

2. New India Network Global and India are presented, which is as follows:

**Table 5.1: Foreign Branches Country and Branches**

| | |
|---|---|
| 1. Japan | • Tokyo<br>• Nagoya<br>• Hiroshima<br>• Okayama<br>• Sappora<br>• Osaka |
| 2. Honkong | • Hongkong |
| 3. Philippines | • Manik |
| 4. Thailand | • Bangkok |
| 5. Australia | • Sydney |
| 6. Fiji | • Sura<br>• Lautoka<br>• Labasa<br>• Nadi |
| 7. Maceritins | • Port Louis |
| 8. U.K. | • London<br>• Ipswich |
| 9. New Zealand | • Auckland |

## Foreign Agencies

### Country and Branches

| | |
|---|---|
| 1. Abu Dhabi | • Abu Dhabi |
| 2. Dubai | • Dubai |
| 3. Bahrain | • Bahrain |
| 4. Kuwait | • Kuwait |
| 5. Oman | • Muscat |
| 6. Dutch Carribheen | • Aruba |
| 7. Netherlands Autives | • Curacao |

### Subsidiary Companies: Country and Branches

| | |
|---|---|
| 1. Nigeria | • Lagos<br>• Kano<br>• Port Harcourt |
| 2. Trinidad & Tobago | • Port of Spain |

3. St. Lucia • Castries
4. Dominica • Roseah
5. St. Maarten • Philipsburg
6. Guyana • Guyana
7. Anguilla • Anguilla
8. Sierra Leone • Freetown

## Representative Offices

1. Myanmar * Myanmar

Associates Companies

1. Singapore 2. Kenya — Nairobi and
3. Saudi Arabia

India:

| | | |
|---|---|---|
| 1. Ahmedabad | 2. Bengaluru | 3. Baroda |
| 4. Bhopal | 5. Bhubaneswar | 6. Chandigarh |
| 7. Chennai | 8. Chennai LCBO | 9. Coimbatore |
| 10. Dehradun | 11. Delhi ROI | 12. Delhi ROII |
| 13. Delhi LCBO | 14. Delhi Auto Hub | 15. Ernakulam |
| 16. Guwahati | 17. Hubli | 18. Hyderabad |
| 19. Hyderabad LCBO | 20. Jaipur | 21. Kanpur |
| 22. Kolkata | 23. Kolkata LCBO | 24. Ludhiana |
| 25. Madurai | 26. Mumbai LCBOI | 27. Mumbai LCBO-II |
| 28. Mumbai ROI | 29. Mumbai ROII | 30. Mumbai RO-III |
| 31. Mumbai ROIV | 32. Mumbai ROV | 33. Nagpur |
| 34. Patna | 35. Pune | 36. Raipur |
| 37. Surat | 38. Visakhapatnam | |

2. New India Assurance 20 Point Action Plan :
   - Each RO/DO/BO to grow @ 25% each LCBO and Broker specialised offices to grow @ 40%.
   - Insured claims ration of every office to come down at least by 5% on earned premium as compared to previous year.
   - Every operating office should show an operating surplus on earned premium basis.
   - Settle non-suit claims expartiously 75% of non-suit claims to be settled in 30 days. Non-suit claims of a quarter to be settled before the end of the next year. No suit claims pending for

more than a year to be personally reviewed by RO/LCBO in charge and settled early.

- Claims hubs to be customer centric and achieve greater levels of customer service. Employees of claims hubs to be trained regularly. Regional incharges should visit both non-suit and TP claims hubs at least once in a year to review their performance.

6. Motor TP claims settlement ratio to be 40%, 50% of those settlements to be compromise settlements through Lok Adalats and other conciliation method settle 20% of pending cases through National Mega Lok Adalats.
7. All pending TP claim files to be classified into fit for unfit after building up the files. All efforts to be made to settle fit files through conciliation. Files where we have valid defences should be contested effectively to win them.
8. Each DO/BO/MO to recruit at least 20 Agents during the year. Agent Managers to play a very important role in recuring, mortering, training and motivating towards better performance. Agency channel should be personally driven, regional incharges to achieve 40% growth.
9. Development officers, AO(D)S, AM(D)S to be fully emergised. They should grow at least 25%. Two training programmes of two days each to be organised during the year. Annual meet at RO level to be organised.
10. Broker relationships to be strengthened and this channel to grow at 40%. Relationship Managers to be active in the market and should visit brokers regularly.
11. Auto tie-up to be enlarged. To cover all declares in all OEM things and also others. No blocking of any patal by close monitoring and better service levels. This channel to grow at 50%.
12. Liaison with all Bank Head Offices for a tie-up when opened up. Each RO to enroll at least 56 operative banks as corporate or micro insurance agents. Bank assurance business to grow at 30%.
13. Micro insurance business including Micro/small/medium Enterprises business as per new Micro Insurance Regulations to be fully tapped through agents and Micro insurance agents. Each RO should recruit atleast 500 micro insurance agents during the year.

14. Each RO to add 10 new Micro offices during the year. The Micro offices to grow at 50% Micro office in changes to be trained twice during the year.
15. Special focus on growth of Retail Health, Miscellaneous (TB, NTB, PA, Liability, Rural) lines of business during the year. Three times to grow at 50%.
16. Every employee to undergo at least one training programme during the year. Regional training centres to be revamped, activated and should have full time incharge. They should be centres of excellence in training and focus on training our employees in a big way.
17. Accounts of each quarter to be finalised before end of the month succeeding the quarter. Annual Accounts to be finalised before the end of April. Audit comments of statutory Auditors to be analysed, resolved and not repeated.
18. Grievances of customers to be resolve within 15 days grievances committee to be active in quick resolution of grievances.
19. Each Regional/Divisional/branch in charge to analyse MIS of his office everyday and take appropriate steps for improving efficiency.
20. All major customers are to be given portals with personal lines of business including motor and health for their employees.

**Our Vision**

To be the most respected, trusted and preferred non-life insurer in the Global markets more operate.

**Our Mission**

To develop General Insurance Business in the best interest of the community.

To provide financial security to Individuals, trade, commence and all other segments of the society by offering insurance products and services of high quality at affordable cost.

(1) Medical claim policy – Attractive cover at affordable price –

| Tax Benefit | Hospital | Get well | 74+Day | Covers |
|---|---|---|---|---|
| 80D | Cash | Benefit | care | entire |
| | | | Procedure | family |

(2) Griha Suvidha Policy – Affordable Home Insurance Plans starting ₹ 1125/- only.

Home Insurance for your valued possessions.

Peace of mind for you.

Coverage under the policy.

| Fire, Flood Earthquake & more | Burglarly House Breaking & Theft | Valuable & Jewellery | Break down of domestic Applicables | Tele-vision & Desktop |
|---|---|---|---|---|

(3) Long term motor two-wheeler package policy.

Save 30% on your 3 years two wheeler Insurance Payable and get peace of mind for 3 years.

(4) Corporate Social Responsibility.

Project Insurance Policy.

**Highlights:**

- Designed for small and big projects against accident materials damages.
- Policies arranged to suit individual needs of clients to provide scamless coverage from start to end.
- Can be extended to cover advances loss of profit due to accident related delays.
- Policy can be designed to provide all risks and customized coverage to address specific needs of the insured.

3. **Achievements:**

   1. Global premium of ₹ 16,050 crores.
   2. Rated 'A-Excellent (stable)' by A.M. Best.
   3. Crisil rating 'AAA (Stable outlook)'.
   4. World-wide presence 28 countries.
   5. Highest Solvency ratio.
   6. Highest Net Worth.
   7. Highest Asset base ₹ 61,720 crores.
   8. Largest motor, health, liability and property insurer.

4. **Office protection shield policy:**

   The following are highlights and trust.

**Highlights:**

1. Multiperil policy to meet each and every requirement of office establishment.

2. Can be given to various professionals like doctors, engineers with modifications.

**Properties Covered**

Covers employees, office furniture, appliances, equipments, etc.

**Period Covered:**

Fire, burglary and Natural calamities and many more risks.

Stay protected and safe.

Subject to terms and conditions.

Trusted by Millions.

1. India's only non-life Insurance Co. Rated 'A-Excellent (Stable), by A. M. Best.
2. Crisis rating 'AAA (Stable outlook),
3. Total assets: ₹ 61,720 crores ($ 9876 Mn)
4. Net worth ₹ 9722 crores ($ 1556 Mn)
5. Gross premium ₹ 16050 crs ($ 2625 (N); and
6. Global network: More than 2200 offices.

5. **Conclusion:**
   (1) It is concluded that the one and only one Indias only non Life Insurance Co. so far.
   (2) Intensive attempts of entrepreneurs to do their business competitively. There are parallel companies have been growing (for life) butter business pattern could be identified in its performance.
   (3) Both local and global commercial activity (commerce) has been on its wings and work restlessly through out the year.
   (4) Finally, we should appreciate the vision and missions work of NiA, which stands as an example to nonlife insurance Co. The network is quite well to continue its business both local and international (Global) level. New India pays ₹ 300 crores as dividend for 2014-15.

# 6

# Growth of E-Commerce in India

***Dr C.S.S.R.L. Hanumanth Rao***
***Dr Ch. Karuna***

## Abstract

*E-commerce is one of the fastest growing segments in the Indian Economy. The rise of the Indian economy has not given millions of Indians the privilege of technology but also enabled them to utilise the internet in a way to have a great shopping experience. Today the business world is dynamic, it is changing almost every minute, the technological advancements and globalisation has caused extensive amounts of competition, bringing the ability of producing better products and services that cater more precise needs and wants of the customers than ever before. With the new advancements that are taking place, people can have easy access to goods and services than ever before, which is because of concept of e-commerce or electronic commerce. E-commerce has brought people and the rest of the world together, creating a lot of opportunities, competition and also challenges. In the present world customers are going online to check reviews, offers, prices and availability of the products to save time. Having online purchases could drive in more business. Ecommerce evolves into an established market worldwide. According to Statistics, in 2017, it was recorded as 1.66 billion people worldwide purchased goods online; in addition to that outstanding statistic, global e-retail sales have reached $2.3 trillion (US). The figure has almost estimated to be doubled by 2021, hitting approximately $4.48 trillion (US). Despite its explosive growth, there are challenges faced by e-commerce namely economic, social, technological and legal challenges. The survival of the e-commerce firms in a highly dynamic environment becomes a challenging task when coupled with the cutthroat competition prevailing in the sector. The onus then lies on the firms to constantly adopt and innovate while providing an information rich and seamless experience to ensure customer loyalty. This study attempts to explore the evolution of e-commerce in India and identifies various challenges to as well the factors responsible for the future growth and development of e-commerce.*

***Keywords:***
*E-commerce, Internet, Growth Issues.*


- Senior Assistant Professor, Department of Statistics, M.R. (A) College, Vizianagaram
- Senior Assistant Professor, Department of Commerce, M.R.P.G. College, Vizianagaram


## Introduction

In today's world, e-commerce has acquired importance. India has been experiencing significant growth in e-commerce, with many small companies mushrooming and a few giants striving to take over the huge Indian e-commerce market. Flipkart, Amazon, Snapdeal, Uber, Ola, etc. are a few examples. Some of them are said to be home-grown, in the sense that their promoters have been Indians. But later they attracted foreign equity, and ultimately are dominated by foreign investors. As per the law of the land, foreign investment is not allowed in e-commerce. So, these companies got foreign investment in the name of the marketplace model. In this way, while running full-fledged e-commerce businesses, they were circumventing the law. Electronic commerce or e-commerce is a business model that lets firms and individuals buy and sell things over the Internet. Propelled by rising smart phone penetration, the launch of 4G networks and increasing consumer wealth, the Indian e-commerce market is expected to grow to US$ 200 billion by 2026 from US$ 38.5 billion in 2017. India's e-commerce revenue is expected to jump from US$ 39 billion in 2017 to US$ 120 billion in 2020, growing at an annual rate of 51%, the highest in the world. The Indian e-commerce industry has been on an upward growth trajectory and is expected to surpass the US to become the second-largest e-commerce market in the world by 2034.

## Objectives of the Study

- To know the concept and the prospects of e–commerce
- To study the market size and the growth of e-commerce in India
- To focus on the issues faced by e-commerce players and the government initiatives

**Research Methodology:** The paper is based on the secondary data. The secondary data was collected from published books, journals, research papers, magazines, newspapers, internet and official statistical documents. The study is qualitative in nature.

## Review of Literature

1. **Gupta (2014):** In his paper "E-Commerce: Role of e-commerce in today's business", presents a comprehensive definition of e-commerce while isolating it from e-business. The paper enlists the different e-commerce models i.e. B2B, B2C, B2G and C2C, narratively analysing the nitty gritties of each.
2. **Rina (2016):** In her articles also elaborated the different applications of e-commerce in "Challenges and Future Scope of E–commerce in India", at the same time, defining the degree to which they are operational in the country.
3. **Dr. Anukrati Sharma (2013):** The article entitled "A study on E-commerce and Online Shopping: Issues and Influences". In this article an attempt is made to study the recent trends, influences, preferences of customers towards E-commerce and online shopping and to give the suggestions for the improvement in online shopping websites. The study found that, most of the people who are engaged in making the decision of purchasing goods are in the age of 21-30 years. While making the websites for online shopping, it must be designed in a strategic way.
4. **Abhijit Mitra (2013):** The article entitled "E-Commerce in India-A review". In this article an attempt is made to study the present status and facilitators of E-Commerce in India, analyzed the present trends of E-Commerce in India and examined the barriers of E-Commerce in India. The study found that, there has been a rise in the number of companies taking up E-Commerce in the recent past. The study also found that, the major Indian portal sites have also shifted towards E-Commerce instead of depending on advertising revenue.
5. **Nisha Chanana and Sangeeta Goele (2012):** The article entitled "Future of E-Commerce in India". In this article an attempt is made to study the overview of the future of E-commerce in India and discussed the future growth segments in India's of E-commerce. The study found that, various factors that were essential for future growth of Indian E-commerce. Further the study also found that, the overall E-commerce will increase exponentially in the coming years in the emerging market of India.
6. **Sarbapriya Ray (2011):** The articles entitled "Emerging Trends of E-commerce in India: Some Crucial Issues Prospects and challenges". In this article an attempt is made to present a snapshot

of the evolution of E-commerce business indicating the chronological order, category of E-commerce business, description of organisations involved in E-business in India. The study found that, the role of government should have to be provided a legal framework for E-commerce so that while domestic and international trade were allowed to expand their horizons, basic rights such as privacy, intellectual property, prevention of fraud, consumer protection etc are taken care of.

## Concept of E-Commerce

1. **Multi Product E-Commerce:** Some internet portals provide almost all categories of goods and services in a single site; they are targeting customers of every possible product or service. Indian E-Commerce portals provide goods and services in a variety of categories like apparel and accessories for men and women, health and beauty products, books and magazines, computers and peripherals, vehicles, collectibles, software, consumer electronics, household appliances, jewellery, audio/video entertainment goods, gift articles, real estate and services, business and opportunities, employment, travel tickets, matrimony etc. Examples: www.indiayplaza.com, www.thebestofindia.com, www.khoj.com., www.sify.com, www.rediff.com, www.indiatimes.com. etc.
2. **Single Product E-Commerce:** Some Indian portals/websites deal in a specialised way or field.

## Examples

In automobiles, the portals are http://www.indiacar.com and http:/www.automatindia.com, on these sites, we can buy and sell four wheelers and two wheelers new as well as old vehicles online. Some of the services they provide are car research and reviews, online evaluation, technical specifications, vehicle insurance, vehicle finance, dealer locator etc.

- In stock and shares markets some of the sites are http:/www/.equitymaster.com,http:/www.5paisa.com. Some of the services offered to the registered members are online buying or dealing of stock and share, market analysis and research, company information, comparison of companies, research on equity and mutual funds, tracking market trends etc.
- In real estate, the portals like http://www.indiaproperties.com. This website facilitate online dealing in real estate, they offer outright purchase or lease of a property through their portal. They also

provide information on new properties as well as for resale. Some of the allied services are housing finance, insurance companies' architects and interior designers, property management consultant services etc.

- In travel and tourism industry a major government of India portal is http://www.tourismindia.com. The tourist destination sites are categorised according to the themes like eco-themes pertains to jungles, flora.

**Phases of Evolution of E-commerce**

The different phases of evolution of e-commerce were presented under first phase and second phase, these are presented in the following paragraphs:

## First Phase (1995 to 2005)

The introduction of internet in India in 1995 marked the beginning of the first wave of e-commerce in the country. Moreover, the economic liberalisation after the launch of reforms in 1991 attracted Multi-National Corporations (MNCs) and caused for a significant growth in Information Technology (IT) industry. The implementation of liberalisation policies led to the demise of the license regime, high taxes and import restrictions and facilitated the growth of Small and Medium Enterprises (SMEs). The IT industry and SMEs were the early adopters of internet that led to the development of B2B, job searches and marital portals are stated in the following paragraphs.

**B2B Directory:** India's first online B2B directory was launched in 1996. The liberalisation of the country's international trade policies was the main factor that enhanced the growth of B2B virtual portals.

**Virtual Marital:** In 1996, the first virtual matrimonial portal was launched in India, which transformed the perceptions about the matchmaking process from "*marriages are made in heaven*" to "*marriages are made in cyber space*".

**Virtual Recruitment:** India's virtual recruitment industry took shape in 1997. The growth of the services sector, following the launch of economic reforms in 1991, resulted in the creation of additional jobs and the internet proved to be an efficient medium that allowed employers and job seekers to connect each other.

The first wave of e-commerce in India was characterised by low internet penetration, a small online shopping user base, slow internet speed, low consumer acceptance of online shopping and inadequate logistics infrastructure. The IT downturn in 2000 led to the collapse of more than 1,000 e-commerce businesses in India, as a result there was a muted activity in India between 2000 and 2005.

## Second Phase (2005 to Present)

After the muted activity during 2000 to 2005, there has been a significant development in e-business, specifically in the areas of travelling, retailing, group purchasing, societal interaction, etc. as presented below.

**Air Travel:** The entry of Low Cost Carriers (LCCs) in the Indian flying sector in 2005 marked the beginning of the second phase of e-commerce in India. Travel developed as the biggest segment and individuals began trusting on internet to search for travel-related information and to book tickets. As a result of which, the success of the online travel segment made consumers comfortable with shopping through online, this paved the way for a massive improvement of online retail.

**Virtual Travel:** The decision of LCCs like Indigo and Spice Jet to sell their tickets online and through third parties enabled the development of Online Travel Agents (OTAs). Prior to the entry of LCCs in 2005-2006, air travel was considered a luxury and meant only for the rich and corporate travel. LCCs changed the scenario by making air travel affordable for a large number of people. They developed their own websites and partnered with OTAs to distribute their tickets online and, thus, contain costs. The Indian Railways had already implemented the e-ticket booking initiative by the time LCCs commenced their online ticket booking schemes.

**Virtual Selling:** The growth of online retail was partly driven by changing urban consumer lifestyle and the need for convenience of shopping at home. This segment established in the second movement in 2007 with the launch of multiple online retail websites. New businesses were driven by entrepreneurs who looked to differentiate themselves by enhancing customer experience and establishing a strong market presence.

**Group Purchasing:** In the initial period of 2010, the group buying and daily deals models became a global trend, Group-buying sites have seen a significant rise in the number of unique visitors and membership which enhanced the e-business.

**Societal Interacting:** In the recent years, social networking gained steam in the Indian online space and it has gone on to become an integral part of people's lives. Initially it is used for staying connected with friends but now social networking websites have emerged as an anchor in any company's digital strategy. Termed as social commerce, it is an important avenue for e-commerce players to reach out to target customers. Companies have started establishing their presence in the social media space for branding activities, connecting with customers for feedback and advertising new product launches.

In this context, it is noticed that e-commerce form of marketing (Rath & Samal, 2013) is a modern technique used by business firms, companies and industries for doing their business work through the e-net system in order to enhance their business plans, strategies for better product promotion as well as increasing economic health of various industries, firms, organisations, etc.

After understanding the concept and evolution of E-commerce, an attempt has been made to review the past studies related to the study to establish the relevance of the study and the same is presented chronologically in brief way in the following paragraphs.

**Types of E-commerce:** The major different types of E-commerce are as follows:

- **Business to Business (B2B):** Business to Business E-commerce refers to the full spectrum of E-commerce that can occur between two organisations B2B. E-commerce includes purchasing and procurement, supplier management, inventory management, channel management, sales activities, payment management, and service and support. A few B2B pioneers are Chemdex (www.chemdex.com), Fastparts (www.fastparts.com) and Free Markets (www.freemarkets.com)
- **Business to Consumer (B2C):** Business to Consumer E-commerce refers to exchanges between Business and Consumer. Direct dealing between Business and Consumer has always existed, but with the E-commerce such transactions have gained further momentum.
- **Traditional B2C model:** Manufacturer ⇒ Retailer ⇒ Consumer
- **Online B2C Model:** Manufacturer/Retailer ⇐ Consumer
- **Examples:** Amazon.com, Yahoo.com and Schwab.com. Similar activities transactions that occur in business to business, E-commerce also take place in the business to consumer context. However, all customer facing activities are typically tracked. These include sales activities, consumer search, service and support.
- **Consumer to Consumer (C2C):** Consumer to Consumers involves transactions between and among consumers. These

exchanges may or may not include third party involvement. Traditionally consumers have had dealings with other consumers, but only few of those activities were in a commercial sense. E-commerce has made it possible to bring together strangers and providing a platform for them to trade on.

- **Consumer to Business (C2B):** Consumer to Business is relatively a new model of commerce and is a reverse of the traditional commerce models. Here, consumers provide service or goods to businesses and create value for the business. Consumers can band together to form and present themselves as a buyer group to businesses in a consumer to business relationship. These groups may be economically motivated as with the demand aggregator. This type of transaction can be seen in internet forums where consumers provide product development ideas and product review; these are used for product advertisement.
- **Business to Business to Consumer (B2B2C):** A variant of the B2B2C model wherein there is an additional intermediary business to assist the first business transact with the end consumer. Here, it is poised to much better in a web based commerce with reduced costs of having an intermediary. ***Example:*** Flipkart is one of the most successful E-commerce portals which provide a platform for consumers to purchase a different variety of products like electronic goods, apparels, books and music CDs.

**Functions of E-Commerce:**

- **Communication function:** Aimed at the delivery of information and/or documents to facilitate business transactions. ***Example:*** *E-Mail.*
- **Process management function:** Covers the automation and improvements of business processes.

  ***Example:*** networking two computers together.
- **Service management function:** Application of technology to improve the quality of service.

  ***Example:*** Federal Express website to track shipments and schedule.
- **Transaction capabilities:** Provides the ability to buy/sell on the internet or some other online services.

  ***Example:*** Amazon.com.

**Prospects of E-Commerce**

- The process of e-commerce enables sellers to come closer to customers that lead to increased productivity and perfect competition. The customer can also choose between different sellers and buy the most relevant products as per the requirements, preferences, and budget. Moreover, customers now have access to virtual stores 24/7.

- E-commerce also leads to significant transaction cost reduction for consumers.
- E-commerce has emerged as one of the fast-growing trade channels available for the cross-border trade of goods and services.
- It provides a wider reach and reception across the global market, with minimum investments. It enables sellers to sell to a global audience and also customers to make a global choice. Geographical boundaries and challenges are drastically reduced.
- Through direct interaction with final customers, this e-commerce process cuts the product distribution chain to a significant extent. A direct and transparent channel between the producer or service provider and the final customer is made. This way products and services that are created to cater to the individual preferences of the target audience.
- Customers can easily locate products since e-commerce will be one store set up for all the customers business needs.
- The growth in the e-commerce sector can boost employment, increase revenues from export, increase tax collection by ex-chequers, and provide better products and services to customers in the long-term.

**Market size of e-commerce in India**

- India has an internet users base of about 450 million as of July 2017, about 40 percent of the population. This number is expected to be 730 million by the end of 2020. Despite being the second-largest user base in world, only behind China. The *penetration* of e-commerce is low compared to markets like the United States of America or France. However, by the end of 2021 it is expected to increase to 829 million but is growing, and adding around 6 million new entrants every month. The industry consensus is that growth is at an inflection point. In 2017, the largest e-commerce companies in India were *Flipkart*, *Snapdeal* and *Amazon*. In 2018, Amazon beat Flipkart and was recorded the biggest e-commerce in India in terms of revenue.

**Number of Internet Population in India**

India is gradually becoming the country with highest number of internet literate population in the world and the internet penetration is largely driven by mobile phones, with some of the cheapest and most basic hand-sets currently offering access to the internet.

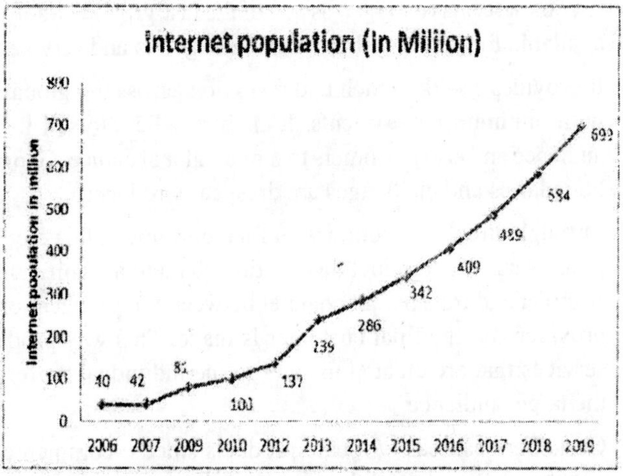


As per data released by Telecom Regulatory Authority of India (TRAI), India's total internet subscribers stood at 238.71 million as of December 31, 2013. Due to high internet penetration in India, the adaptability of online shopping and better shopping experiences offered by the e-commerce websites among Indians have increased

***Indian E-Commerce market size.***

*Source:* Govt. CISCO.

rapidly. The above graph represents the year-wise internet users in India, growing at a CAGR (Compound Annual Growth Rate) of 20 percent. And as a result the numbers of internet users is expected to reach the figure of 700 million by 2019.

The above figure shows the key market and technology trends in e-commerce which indirectly will lead to the increasing growth of e-commerce in India:

1. Online retailers would have to leverage technology to the fullest, and by developing strategies through analytics produced using big data would help in making customers feel special and increase brand loyalty.
2. Cash on Delivery (CoD) accounts for up to 60 percent of transactions, according to Internet and Mobile Association of India.
3. The increasing adoption and use of Smartphone's enable businesses to collect large amount of data on consumers for utilisation to perform target-based marketing and advertising.
4. Product and service feedback via social madia channels have an impression and good effect on the minds of the larger customer base.
5. It is necessary to create high quality and SEO-friendly e-commerce site for building long relationship with customers with exclusive content help to increase the profit volume ratio.
6. The service of providing 24 hours chat assistance to give instance response and guidance to customers has raised the quality of online shopping experience.

Mobile advertising route has the potential to increase online shoppers as they are more comfortable with using mobile devices for browsing and shopping, they are now more open to getting messages from brands via their mobiles.

## Key Drivers in Indian E-commerce Growth are

- **Increased Usage of Internet** – According to the Internet and Mobile Association of India (IAMAI), the Internet user base in the country stood at 190 million at the end of June 2013. With more and more people accessing the web through mobile phones, the Internet user base in the country is projected to touch 243 million by June 2014, a year-on-year growth of 28 percent. The growth of Internet users has also led to a substantial growth of other digital industries such as e-commerce and digital advertising.

- **Rising Educational Level in Computer** – The Government of India has put in new horizontal efforts in the educational tools and techniques of computer studies. The students of urban areas, rural areas and business persons are attracted towards the advanced computer technologies. The development of educational standards has enabled or enhanced a great demand in the market.
- **Busy Lifestyle** – The powerful influence of various social media tools such as Pinterest or Facebook allows consumers to organise their favourite items and segment it into themed collections to share it with others. This fuels personal expression in shopping and makes others reflect on their purchase decisions.
- **Rising middle class with disposable income** – With the rise of small and medium enterprises, foreign direct investment (fdi), and India's own powerful multinational corporations creating millions of new jobs, a new generation of globally-minded Indian consumers have been created. With the growing job opportunities, the income sources have also been increased. Because of high purchasing power, the customers are going for online shopping.
- **Awareness of Porducts** – People are aware of the availability of various products in the markets through the help of television, newspaper, website etc. Hence the availability of a new product and its price and other features could be known easily.
- **Easy to Find the Review of Products** – It is quite easy to find the review of products with the help of online shopping. E-commerce has made it simpler to get information regarding the product and the customers can purchase the products after getting reviews and feedback of the product.

## E-Commerce Companies in India

| | | | |
|---|---|---|---|
| (1) American Swan | (6) Health Kart | (11) Ola Cabs | (16) Carat lane |
| (2) Bata Shoes | (7) IRCTC | (12) Paytm | (17) Tradus |
| (3) Bro4u | (8) Instamojo | (13) Snapdeal | (18) Jabong |
| (4) Flipkart | (9) Myntra | (14) Shop Clues | (19) HomeShop |
| (5) Ebay India | (10) Mobi Kwik | (15) Zomato | (20) Naaptol |

## Few E-Commerce websites

| | | | |
|---|---|---|---|
| (1) Filpkart.com | (13) Smartshoppers.in | (25) Themobilestone.in | (37) Egully.com |
| (2) Infibeam.com | (14) Homeshop18.com | (26) Adexmart.com | (38) Bitfang.com |
| (3) Ebay.in | (15) Yebhi.com | (27) Zoomin.com | (39) Bigcmobiles.in |
| (4) Thelwares.com | (16) Univerceli.in | (28) Ratetag.com | (40) Seventymm.com |
| (5) Futurebazaar.com | (17) Mediahome.in | (29) Deltapage.com | (41) JJMehta.com/ shop/ |
| (6) Lynx-india.com | (18) Primeabgb.com | (30) Ezoneonline.in | (42) Indiaplaza.com |
| (7) Timtara.com | (19) Next.co.in | (31) Gadgetsuru.com | (43) Theitdepot.com |
| (8) Shopping.rediff.com | (20) Royalimages.in | (32) Machpowertools .com | (44) Gadgets.in |
| (9) Edigiworld.com | (21) Cromaretail.com | (33) SMCinternational .in | (45) Bigadda.com |
| (10) Letsshop.in | (22) Rightshopping.in | (34) Smartshoppers.in | (46) Tradus.com |
| (11) Buytheprice.com | (23) Pristinenote.com | (35) Storeji.com | (47) Vijayasales.com |
| (12) Shopbychoice.com | (24) Theelectro.com | (36) Zapstore.com. | (48) buytheprice.com |
| (49) Computerwarehousepricelist.com | | (50) Shopping.indiatimes.com | |

- **Issues of e-commerce players:** Ecommerce in spite of opportunities, hoopla and hype, also bears the connotations of issues at he same time.
- ***Infrasturctural Problems:*** Internet is the backbone of e-commerce. Unfortunately, internet penetration in India is so far dismally low at 0.5 percent of the population against 50 percent in Singapore. Similarly, penetration of personal computer (PC) in India is as low as 3.5 per thousand of population compared to 6 per thousand in China and 500 per thousand in US. Internet is still accessible through PCs with the help of telephone lines. Given the penetration of telephone only 2.1 percent of population, e-commerce remains far away from the common man. It is difficult for e-commerce to reach to 1,000 million population spread over 37 million households in 6,04,374 odd villages and 5,000 towns and cities. Besides, both cost of PCs and internet access in India are quite high.
- ***Absence of Cyber Laws:*** Other big challenge associated with e-commerce market is the near absence of cyber laws to regulate transactions on the Net. WTO is expected to enact cyber laws soon. The India's Information Technology (IT) Bill passed by the Indian Parliament on May 17, 2000 intends to tackle

legislatively the growing areas in e-commerce. The Bill also intends to facilitate e-commerce by removing legal uncertainties created by the new technology. As it stand today, the Bill deals with only commercial and criminal areas of law. However, it does not take care of issues such as individual property rights, content regulation to privacy and data protection specific legislation.

- ***Privacy and Security Concern:*** As of to-day, quite vulnerable issues related to e-commerce are privacy and security. So far, there is no protection offered either by Website or outside watchdogs against hazard created by exploiting one's privacy.
- ***Payment and Tax Related Issues:*** Issues related to payment and tax is yet another problem continuously hinting e-traders. The electronic payment is made through credit card or plastic money which could, however, not become popular so far in India mainly due to two reasons. First, the penetration of credit card in India is very low (two percent of the population). Second, the Indian customers are quite sceptical of paying by credit card with the increasing threat of fraud played by hackers. Like elsewhere, credit card could not gain growth in India mainly because of authentification and recognition problems of electronic signatures (Dahiya and Singh, 2000: 70). Similarly, tax administration is yet another complex problem in this seamless worldwide e-commerce. As establishing incidence of tax in case of e-commerce transactions becomes difficult, this, thus, provides ample scope for tax evasion. How to get rid of this? Some suggest total tax holiday till 2010 for e-commerce in the country.
- ***Digital Illiteracy and Consumer Psyche:*** At present, digital illiteracy is one of the formidable problems of e-commerce is facing in India. On the other hand, the continuous exodus of skilled computer engineers to other countries has denuded India of software engineers. This has posed a real threat to the Indian IT industry. Obviously, solution to this problem lies in curbing the computer brain - drain and uses the same in the country. The Indian consumer is also characterised by his unique psyche. Usually, the Indian consumer does not go long distances for having any goods of his choice when a neighbourhood store provides him whatever he wants. That is why the consumer does not browse the Net knowing

the consequent hassles of connectivity and other botherations. Added to this is that building trust on the electronic media also takes long time more especially when the vendor is situated at a very far off place.

- ***Virus Problem:*** That computer virus is also a formidable problem in the execution of e-transactions is confirmed by the computer virus originated in Manila. A computer virus lagged 'I Love You' originated in Manila, Philippines on May 5, 2000 rippling across world, inflected millions of computer files causing colossal loss of US $7 billion to the governments and businesses. The offenders causing 'virus' must be awarded deterrent punishment, otherwise similar assaults in future can cause lasting blows to the quite young e-commerce in India as well.
- **English Specific:** Last but not the least, the software so far in the country is English specific. But, in order to make e-commerce reach to the small enterprises, it needs to be available in the languages (regional) of the owners of the small enterprises to enable them to adapt e-commerce processes in their operations. Sooner it is done, better will be it for small enterprises to adapt e-commerce.

## Key points for effective E-Commerce business

1. **It must be Secure** – Every customer wishes for safe and secure transactions during purchasing goods online. If the website is secure, customers will tend to purchase more from it. Secure Sockets Layer (SSL) is a standard security technology for establishing an encrypted link between the web server and a browser. E-commerce websites with the SSL certificate are able to prevent and protect the users' information when customers access their websites.
2. **There must be Easy and Understandable Content** – The website for online shopping should be in an understandable language. The language should be kept simple while making the website, and if possible the translation of the content must be given on the website in simple languages.
3. **Effectiveness and cost-efficiency should be of concern** – Internet marketing is one of the most effective and cost-efficient methods of advertisement. It is effective because it creates a better chance to see the impact of internet marketing on your

online business almost immediately. It is cost-efficient because the costs associated with starting a website, and then, using marketing articles or social media to establish an online presence is minimal when compared to the costs of traditional forms of advertising.

4. **Choose a reliable hosting provider** – Do analyze and opt for the most reliable and cost effective choice of servers for your business. The most important things to measure while selecting are choosing a hosting provider that is tried and tested, guaranteed uptime, response times of the servers, security and the level of support and customer care provided.
5. **Prompt Delivery and Quick Quality Services** –The processing of delivery and quick quality services of the product is an important feature to make the online shopping websites better than others. It must be quick with regard to home delivery services and payment etc.
6. **Improve business credibility through online branding** – Internet marketing campaign will help your business increase product awareness and brand loyalty. Maintaining an online presence via internet marketing is a great way to keep up with the time and provide consumers with all of the opportunities they need 24 hours a day. As consumers browse the web, they may come across your business name or logo and become interested in what your business has to offer.

## Futuristic trends in the growth of E-Commerce

Some futuristic trends in the growth of e-commerce can be studied as follows:

1. **Omnichannels** – The future lies not in a market where traditional brick and mortar stores are dominated by e-commerce websites, but, in a business environment where offline stores are perfectly complemented by their online counterparts. (Nuberger & Renhank, 2005). With the number of online vendors, with similar offerings of goods and services increasing everyday, the consumers are becoming largely fickle with respect to their preferences, turning everytime to the website offering more discounts and offers. In such a scenario, survival becomes difficult and can only be sustained by increasing the number of touch points with the consumers, so as to expand the seller's visibility. In May 2015, India's largest fashion portal, Myntra shut down its desktop website

to become an app only marketplace, but, had to relaunch it in June 2016 owing to customer attrition. Thus, the convergence of bricks and clicks projects a more sustainable ecosystem.

2. **Niche Businesses** – A study conducted by Deloitte, "Future of e-commerce: Uncovering Innovation", notes the rising culture of start-ups focussing on niche areas, that tend to serve everyday purposes of the customers. In the era of giant marketplaces like Amazon and Flipkart, which focus on adding more products to their existing basket, firms like Bluestone, Lenskart, Pepperfry, UrbanClap, OlaCabs etc. Target a niche area, so as to offer a unique proposition.

3. **Focus on Services** – In the light of increasing number of e-commerce firms coming up with similar offerings, services will provide the cutting edge to the firms to improve their performance metrics. Services can act as a differentiating factor for the firms, who can tap into the potential of increasing customer base by serving them better than their competitors. Social Media, while being an import data source and advertising avenue for e-commerce firms, also serves as a platform for the customers to vent out their frustration in case of bad shopping experience, an event which can prove detrimental to the image of the online vendor or marketplace. Firms can avoid the same by ensuring constant order and delivery updates, immediate redressal of grievances, in addition to product quality.

4. **Internet Marketing** – Internet Marketing has an important role to play, to provide an enhanced customer experience, as well as, to generate and retain more traffic on the website. Attractive design and user friendliness of the website would play key roles in the consolidation of a firm in e-commerce market. "Search engine marketing (SEM) is a form of web advertising that companies use to promote their products and services on search engine results pages." (Gangeshwer, 2013). SEM, which places ads on search engine result pages is evolving as an important customer acquisition strategy. Similarly, companies can make use of effective SEO (Search Engine Optimization) to increase its online visibility and hence, generate more traffic.

5. **Tapping Rural Markets** – With the smartphone penetration (through low priced devices) to rural areas, the potential of rural markets cannot be tapped unless it is followed by a penetration of network services. According to "India@Digital, Bharat" Report by BCG and

IAMAI, the share of rural Internet user base will increase in 2018. The rural internet user base is estimated to increase from 60 million in 2014 to 280 million in 2018, growing at a rate of 40 percent per annum. In the light of these projections, firms can initiate content development in vernacular languages to effectively exploit the opportunities in rural markets, at the same time improve its logistics capability so as to ensure last mile connectivity.

6. **Better Infrastructure** – With a large proportion of the online traffic moving from desktop mobile, e-commerce firms need to introduce apps that consume less data and light mobile websites that provide a seamless shopping experience to its customers.
7. **Rise in the share of Digital Payments** – Cash on Delivery has forever been the default payment option for most buyers due to convenience and privacy issues. Though, COD has played an important role in driving sales, it has also adversely affected the merchants by adding to the costs and leading to reverse logistics. Firms have tried to curb the use of COD by adding delivery charge and offering additional discounts on the use of digital payments, but the reluctance of the customers to share information owing to security concerns has hindered the growth of digital payments. However, in the aftermath of demonetisation, implemented by the government of India in November 2016, the culture of cashless payments is set to rise: evidence from the fact that many e-commerce firms reported a decline in the share.
8. **Mergers and acquisitions** – Another emerging trend in the e-commerce market is acquisition of smaller firms by the market leaders, which helps to curb competition and ensures the survival of the fittest. The past years have been marked by significant acquisitions, which have enabled firms like Flipkart, Snapdeal, Ola and others to grow inorganically. Snapdeal has made around 12 acquisitions since its inception. Similarly, Ola Cabs, BookMyShow, Pepperfry etc. have taken over lesser known players in the same product category to consolidate their position in the market.
   - According to a report by Grant Thronton, as much as US$2.1 billion worth of mergers and acquisitions were inked in 2017 in the booming Indian e-commerce industry. Here is the list of Mergers and Acquisitions which happened in India over a period of time:

**Table 6.3: Mergers and Acquisitions in Indian E-commerce Market**

| *Date* | *Merger/Acquisition* | *Companies Involved* | *Cost* | *Refs* |
|---|---|---|---|---|
| May 2014 | Acquisition | *Flipkart* acquires *Myntra* | US$300 million | |
| March 2015 | Acquisition | *Snapdeal* acquires *Unicommerce* | Undisclosed | [58][59] |
| April 2015 | Acquisition | *Snapdeal* acquires *Free Charge* | US$400 million | [60] |
| April 2016 | Acquisition | *Flipkart* acquires *PhonePe* | Undisclosed | [61][62] |
| June 2016 | Acquisition | *Myntra* (owned by Flipkart) acquires *jabong* | US$70 million | [63] |
| July 2017 | Acquisition | *Axis Bank* acquires *FreeCharge* | US$60 million | [64] |
| May 2018 | Acquisition | *Walmart* acquires *Flipkart* | US$16 billion | [65] |
| January 2020 | Acquisition | *Zomato* acquires *Uber Eats* | US$350 million | [66] |

## E-commerce Market size

Propelled by rising smartphone penetration, launch of 4G network and increasing consumer wealth, the Indian E-commerce market is expected to grow to US$ 200 billion by 2026 from US$ 38.5 billion in 2017. Online retail sales in India is expected to grow 31 percent to touch US$ 32.70 billion in 2018, led by Flipkart, Amazon India and Paytm Mall.

Smartphone shipments in India increased eight percent y-o-y to reach 152.5 million units in 2019, thereby making it the fastest among the top 20 smartphone markets in the world.

Internet penetration in India grew from just four percent in 2007 to 52.08 percent in 2019, registering a CAGR of 24 percent between 2007 and 2019. The number of internet users in India is expected to increase from 687.62 million as of September 2019 to 829 million by 2021.

## Investments/Developments

Some of the major developments in the Indian e-commerce sector are as follows:

- In Agugust 2020, Reliance Industries (RIL) acquired 60 percent stake in Netmeds, an online pharmacy, for ₹ 620 crore (US$ 84.61 million). This acquisition gives RIL's retail unit, Reliance Retail, entry into a vertical e-commerce space.

- In January 2020, Divine Solitaires launched its E-commerce platform.
- In February 2020, Flipkart set up a 'Furniture Experience Center' in Kolkata, its first offline presence in eastern India.
- In April 2020, Reliance Industries (RIL) started home delivery of essentials in partnership with local kirana stores in Navi Mumbai, Thane and Kalyan.
- In April 2020, Swiggy received an additional US$ 43 million funding as part of its ongoing Series I round.
- In May 2020, PepsiCo India partnered with Dunzo for its snack food brands that include Lay's Kurkure, Doritos and Quaker.
- In May 2020, chocolate maker Hershey India partnered with Swiggy and Dunzo to launch their flagship online store in order to increase reach.
- In Union Budget 2020-21, Government has allocated ₹ 8,000 crore (US$ 1.24 billion) to BharatNet Project to provide broadband services to 150,000-gram panchayats.
- In August 2019, Amazon acquired 49 percent stake in a unit of Future Group.
- Reliance will invest ₹ 20,000 crore (US$ 2.86 billion) in its telecom business to expand its broadband and E-commerce presence and to offer 5G services.
- In September 2019, PhonePe launched super-app platform 'Switch' to provide a one stop solution for customers integrating several other merchants apps.
- In November 2019, Nykaa opened its 55th offline store marking success in tier II and tier III cities.

**Government Initiatives Regarding e-Commerce in India:** Since 2014, the Government of India has announced various initiatives, namely Digital India, Make in India, Start-up India, Skill India and Innovation Fund. The timely and effective implementation of such programmes may likely support growth of E-commerce in the country. Some of the major initiatives taken by the Government to promote E-commerce in India are as follows:

- **In February 2019, a draft National e-Commerce policy** has been prepared and placed in the public domain, which addresses six broad issues of the e-commerce ecosystem viz. e-commerce marketplaces; regulatory issues; infrastructure development; data;

stimulating domestic digital economy and export promotion through e-commerce.

- The Department of Commerce initiated an exercise and established a Think Tank on 'Framework for National Policy on-e-Commerce' and a Task Force under it to deliberate on the challenges confronting India in the arena of the digital economy and electronic commerce.
- The Reserve Bank of India (RBI) has decided to allow "interoperability" among Prepaid Payment Instruments (PPIs) such as digital wallets, prepaid cash coupons and prepaid telephone top-up cards. RBI has also instructed banks and companies to make all know-your-customer (KYC)-compliant prepaid payment instruments (PPIs), like mobile wallets, interoperable amongst themselves via Unified Payments Interface (UPI).
- **FDI guidelines for e-commerce by DIPP:** In order to increase the participation of foreign players in the e-commerce field, the Government has increased the limit of foreign direct investment (FDI) in the e-commerce marketplace model for up to 100 percent (in B2B models).
- Government e-Marketplace (GeM) signed a Memorandum of Understanding (MoU) with Union Bank of India to facilitate a cashless, paperless and transparent payment system for an array of services in October 2019.
- The heavy investment of Government of India in rolling out the fibre network for 5G will help boost e-commerce in India.
- In the Union Budget of 2018-19, the government has allocated ₹ 8,000 crore to **BharatNet** Project, to provide broadband services to 150,000-gram panchayats.
- In February 2019, the Government of India released the Draft National e-Commerce Policy which encourages FDI in the marketplace model of E-commerce.
- In order to increase the participation of foreign players in E-commerce, Indian Government hiked the limit of FDI in E-commerce marketplace model to up to 100 percent (in B2B models).
- Heavy investment made by the Government in rolling out fiber network for 5G will help boost E-commerce in India.
- As of August 2018, the Government has been working on the

second draft of E-commerce policy, incorporating inputs from various industry stakeholders.

## Road Ahead

Today E-commerce has become an integral part of everyday life. Accessibility to E-commerce platform is not a privilege but rather a necessity for people, particularly people who are staying in urban areas. Due to fast adoption of internet enabled devices like Smartphone and Tablets, it is examined that an unparalleled growth in E-commerce. The telecommunication technology has completely changed the way of our living, communication methods, shopping etc. It has a huge impact on how we communicate with friends and relatives, how we travel, how we access the information and the way we buy or sell products and services. The growth of E-commerce volumes in India is attracting the attention of players around the globe, E-commerce creates new opportunities for business it also creates new opportunities for education and academics. It appears that there is tremendous potential for providing E-business education. The growth in E-commerce sector will also boost employment, increase revenues from export, increase tax collection by ex-chequers, and provide better products and services to customers in the long-term. Rise in smart phone usage is expected to rise 84 percent to reach 859 million by 2022.

## References

1. Dr. Anukrati Sharma, "A Study on E-Commerce and Online Shopping: Issues and Influences," in International Journal of Computer Engineering and Technology, Volume 4, Issue 1, January-February 2013, pp. 364-376.
2 Himani Grewal & Shivani, "A Study of Ethical and Social Issues in E-Commerce," in International Journal of Advanced Research in Computer Scinece and Software Engineering, Volume 2, Issue 7, July 2012, pp. 167-174.
3. Lotfollah Forouzandeh Dehkordi, Ali Shahnazari, Ali Noroozi, "A Study of the Factors that Influence the Acceptance of e-Commerce in Developing Countries: A Comparative Survey between Iran and United Arab Emirates," in Interdisciplinary Journal of Research in Business, Vol. 1, Issue 6, June 2011, pp. 44-49.
4. Niranjanamurthy M, Dr. Dharmendra Chahar, 2013, The study of E-Commerce Security Issues and Solutions "in International Journal of Advanced Research in Computer and Communication Engineering", Vol. 2, Issue 7, July 2013, pp. 2885-2895.
5. Tryambak Hiwarkar, 2013, E-Commerce impact on Indian Market: a Survey on social impact "in International Journal of Advanced Research in Computer Engineering & Technology (IJARCET)", Volume 2, Issue 3, March 2013, pp. 870-874.

6. IAMAI/articleshow/29563698.cms.

7. Growth of internet users in India and impact on country's economy, http://www.dartconsulting.co.in/DARTBlogs/growth-of-internet-users-in-india-and-impact-on-countrys-economy/

8. Zurak-Owezarek C., E-business on global and local scales. Analysis and an evaluation attempt [in Polish], Lodz 2013, p. 16.

9. Benicewicz-Miazda A., *E-business on the Internet and in multimedia* [in Polish]. MIKOM, 2003, pp. 6-8.

10. Benicewicz-Miazda A., *E-business on the Internet and in Multimedia* [in Polish]. MIKOM, 2003, pp. 6-8

11. Mac, R. (2014, October). Retrieved from https://www.google.co.in/amp/www.forbes.com/sites/ryanmac/2014/10/28/softbank-betsbig-on-india-with-627-million-snapdeal-investnment/amp/

12. Mishra, S.V., & Kotkar, D.S. (2015, February). A Study on Current Status of E-Commerce in India: A Comparative Analysis of Flipkart and Amazon. International Journal of Advance Research in Computer Science and Management Studies, 3(2), 133-137.

13. Numberger, S., & Renhank, C. (2005). The Future of B2C E-Commerce. Electronic Markets 269-282.

14. Reghunath, A., & Panga, M.D. (2013). Problem and Prospects of E-Commerce. International Journal of Research and Development-A Management Review, 2(1), 59-68.

15. Ray, S. (2011). Emerging Trend of E-Commerce in India: Some Crucial Issues, Prospects and Challenges. Computer Engineering and Intelligents Systems, 18-36.

16. Rina, D. (2016, March-April). Challenges and Future Scope of E-commerce in India. International Journal of Emerging Trends & Technology in Computer Science, 5(2), 232-235.

17. Shankar, S. (2016, May). Retrieved from http://economictimes.indiatimes.com/small-biz/sme-sector/b2b-e-commerce-market-6-times-larger-than-b2c-sme-lenders/articleshow/52499816.cms.

18. Gupta, A. (2014, January). E-Commerce: Role of E-Commerce in Today's Business. International Journal of Computing and Corporate Research, 4(1).

# C. Industry and Trade

# 7

# International Trade and Economic Development in India

*Dr A Venkata Rayudu*

This Chapter is divided into five Parts. Part-I briefly introduces the importance of International Trade in a country's economic development. Later, the steps initiated by the Govt. of India to control imports and to promote exports are briefly discussed. Then, the trade gap that arose between India's imports and exports is presented. Under Part-II, the direction of India's imports from and exports to different regions and countries across the Globe are studied. As part of this, India's imports and exports to top ten (10) countries in the world are also briefly analyzed. Part-III examines, in detail, the importance of top ten principal import items of India. Similar exercise is carried out in respect of top ten export items of India's in Part-IV. Summary of conclusions is presented in Part-V.

## I. Introduction

International trade may be defined as an exchange of goods and services between countries. Goods include both consumer and capital in nature. Services include banking, consulting, tourism, transportation, etc. It is an established fact that trade is primarily conducted for the purpose of providing a nation commodities and services it lacks in exchange for those that it produces in abundance. Trading globally may, therefore, give consumers and countries an opportunity to be exposed to new markets and products. As such, it plays a key role in an increasingly interconnected and interdependent world in the form of export and import of goods or services, including acquisition of new technologies. Further, it acts as an engine of growth in terms of employment generation, an increase in savings and investment capacities and reduction in poverty and employment inequalities.

Careful manipulations of trade, therefore, boost economic development and create absolute gains amongst trading partners.

In Indian context, International trade had been playing a very crucial role in its economic development. Soon after independence, India was seen mainly as an exporter of foodstuffs and raw materials to the industrialised countries and an importer of manufactured items. Later, it gave importance for establishing heavy industries, particularly since the inception of II Five Year Plan, with a view to increase its production capacity in the manufacturing sector too. Subsequently, the imposition of severe import restrictions badly affected the process of industrialisation in the country. On the other hand, India's exports faced supply and demand inelasticity, besides other accompanied adverse affects such as secular deterioration in terms of trade, international demonstration affect etc., and thereby caused, at times, the balance of payments crisis. Against this background, the post 1991 period witnessed a major shift in India's trade policy in terms of 'Liberalisation' i.e., simplification of procedures, lessening quantitative restrictions and substantial reduction in import tariffs. 'Globalisation' too played its part in finding new international opportunities/markets. In order to substantiate the persistent trade gap across the border, the value of India's exports and imports are presented covering the period broadly from 1960-61 to 2018-19 in Table 1:

**Table 1. Exports, Imports and Trade Gap of India**

***(Values in US $ Million)***

| *Year* | *Exports* | *Imports* | *Trade gap* |
|---|---|---|---|
| 1960-61 | 1346 | 2353 | -1007 |
| 1970-71 | 2031 | 2162 | -131 |
| 1980-81 | 8486 | 15869 | -7383 |
| 1990-91 | 18143 | 24075 | -5932 |
| 2000-01 | 44076 | 49975 | -5899 |
| 2010-11 | 249816 | 369769 | -119953 |
| 2011-12 | 305964 | 489319 | -183355 |
| 2012-13 | 300401 | 490737 | -190336 |
| 2013-14 | 314405 | 450200 | -135795 |
| 2014-15 | 310338 | 448033 | -137695 |
| 2015-16 | 262291 | 381008 | -118717 |
| 2016-17 | 275852 | 384357 | -108505 |
| 2017-18 | 303526 | 465581 | -162055 |
| 2018-19 | 330078 | 514078 | -184000 |

*Source:* Adopted from Economic Survey 2019-20 (Statistical Appendix), pp. A 103 & A 104.

It is evident from Table 1 that there is a quantum jump both in exports and imports since 1990-91, reflecting the impact of the reforms introduced in India's trade policy as stated above. It can be observed that India's imports dominated the foreign trade Sector compared to its exports resulting in a continuous widening trade gap at the cost of domestic consumer. It can also be observed that the ever increasing trade gap reached its peak during 2012-13 and thereafter showed a declining trend till 2016-17 and then took an upward direction due to essential domestic requirements. In regard to exports, they were more or less stagnant since 2011-12 calling for renewed efforts to promote them.

## II. Direction of India's Imports and Exports

Against the above background it is proposed to study broadly the direction of India's imports and exports to various regions and countries

**Table 2. Direction of India's Imports and Exports by Regions and Countries (2018-19)**

***(Value in US $ Million)***

| *Sl. No.* | *Region* | *No. of Countries* | *Imports* | *%share in Total Imports* | *Exports* | *% share in Total exports* | *Trade Gap* |
|---|---|---|---|---|---|---|---|
| **1** | Europe | 38 | 79357 | 15.44 | 64375 | 19.50 | -14982 |
| **1.1** | EU countries | 28 | 58431 | 11.37 | 57204 | 17.33 | -1227 |
| **1.2** | EFTA | 4 | 18466 | 3.59 | 1534 | 0.46 | -16932 |
| **1.3** | Other European countries | 6 | 2459 | 0.48 | 5637 | 1.71 | 3178 |
| **2** | Africa | 54 | 41128 | 8.00 | 28541 | 8.65 | -12587 |
| **2.1** | South African Customs union (SACU) | 5 | 7555 | 1.47 | 4378 | 1.33 | -3177 |
| **2.2** | Other S.A. countries | 4 | 5643 | 1.10 | 1856 | 0.56 | -3787 |
| **2.3** | West Africa | 22 | 20084 | 3.91 | 7698 | 2.33 | -12386 |
| **2.4** | Central Africa | 7 | 554 | 0.11 | 1342 | 0.41 | 788 |
| **2.5** | East Africa | 10 | 1563 | 0.30 | 7378 | 2.24 | 5815 |
| **2.6** | North Africa | 6 | 5728 | 1.11 | 5889 | 1.78 | 161 |
| **3** | America | 46 | 65190 | 12.68 | 68861 | 20.86 | 3671 |
| **3.1** | North America | 3 | 44643 | 8.68 | 59121 | 17.91 | 14478 |
| **3.2** | Latin America | 43 | 20547 | 4.00 | 9741 | 2.95 | -10806 |
| **4** | Asia | 50 | 318762 | 62.01 | 161216 | 48.84 | -157546 |
| **4.1** | East Asia | 12 | 13914 | 4.00 | 4027 | 1.22 | -9887 |
| **4.2** | ASEAN | 10 | 59326 | 11.54 | 37477 | 11.35 | -21849 |
| **4.3** | West Asia-GCC | 6 | 79718 | 15.51 | 41622 | 12.61 | -38096 |
| **4.4** | Other West Asia | 7 | 39016 | 7.59 | 10761 | 3.26 | -28255 |
| **4.5** | North East Asia | 8 | 122426 | 23.81 | 41981 | 12.72 | -80445 |
| **4.6** | South Asia | 7 | 4363 | 0.85 | 25349 | 7.68 | 20986 |
| **5.** | CIS & Baltics | 12 | 9443 | 1.84 | 3467 | 1.05 | -5976 |
| **5.1** | Cars Countries | 5 | 863 | 0.17 | 442 | 0.13 | -421 |
| **5.2** | Other CIS Countries | 7 | 8580 | 1.67 | 3025 | 0.92 | -5555 |
| **6** | Unspecified Region | - | 199 | 0.04 | 3617 | 1.10 | 3418 |
| | **Total** | **200** | **514078** | **(100)** | **330078** | **(100)** | **-184000** |

*Source:* Worked out from Economic Survey 2019-20 (Statistical Appendix), pp. A 113 to A 130.

across the Globe during 2018-19 in order to understand the focused areas in the international trade sector. The Table 2 presents the direction of India's imports and exports to various regions and countries:

It is evident from Table 2 that there are five regions consisting of 200 countries, excluding unspecified region under serial number-6. About 62 percent of India's imports were originated from the countries of Asian region only, followed by about 15 percent from European region and about 13 percent from American region. Among the countries of Asia, those under North East Asia, West Asia and ASEAN, account for more than 50 percent of India's imports. In regard to exports also, it is evident that more than 50 percent of the total exports are moving to the regions and countries located in Asia only. It can also be noticed that America and Europe regions account for around 20 percent exports each. Further, it can be noticed from the table that both imports and exports are more directed to the regions and countries located in Asia, Europe, America, Africa and CIS & Baltic's

**Table 3. India's Imports and Exports to Top Ten Countries(2018-19)**

***(Value in US $ Million)***

| *Sl. No. (1)* | *Country (2)* | *Imports (3)* | *Col.3 as % in Total Imports (4)* | *Exports (5)* | *Col.5 as % in Total Exports (6)* |
|---|---|---|---|---|---|
| 1 | China P Rp | 70320 | (13.68) | 16753 | 5.08 |
| 2 | USA | 35550 | (6.92) | 52428 | 15.88 |
| 3 | UAE | 29787 | (5.79) | 30127 | 9.13 |
| 4 | Saudi Arbia | 28479 | (5.54) | - | - |
| 5 | Iraq | 22372 | (4.35) | - | - |
| 6 | Switzerland | 18088 | (3.52) | - | - |
| 7 | Hong Kong | 17987 | (3.50) | 13002 | 3.94 |
| 8 | Korea Rp | 16759 | (3.26) | - | - |
| 9 | Singapore | 16282 | (3.17) | 11572 | 3.51 |
| 10 | Indonesia | 15854 | (3.08) | - | - |
| 11 | U.K. | - | | 9330 | 2.83 |
| 12 | Bangladesh PR | - | | 9210 | 2.79 |
| 13 | Germany | - | | 8904 | 2.70 |
| 14 | Netherlands | - | | 8814 | 2.67 |
| 15 | Nepal | - | | 7766 | 2.35 |
| | **Sub-total** | **271478** | **52.81** | **167906** | **50.87** |
| | **Total** | **514078** | | **330078** | |

*Source:* Worked out from Economic Survey 2019-20 (Statistical Appendix), Govt. of India, pp. A 113 to A 130.

in that order. In continuation of the above, it is proposed to study the imports and exports to top ten (10) countries from India's point of view in order to understand their importance in the foreign trade sector. Table 3 presents the position in regard to India's imports and exports for the year 2018-19:

It is evident from the Table 3 that India's imports and exports to the top ten countries as a percent in their respective totals are a little over 50 percent revealing their importance in the foreign trade sector of the country. In fact, imports are more compared to exports in any given year as established supra. It can be seen that imports, mostly originated from China followed by USA, UAE, South Africa, Iraq and the remaining five countries in that order as presented in col. (3) & (4) during 2018-19. The imports in the given year from Switzerland, Hong Kong, Korea RP, Singapore and Indonesia range between three and four percent. In regard to India's exports, they are more directed towards USA followed by UAE, China, Hong Kong and Singapore in the year under reference. In regard to the remaining five countries, their percentage share in total exports ranges between two and three percent only.

## III. India's Principal Imports

As per the Economic Survey-2019-20 of the Govt. of India, the principal import items are broadly categorised into three Groups and they are (i) Food and live animals, chiefly for food (excluding cashew raw), (ii) Raw materials and intermediate manufactures, and (iii) Capital goods. Among the three, the import items under the second group occupies major percentage share ranging from 46.96 percent in 1960-61 to 86.13 percent in 2018-19, followed by third 13.82 percent and first group 0.04 percent. The percentage share of the second group in the first half year of 2019-20 also confirms to that of 2018-19 and remaining two groups follow in suit the same order. Therefore, import of raw materials and intermediate manufactures occupies prime place for the country's essential developmental requirements.

In this connection, it is proposed to assess the magnitude of top ten principal import items as percentage shares in respective total imports covering the period broadly from 1960-61 to 2019-20. Accordingly, Table 4 presents the percentage share of top ten (10) import items of India in their respective total imports during the years under reference:

**Table 4. Top Ten Import Items of India During 1960-61 to 2019-20**

***(Value in US $ Million)***

| *Sl.No.* | *Item* | *1960-61* | *1970-71* | *1980-81* | *1990-91* | *2000-01* | *2010-11* | *2018-19* | *2019-20** |
|---|---|---|---|---|---|---|---|---|---|
| 1 | Cereals and its preparations | 380 (16.15) | 282 (13.04) | | | | | | |
| 2 | Fibers | 212 (9.01) | 168 (7.77) | | | | | | |
| 3 | Raw cotton | 172 (7.31) | 131 (6.06) | | | | | | |
| 4 | POL | 145 (6.16) | 180 (8.33) | 6656 (41.94) | 6028 (25.04) | 15650 (3044) | 105964 (28.66) | 140921 (27.41) | 65106 (26.37) |
| 5 | Edible oils | - | - | 857 (5.40) | | 1334 (2.59) | 6551 (1.77) | 9890 (1.92) | 4741 (1.92) |
| 6 | Fertilizers and its manufacturing | - | 113 (5.23) | 1034 (6.52) | 984 (4.09) | 664 (1.29) | 6885 (1.86) | | |
| 7 | Chemical elements and compounds | 82 (3.48) | 90 (4.16) | 453 (2.85) | 1276 (5.38) | | | 31535 (6.13) | 15397 (6.24) |
| 8 | Plastic material etc. | - | - | | 610 (2.53) | 558 (1.09) | 6874 (1.86) | 15682 (3.05) | 7765 (3.14) |
| 9 | Pearls, Precious stones etc. | - | - | 527 (3.32) | 2083 (8.65) | 4838 (9.41) | 34620 (9.36) | 27076 (5.27) | 11425 (4.63) |
| 10 | Iron and Steel | 258 (10.96) | 194 (8.97) | 1078 (6.79) | 1178 (4.89) | 781 (1.52) | 10376 (2.81) | 12582 (2.45) | 6411 (2.60) |
| 11 | Non-ferrous metals | 99 (4.21) | 158 (7.31) | 604 (3.81) | 614 (2.55) | 539 (1.05) | 46677 (12.62) | 51391 (10.00) | 24723 (10.01) |
| 12 | Non-electric machinery | 426 (18.10) | 341 (15.77) | 1377 (8.68) | 2363 (9.82) | 3703 (7.20) | 2611 (7.06) | 19670 (3.83) | 9975 (4.04) |
| 13 | Electrical machinery | 120 (5.10) | 93 (4.30) | 328 (2.07) | 949 (3.94) | 487 (0.95) | 3845 (1.04) | 18182 (3.54) | 9697 (3.93) |
| 15 | Transport equipment | 151 (6.42) | - | 597 (3.76) | 931 (3.87) | 953 (1.85) | 11467 (3.10) | 24776 (4.82) | 10855 (4.40) |
| 16 | Sub-total (0 to 15) | 2045 (86.91) | 1750 (80.94) | 13511 (85.14) | 17016 (70.68) | 29506 (57.39) | 259370 (70.14) | 351705 (68.41) | 166095 (67.26) |
| **Total Imports** | | **2353** | **2162** | **15869** | **24075** | **51413** | **369769** | **514078** | **246931** |

**April-September (P).*

**Pl. Note:** Figures in the parentheses indicate percentage in their respective total imports.

*Source:* Economic Survey 2019-20 (Statistical Appendix), pp. A 105-A107.

The Table 4 contains a total of sixteen (16) principal import items; with a view to present top ten import items for each reference year based on their value. It is evident from Table 04 that the percentage share of the ten (10) principal import items in their respective total imports range between 57.39 percent in 2000-01 and 86.91 percent in 1960-61, revealing that the percentage share of the top ten import items in the total imports on an average is nearly 69 percent during the eight year period under consideration. Though the import items at Sl. Nos. one to three appeared during the first two reference years, they gave place to new items like edible oils, pearls and transport equipment. Out of the ten, five items such as POL, iron and steel, non-ferrous metals, non-electric machinery and electric machinery consistently find place among the top ten import items. It can be observed that importation of edible oils, fertilizers, iron and steel, both non-electric and electric machinery showed gradually declining trend during the reference years. Though find place consistently in all the eight year period, the import of non-ferrous metals increased suddenly since 2010-11. Over all, India's imports, though marginally declined by 1970-71, increased phenomenally since 1980-81 to meet the essential developmental requirements.

## IV. India's Principal Exports

Based on the Economic Survey (2019-20), Govt. of India, the principal export items are broadly categorised into four. They are (i) Agriculture and allied products, (ii) Ores and minerals (excl. Coal), (iii) Manufactured goods, and (iv) Mineral fuels and lubricants (incl. Coal). The first category contains 13 export items, the second is only with two items, the third is with eight; items including gems and jewellery and the fourth category contains with only one export item. These four categories of export items along with their percentage shares in total exports are presented covering the period broadly from 1960-61 to 2019-20 in Table 05:

**Table 5. Category-wise Principal Export Items of India During 1960-61 to 2019-20**

***(Value in US $ Million)***

| *Sl.No.* | *Category* | *1960-61* | *1970-71* | *1980-81* | *1990-91* | *2000-01* | *2010-11* | *2018-19* | *2019-20** |
|---|---|---|---|---|---|---|---|---|---|
| I | **Agriculture and allied products** | 596 (44.28) | 644 (31.71) | 2601 (30.65) | 3521 (19.41) | 6256 (14.19) | 24448 (9.73) | 38829 (11.76) | 16875 (10.60) |
| II | **Ores and minerals (excl. Coal** | 109 (8.10) | 217 (10.68) | 523 (6.16) | 834 (4.60) | 906 (2.06) | 8581 (3.42) | 5928 (1.80) | 3526 (2.21) |
| III | **Manufactured goods** | 610 (45.32) | 1021 (50.27) | 4738 (55.83) | 13229 (72.92) | 35181 (79.82) | 173263 (68.99) | 231951 (70.27) | 113989 (7157) |
| IV | **Mineral fuels and lubricants (incl. Coal)** | 15 (1.11) | 17 (0.84) | 35 (0.41) | 528 (2.91) | 1931 (4.38) | 42280 (16.84) | 47885 (14.51) | 22115 (13.89) |
| | **Total exports** | **1346 (100)** | **2031 (100)** | **8486 (100)** | **18143 (100)** | **44076 (100)** | **251136 (100)** | **330078 (100)** | **159269 (100)** |

***April-September (P)**

**Pl. Note:** Figures in the parentheses indicate percentage in their respective total imports.

*Source:* Economic Survey 2019-20 (Statistical Appendix), pp. A 109-A 111, Govt. of India.

It is evident from Table 5 that the share of manufactured goods steadily increased from 45.32 percent in 1960-61 to 70.27 percent in 2018-19. The same trend continued in the first half of financial year 2019-20 also. Though the export potential of agriculture and allied products declined from 44.28 percent in 1960-61 to 30.05 percent by 1980-81, they witnessed very sharp decline in the post liberalisation period. It can also be observed that ores and minerals, under category two, exhibited a gradually declining share in exports except in 1970-71. In regard to mineral fuels and lubricants, though their share in total imports started increasing since 1980-81, coincides with liberalised trade policy in the country. On the whole, the table reveals the dominance of manufactured goods in the export basket of India.

In order to amplify the conclusions drawn under Table 5, it is proposed to study briefly the principal export items of India. For which, Table 6

**Table 6. Top Ten Export Items of India During 1960-61 to 2019-20**

***(Value in US $ million)***

| *Sl. No.* | *Export Item* | *1960-61* | *1970-71* | *1980-81* | *1990-91* | *2000-01* | *2010-11* | *2018-19* | *2019-20** |
|---|---|---|---|---|---|---|---|---|---|
| 1 | Tea and mate | 260 (19.32) | 196 (9.65) | 538 (6.34) | 596 (3.29) | - | - | - | - |
| 2 | Oil cakes | - | 73 (3.59) | - | - | 448 (1.02) | - | - | - |
| 3 | Tobacco | 34 (2.53) | - | | | | | | |
| 4 | Cashew kernels | 40 (2.97) | 76 (3.74) | - | - | - | - | - | - |
| 5 | Spices | 36 (2.67) | - | - | - | - | - | - | 1959 (1.23) |
| 6 | Sugar and molasses | 60 (4.46) | - | - | - | - | - | - | - |
| 7 | Raw cotton | - | - | - | 471 (2.60) | - | 2710 (1.16) | - | - |
| 8 | Rice | - | - | 283 (3.33) | - | 644 (1.46) | - | 7751 (2.35) | 3049 (1.91) |
| 9 | Fish and its preparations | - | - | 274 (3.23) | 535 (2.95) | 1394 (3.16) | 2623 (1.04) | 6803 (2.06) | 3356 (2.11) |
| 10 | Meat and it's preparations | - | - | - | - | - | - | 3716 (1.13) | |
| 11 | Iron ore (excl. Coal) | 36 (2.67) | 155 (7.63) | 384 (4.53) | 585 (3.22) | - | 4715 (1.88) | - | - |
| 12 | Cotton yarn, fabrics, made-ups etc. | 136 (10.10) | 188 (9.26) | 516 (6.08) | 1170 (6.45) | 3509 (7.96) | 2910 (1.16) | 9843 (2.98) | 4303 (2.70) |
| 13 | Readymade garments of all textile materials | - | - | 696 (8.20) | 2236 (12.32) | 5577 (12.65) | 11614 (4.62) | 16138 (4.09) | 7873 (4.74) |
| 14 | Jute manufactures incl. Twist and yarn | 283 (21.03) | 252 (12.41) | 417 (4.91) | - | - | - | - | - |
| 15 | Leather & leather manufactures etc. | 59 (4.38) | 106 (5.22) | 493 (5.81) | 1449 (7.99) | 1951 (4.43) | 3909 (1.56) | 5141 (4.56) | 2424 (1.52) |
| 16 | Gems and jewellery | | 59 (2.90) | 782 (9.22) | 2924 (16.12) | 7384 (16.75) | 40509 (16.13) | 40251 (12.19) | 19264 (12.32) |
| 17 | Chemicals and allied products | - | - | 284 (3.35) | 1176 (6.48) | 5002 (11.35) | 28905 (11.51) | 31479 (9.54) | 18861 (11.84) |
| 18 | Machinery, transport & metal manufactures, etc. | 46 (3.42) | 261 (12.85) | - | 2158 (11.89) | 6976 (15.83) | 49815 (19.84) | 81191 (24.60) | 45418 (28.52) |
| 19 | Mineral fuels and lubricants (incl. Coal) | | - | - | - | 1931 (4.38) | 42280 (16.84) | 47885 (14.51) | 22115 (13.89) |
| | **Sub-total** | **990 (73.55)** | **1462 (71.98)** | **4667 (55.00)** | **13300 (73.31)** | **34816 (78.99)** | **190190 (75.73)** | **250198 (75.80)** | **128622 (80.76)** |
| | **Total Exports** | **1346** | **2031** | **8486** | **18143** | **44076** | **251136** | **330078** | **159269** |

***April-September (P).**

**Pl Note:** Figures in the parentheses indicate percentage in their respective total imports

*Source:* Indian Economic Survey 2019-20 (Statistical Appendix).

presents the percentage share of top ten (10) export items in their respective total exports covering the period broadly from 1960-61 to 2019-20.

The Table 6 contains a total of 19 export items. But only top ten export items are presented for each reference year based on their export earnings. The first ten items represent agriculture and allied products under category-I. Item number eleven pertains to category-II. The export items at Sl. Numbers 12 to 18 are under the category-III of manufactured goods. Item number nineteen is the only item in category-IV. Among the four categories of export items, manufactured goods and mineral fuels, etc., are contributing more in terms of their percentage share in total exports.

It is evident from Table 6 that all the items under agriculture and allied products could not sustain their presence as top ten export items during the entire eight year period under reference. It can be seen that tea and mate remained among top ten export items only till the introduction of reforms in trade policy in 1991. Fish and its preparations became part of the top ten export group since 1980-81 but could not improve its percentage share in the total exports of respective years. The only item represented under category II, i.e., iron ore (excl. Coal) continued as a principal export item between 1960-61 to 1991-92 and thereafter lost its significance except in 2010-11. Among the manufactured goods under category-III, only two items. i.e., cotton yarn and leather made their presence consistently as principal export items, though their percentage shares declined, during the period under reference. Gems and jewellery, and chemical and allied products have become reliable export earners. Besides, mineral fuels and lubricants (incl. Coal) under category IV too joined the club of top ten export items since 2000-01 and its percentage share in total exports is quite promising. On an average, the table reveals that the top ten (10) export items contributed 76.64 percent share to the total exports. The table further indicates that there is a gradual transformation in India's export items from traditional agricultural products to manufactured goods.

## V. Conclusions

The study reiterated the importance of International trade in a country's economic development in general and in particular with reference to India. It also brought out clearly the ever growing trade gap between imports and exports i.e., the former are in excess of the latter over a period of time. It reveals that about 62 percent of India's imports during 2018-19 are from the countries of Asian region only, followed by 15 percent from European region and about 13 percent from American region. Similarly, it also establishes that nearly 49 percent of the India's exports are directed to the regions and countries located in Asia only, followed by American region (20.86%) and European region (19.50%).

Among the three categories of import items (i) Food and live animals, chiefly for food (excluding cashew raw), (ii) Raw materials and intermediate manufactures, and (iii) Capital goods- the import of raw materials and intermediate manufactures occupies prime place for the country's essential developmental requirements. The study further reveals that the percentage share of top ten import items in total imports, on an average, is nearly 69 percent during the period under review. POL remained as an important import item. The study observed a sharp increase in the importation of non-ferrous metals since 2010-11. It also observed a gradual reduction in the imports of iron and steel and non-electric machinery. It further reveals that the import of transport equipment as percent in total imports is revolving around four percent. In regard to top ten export items, the study reveals that the percentage share of manufactured goods steadily increased from 45.32 in 1960-61 to 70.27 in 2018-19. Though the export potential of agriculture and allied products declined from 44.28 percent in 1960-61 to 30.65 percent by 1980-81, they witnessed further sharp decline in the post liberalisation period. Among the manufactured goods, only two items i.e., cotton yarn and leather made their presence consistently as principal export items, though their percentage shares declined, during the period under reference. Gems and jewellery, and chemical and allied products have become reliable export earners. Besides, mineral fuels and lubricants (incl. Coal) too joined the club of top ten export items since 2000-01 and its percentage share in total exports is quite promising. Further, it reveals that the top ten (10) export items contribute nearly 77 percent share in the total exports. Also, the study confirms the dominance of manufactured goods in the export basket of India. Finally, the study concludes that there is a gradual transformation in India's export items from traditional agricultural products to manufactured goods.

## References

1. International Trade and Development nexus, Great Insights, Volume 2, Issue 8, Nov. 2013-by Dr. Mukshisa Kituyi, Secretary General, UNCTAD.
2. WTO-trade and Development, The Center for Global Development, 1776, Massachusetts.
3. International Economics & Trade – India: Foreign Trade policy, World Bank, Org. 2011.
4. Foreign Trade in India by Sheshan Pradhan, July 10, 2019.

5. Impact of Services Trade on India's Economic Growth and Current Account Balance: Evidence from Post-Reform Period – by Mini P. Thomas, Research Scholar, ISEC, Bangaluru.
6. An appraisal of the Impact of International trade on Economic Growth of India: An ARDL Approach by Attahir Babaji Ambubakar, S.R.M university, Tamil Nadu.
7. Wikipedia, an online source.
8. Economic Survey 2019–20, Govt. of India.

# 8

# Scope of the Micro, Small and Medium Scale Enterprises (MSME's) in Telangana State

***Dr Parupally Anjaneyulu,***
***Prof. S. Ramakrishna***

1. **Introduction:** In the world, the Micro, Small and Medium (MSME's) Scale industries have been playing crucial role to economic growth and creating nearly 50 percent employment in developing countries which are also doing 90 percent of the business. The World Bank estimated, nearly 600 million people will need jobs by 2030, in this regard there is need to strengthen the MSME's for creating jobs. According to the International Finance Corporation (IFC), total 6.5 crores MSME's firms are registering in the developing countries and it needed 5.2 trillion dollar every year. Compare to present situation, it will 1.4 times more of the world MSME lending.

The MSME's sector has emerged as vibrant and dynamic sector, and an engine of growth for the present millennium. Past six decades, the sector has been playing crucial role in the socio-economic development of the people as well as the nation. In India, establishment of the MSME sector is very easy, innovative and flexible. Both, State and Central Governments are also giving priority to the MSME sector through the different aspects like; providing loans and day to day monitoring etc. The sector has been taken upswing during the father of Indian Economic Reforms i.e. P.V. Narasimha Rao period (1991-96). During this period, Dr Manmohan Singh (Finance Minister) was lunched Globalisation perspective through the implementing the International Monetary Fund (IMF) policies to save the country. Later on, the other Prime Ministers of the India have been continuing the same, till today.

1.1. **Objectives:** In this paper, the following objectivs are discussed.

1. To analyse the industrial policy of the Telangana;
2. To understand the MSME's sector situation in the state;
3. To discuss the scope for the establishment of MSME's across the districts.

1.2 **Methodology:** The paper has done purely based on the secondary data which is collected from the various official websites like MSME, and Industrial websites, reports and newspapers/ magazines.

2. **Industrial Policies:** There were several Industrial policies announced by the Government of India, during the period 1956-2015. They are, 1948 First Industrial Policy (outlines the strategy in industrial activities), Coir Industry Act, 1953 and 1956 (industry sector categorisation; Schedules A, B & C), Khadi and Village Industries Commission Act, 1956, 1977 (Janata Industrial Policy to boost Small Scale Industries), 1980 (Indira Gandhi's Policy gradual liberalisation) and 1991 Policy (radical changes in LPGM policies; Liberalisation, Privatisation, Globalisation and Marketisation and eases licensing constraints) Up to 1990's period, the industrial sector was not recorded high growth rate in Telangana. In Nizam period, the industrial seeds were grown but after independence the growth of the sector was declined. From 1991, due to liberalisation and boom in the Information Technology (IT), huge investment was made in the Hyderabad city of infrastructure sector. The growth of infra, attracted major Software Industry stakeholders to establishment of their main centres in Hyderabad. During 2000 to 2010 periods, Hyderabad became the central location for IT companies, drugs and pharmaceutical, poultry farms, spices, minerals, textiles, apparels and automobiles which are located in around the Hyderabad.

As per the Micro, Small and Medium Enterprises Development (MSMED) Act, 2006, Government of India enhanced investment limits for Micro and Small enterprises. The main objective of the policy to achieving 15 percent annual growth rate, increasing employment generation, creating congenial and hassle-free environment, help SSI sector to acquire new technologies and skills, improve export performance, promote linkage between Large and Small Sector and to promote appropriate institutional mechanism to revive sick industries. During the 2001 to 2014 period, there were 36,993 MSM Enterprises were established with an investment of ₹ 20,561.28 crores providing employment to 5,20,996 persons (MSME reports).

**Table 1. Classification of the MSME**

| *Classification* | *Investment in Plant and Machinery or Equipment* | *Annual Turnover* |
|---|---|---|
| Micro | Not more than ₹ 1 crore and | Not more than ₹ 5 crore |
| Small | Not more than ₹ 10 crore | Not more than ₹ 50 crore |
| Medium | Note more than ₹ 10 crore | Not more than ₹ 250 crore |

***Source:*** Ministry of Micro, Small & Medium Enterprises, Govt of India, 2020.

**3. Classification:** The Central Government has revised to MSME's which is effect from 01.07.20. As per this, the MEME's classification has done based on the Investment in Plant and Machinery/equipment and Annual Turnover. Each of the industry described below:

(a) **Micro enterprise:** It means where the investment in Plant and Machinery or Equipment does not exceed 1 crore rupees and turnover does not exceed 5 crore rupees;

(b) **Small enterprise:** It means where the investment in Plant and Machinery or Equipment does not exceed 10 crore rupees and turnover does not exceed 50 crore rupees;

(c) **Medium enterprise:** It means where the investment in Plant and Machinery or Equipment does not exeed 50 crore rupees and turnover does not exceed 250 crore rupees.

4. **Influenced factors:** Industrial sectors need strong marketing strategy, easy funding, skilled labour forces, training programmes and Government incentives for the long run and better performance.

4.1 **Marketing Strategy:** Marketing is most important factor for the success of any enterprise especially MSME's. It is one of the weakest areas wherein MSMEs face major problems in the present competitive era. Due to lack of information, scarcity of resources unorganised way of selling/marketing is very less opportunities. MSME sector finds problems in exploiting new markets.

4.2 **Funding:** Initially, to launch MSM Entrepreneurs are not lending money from the bankers or other registered sources, but they start firms by using the own money or adjust from the relatives or friends. For the upliftment of he MSME's the State Government has been providing incentives and also increased allocations in budget from 21.55 crore to 1132 crores. As per budget reports, the establishment expenditure for Industries and Commerce department has increased from ₹ 178.74 crore to ₹ 329.98 crore during the financial years 2019-20 and 2020-2021.

4.3 **Labour Force:** Telangana State has huge labour force in rural areas as well as urban areas. Based on the district resources, Government has promoted Technical Education as well as normal educational institution like ITI's, Polytechnics and Engineering Colleges and vocational courses to create labour force across the state. The employment opportunities in the industries are attracting to other state's people like Andhra Pradesh, Bihar, Karnataka, Odisha, Rajasthan, and Tamil Nadu etc. which means more in migration is noted in the State.

4.4 **Training Programmes:** In Telangana State, MSME's Development Institute conducts Training Programmes like Industrial Motivation Campaigns (IMC); Entrepreneurship Development Programmes (EDP), Entrepreneurship Skill Development Programmes (ESDP) and Management Development Programmes (MDP).

4.5 **Government Initiatives:** The State Government has been providing estimates for assistance to Telangana Khadi and Village Industries Board, 'prevention of sickness to SMEs' and others. In 2020-2021 budgets, the Govt also prposed ₹ 1500 crores incentives towards industrial and 1988 crores are proposed for the industrial sector development. The Govt is also providing funds through the Pavalavaddi Scheme for the all food processing units. According to MSME Ministry report 2019-20, a total 26.05 lakh MSME's are located in the Telangana State. Among all, 25.94 lakh (99.5%) from the Micro-Enterprises, 10,000 are from small units and remaining 1000 belongs to medium units. Presently, some of the MSME's from Telangana State also registered on the Stock Exchange.

5. **Prestigious Schemes:** Telangana State Government has taken good programmes and many schemes for the upliftment of the MSME's. The following scheme like NMCP, ISO, and Cluster Development Programmes. Credit Guarantee Scheme for collateral free loan; Credit linked Capital Subsidy scheme for technology upgradation; ISO 9000/14000 expenses reimbursement scheme; Participation in International Trade Fairs; MSE-Cluster Development Scheme; National Awards. It also introduced

one digital links i.e. Global Linker portal to support growing business of the MSME's. It is completely free e-commerce store with payment gateway and logistics capabilities, buyers-sellers connect, and support for export. Some of the main schemes or policies have discussed below.

5.1 **T-IDEA:** The State Government has framed the new industrial policy in 2014 which is called Telangana State Industrial Development and Entrepreneur Advancement (T-IDEA). The main objective is to provide sustainable industrial development; to create gainful employment opportunities. Under this scheme, Govt is providing incentives like Fixed power cost reimbursement @ ₹ 1.00/ unit for five years from the date of commencement of commercial production; 15 percent investment subsidy on fixed capital investment subject to a maximum of ₹ 20.00 lakhs; VAT reimbursement; Interest subsidy; 100 percent Stamp duty reimbursement; 25 percent rebate in land cost limited to ₹ 10.00 Lakhs in Industrial Parks; Land conversion cost; Seed capital for 1st generation entrepreneur; Training and skill development cost reimbursement; Reimbursement of infrastructure development costs; Interest subsidy under Pavala Vaddi Scheme etc. Women owned Enterprises are also benefiting under the scheme.

5.2 **T-Pride:** It is a scheme of new industrial enterprises in the state for SC/ST a entrepreneur which is called (T-PRIDE) Telangana State Programme for Rapid Incubation of Dalit Entrepreneurs incentive scheme. The new industrial policy created a number of additional supports to increase the SC/STs entrepreneurs. Under this scheme, all manufacturing activities set up by SC and ST entrepreneurs after 1/11/2014 are eligible for availing incentives/concessions under this policy. SC/ST owned Enterprises. The one of the main goal of this scheme is to create minimum 200 SC/ST contractors over a five years period.

5.3 **IIPP:** Another incentive for the state entrepreneurs is Industrial Investment Promotion Policy (IIPP) – Extension of time period for availing incentives in respect of Micro and Small Enterprises and Textile Units (2010-2015). Past five years, for incentives many requests are received by the Government from the SC/ST entrepreneurs who were established during the period of 2010-2015. Under IIPP they are eligible to reimbursement of Sales Tax, Pavala Vaddi Incentive and reimbursement of Power cost for the remaining period under the old policy + one additional year under the T-IDEA Policy 2014.

5.4 **TS-iPass:** Telangana Government was introduced Telangana State Industrial Project Approval and Self Certificate System (TS-iPass) in 2014. The Main objective is speedy processing of applications for issue of various clearances required for setting up of industries at a single point based on the self-certificate provided by the entrepreneur and also to create investor friendly environment in the State. It is also one of the best schemes in the country and also major scheme to accomplish the mandate minimum inspection and maximum facilitation and also attracting investments in the state.

**Table 2. Industrial Status in Telangana State-T.S. iPass**

| *Financial Years* | *No. of Industries* | *No. of ind. Manufacturing* | *No. of ind. Service Sector* | *Total Investment (₹ Crores)* | *Total Employment* |
|---|---|---|---|---|---|
| 2014-2015 | 174 | 174 | 0 | 1806 | 5051 |
| 2015-2016 | 1536 | 1536 | 0 | 28990 | 94454 |
| 2016-2017 | 1710 | 1578 | 132 | 34484 | 98794 |
| 2017-2018 | 2811 | 2496 | 315 | 57423 | 274248 |
| 2018-2019 | 2821 | 2458 | 363 | 34830 | 604679 |
| 2019-2020 | 3091 | 2741 | 350 | 40526 | 316433 |
| 2020-2021 | 2003 | 1807 | 196 | 8741 | 61496 |
| **Total** | **14146** | **12790 (90.4%)** | **1356 (9.6%)** | **206800** | **1455155** |

*Source:* TS-iPass, 2020.

Regarding MSME's, a total 14146 industries have been registered under TS-iPass from 2014-15 to 2020-21 period. Among all the industries, the

**Table 3. Year-wise Details of Manufacturing and Service Sector in Telangana State**

| *Financial Year* | *Manufacturing Sector* | | | | | *Service Sector* | | | | |
|---|---|---|---|---|---|---|---|---|---|---|
| | *Micro* | *Small* | *Medium* | *Total* | *%* | *Micro* | *Small* | *Medium* | *Total* | *%* |
| 2014-15 | 42 | 86 | 23 | 151 | 86.8 | 0 | 0 | 0 | 0 | 0 |
| 2015-16 | 483 | 764 | 105 | 1352 | 88.0 | 0 | 0 | 0 | 0 | 0 |
| 2016-17 | 841 | 635 | 25 | 1501 | 95.1 | 64 | 40 | 10 | 114 | 86.4 |
| 2017-18 | 1336 | 955 | 44 | 2335 | 93.5 | 155 | 92 | 23 | 270 | 85.7 |
| 2018-19 | 1477 | 854 | 42 | 2373 | 96.5 | 158 | 98 | 12 | 268 | 73.8 |
| 2019-20 | 1746 | 850 | 43 | 2639 | 96.3 | 204 | 97 | 7 | 308 | 88.0 |
| 2020-21 | 1332 | 414 | 23 | 1769 | 97.9 | 146 | 29 | 4 | 179 | 91.3 |
| **Total** | **7257 (59.8%)** | **4558 (37.6%)** | **305 (2.5%)** | **12120 (100)** | **94.8*** | **727 (63.8%)** | **356 (31.2%)** | **56 (4.9%)** | **1139 (100)** | **84.0*** |

Source: TS-iPass, 2020 *MSME share to the total industries which includes large and mega industries

share of the manufacturing sector is above 90 percent and the rest of the 10 percent share from the service sector. During the 2019-20, the highest (3091) industries are recorded while lowest (174) is in 2014-15 year. From 2014 to 2020, a total 206800 crores have been invested and created 14.55 lakh jobs for the eligible persons. Up to February -2020, there are 12427 industries are obtained permission from TS-iPass. Under these industries, attracted to 204000 crores of investments and created opportunities for 14 lakhs people, said by the State Finance Minister.

According to the G.Alivelu (2013) from CESS, share of the manufacturing sector (registered and unregistered) in SDP declined in 2006-07 vis-à-vis 1993-94 in Telangana and the share of service sector in SDP increased in Telangana in 2004-05 over 1993-94. In the growth centres, share of the registered manufacturing sector in DDP in Hyderabad registered a large decline in the share of manufacturing sector in SDP (34 percentage points) in 2006-07 compared to 1993-94. It is interesting to note that the share of the service sector in SDP in 2006-07 increased in Hyderabad district by as high as 13 percentage points over 1993-94.

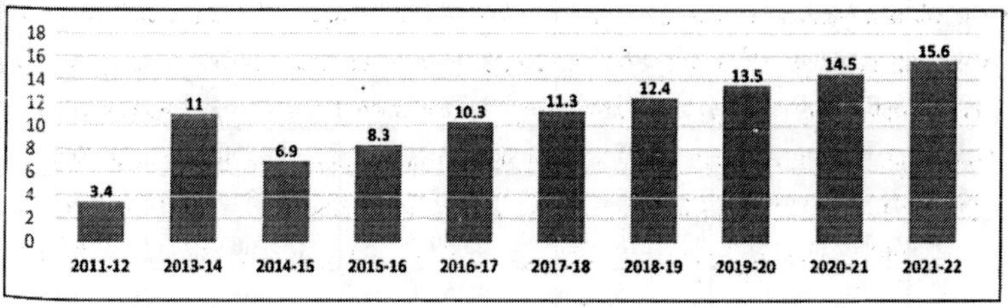


Source: TS-iPass, Annual report-2017.

The manufacturing sector is dominating in the state compare to the service sector. As per the TS-iPass data from 2014-2020, total 12120 MSME's are registered in manufacturing sector. Among the all, micro industries share is higher than the other two industries such as small (37.6%) and medium (2.5%) scale industries. When we see the service sector data, very less. Regarding to service sector, micro industries are dominating to the other two industries of small and medium scale. The Table 2 explains the manufacturing and service sector of MSME's. A total 94.8 percent of the MSME's industries are registered and rest of the 5.2 percent is from the large and mega industries and same in service sector also MEME's registered 84 percent and rest of the 16 percent is from the large and mega industries.

**Graph 2: No. of industries across the 31 districts of the State** (Jan-2015 to Mar-2017)

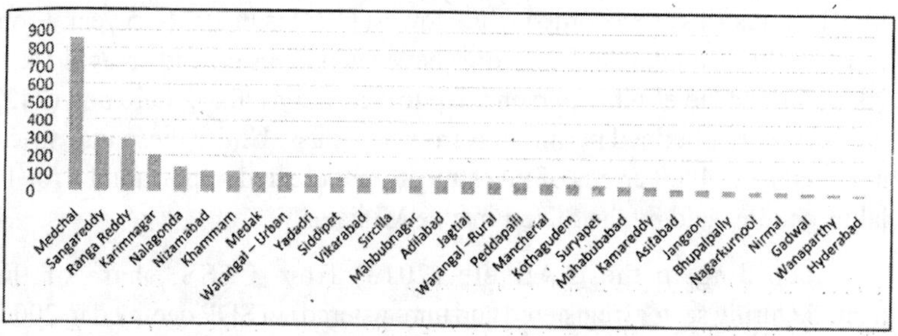


*Source:* TS-iPass Annual report-2017.

**Total 4. District-wise Report – Effect of TS-iPASS on Setting up of New Industries**

| *S.No.* | *Districts* | *No. of Industries* | *Investment (₹ In Crores)* | *Total Employment* | *Share to the Total Industries* |
|---|---|---|---|---|---|
| 1 | Medchal | 853 | 4481.13 | 28214 | 24.7 |
| 2 | Sangareddy | 300 | 5858.63 | 23384 | 8.7 |
| 3 | Ranga Reddy | 293 | 9329.55 | 96164 | 8.5 |
| 4 | Karimnagar | 207 | 3460.99 | 4250 | 6.0 |
| 5 | Nalgonda | 138 | 892.21 | 3339 | 4.0 |
| 6 | Nizamabad | 118 | 257.99 | 7663 | 3.4 |
| 7 | Khammam | 118 | 5415.51 | 4695 | 3.4 |
| 8 | Medak | 110 | 1563.53 | 6306 | 3.2 |
| 9 | Warangal–Urban | 110 | 143.68 | 1402 | 3.2 |
| 10 | Yadadri | 103 | 489.42 | 3601 | 3.0 |
| 11 | Siddipet | 88 | 1037.08 | 5623 | 2.5 |
| 12 | Vikarabad | 84 | 566.42 | 1520 | 2.4 |
| 13 | Sircilla | 80 | 93.68 | 1114 | 2.3 |
| 14 | Mahbubnagar | 78 | 2141.35 | 4661 | 2.3 |
| 15 | Adilabad | 76 | 631.11 | 1251 | 2.2 |
| 16 | Jagtial | 72 | 14.99 | 438 | 2.1 |
| 17 | Warangal – Rural | 68 | 68.82 | 829 | 2.0 |
| 18 | Peddapalli | 66 | 7865.21 | 1407 | 1.9 |
| 19 | Mancherial | 63 | 5676.31 | 1644 | 1.8 |

*Conted...*

| | | | | | |
|---|---|---|---|---|---|
| 20 | Kothagudem | 61 | 2067.6 | 2970 | 1.8 |
| 21 | Suryapet | 53 | 371.56 | 996 | 1.5 |
| 22 | Mahabubabad | 50 | 57.57 | 610 | 1.4 |
| 23 | Kamareddy | 50 | 219.2 | 1699 | 1.4 |
| 24 | Asifabad | 40 | 36.81 | 277 | 1.2 |
| 25 | Jangaon | 37 | 3261.19 | 2077 | 1.1 |
| 26 | Bhupalapalli | 32 | 34.89 | 459 | 0.9 |
| 27 | Nagarkurnool | 28 | 592.95 | 667 | 0.8 |
| 28 | Nirmal | 27 | 417.44 | 227 | 0.8 |
| 29 | Gadwal | 22 | 827.5 | 12423 | 0.6 |
| 30 | Wanaparthy | 16 | 345.13 | 548 | 0.5 |
| 31 | Hyderabad | 10 | 121.68 | 300 | 0.3 |
| | **Total** | **3451** | **58341.13** | **220758** | **100.0** |

*Source:* TS-iPass Annual report-2017.

According to the TS-iPass 2017, Medchal district received highest no. of industries, followed by the Sangareddy and Rangareddy districts. After this, Karimnagar, Nalgonda and Nizamabad districts are attracting more number of industries. From bottom level, undivided Mabhubnagar districts namely; Gadwal and Wanaparthy are existed. Hyderabad district is also recorded only 10 industries during the same period. The Table 4 giving detailed statistics in terms of number of units set up, total investment and employment of all the 31 districts. If we look into the state-wise statistics, a total 3451 industries are located with 58341.13 crores investments and created 220758 jobs for the people.

**5.5 Special Economic Zones:** Telangana Industrial Infrastructure Corporation (TIIC) of State is the nodal agency for the development of SEZs on behalf of the Government whereas the other SEZs in the private sector are to be developed by the respective promoters themselves. Six SEZs in the fields of IT, Aerospace, Biotech, Formulations in Telangana developed so far. As a part of Government initiative of developing IT Park in tier-2 cities, the State IIC has developed SEZ at Madikonda village in Warangal District which is proving employment to the local people. As a major IT cluster, Raheja IT Park at Madhapur, APIIC has developed to the FAB city SEZ at Srinagar and Ravirala to Semi-Conductor Industries; some of the other TIIC assisted projects out of the 13 industries under Special Economic Zone are Hyderabad Gems SEZ for Gems and Jewellery, Infosys,

Pocharam for IT Facility and Divya Sree NSL Infrastructure. Knowledge based industries such as IT; Pharma and Engineering components have a strong presence in Telangana. They are largely located in Hyderabad and erstwhile Ranga Reddy districts which have strong infrastructure such as SEZs, availability of skilled manpower and research institutions.

**Table 5. Existing and Proposed Industrial Zones of Telangana State**

| *Ind. Zones* | *Existing industrial sector* | *Proposed Industrial sector* |
|---|---|---|
| **Jeeddimetla** | Automotive based Industries, General Engineering, Steel Rerolling, R & D of Biotech, Pharmaceuticals, vaccines, Chemicals, Paints, Pesticides, Bulk Drugs | Parma, Food processing, Chemicals, Engineering |
| **Karimnagar** | General engineering, Rice mills, Oil mills, and other agro based industries, Pipes, Paints, Granite etc. | Fertilizer, Power, Cement, Textiles, Paper, Minerals and Food processing |
| **Patancheru** | Pharmaceutical, Chemical, Textile, Logistics and warehousing, Edible Oils; General Engineering, Steel rolling, Paints, Rubber and Tyre | Chemicals, Engineering, Automobiles and Pharmaceuticals |
| **Shamshabad** | Pharmaceutical, Auto ancillary, chemicals, Warehousing, Food processing and Beverage industry, Aerospace, Solar Equipment, Electronic Hardware, Bulk Drugs | IT, Pharma, Food proceesing, Defence and Aerospace, Textiles, Consumer products |
| **Warangal** | General Engineering, Agro based industries, Plastic, granite based, Warehousing | Mineral, Food processing, Textile and Leather, Cement, Pharma, Granite, Power, Metallurgy Paper |
| **Cyberabad** | IT & ITeS (Information Technology & Information technology enabled services) | IT and ITeS |

*Source:* TS-iPass and Industrial Growth of Telangana State.

The above analysis is giving clear picture on the MSME's situation in Telangana State. It clearly mentioned that, Telangana State has a lot of scope to investment MSME's in all sectors. Compare to the large and mega projects, the MSME's are giving large amount of fruits to the society of Telangana State. Before going to discuss scope of the industrial units across the Telangana, we need to understand the Telangana State Profile.

6. **Telangana State:** After bifurcation of the erstwhile Andhra Pradesh, the geographical area of the Telangana State is 1,12,077 sq. kms, with a population of 3,50,03,674 comprising 83,03,612 households with 1,76,11,633 males and 1,73,92,041 females. The sex ratio of the state is 988. In the state, 61.1 percent of the population are living in rural areas and the rest of the population (38.8%) is living in urban areas. The density of

the population is 312. In terms of the literacy by gender, it is 75.04 percent of males against 57.9 percent females. Of the total population in the State, Scheduled Castes (SC's) constitute 15.4 percent and the Scheduled Tribes (ST's) 9.08 percent. Each district has its own geographical importance like soils, cropping pattern, and water facility (domestic and irrigation), and mineral resources. Based on the all sources, we can assume the strength of the districts. Northern and North-Eastern part of Telangana covered with thick forest and Godavari River catchment area. Southern Telangana area drained by the Krishna River and part of the Nagarkurnool and Wanaparthy covered with Nallamala forest. The Central Telangana covered with Musi and Manjeera rivers which are indicates the opportunities for the investors.

6.1 **Agriculture based Industries:** The state is producing a large amount of agro products like seeds and poultry. Based on the agro based productions, there is a huge opportunity to add value to agro-products and expand the existing strengths. The state government has promoting greenhouse cultivation, mechanisation, crop loan or Raitu Bandu scheme for the investment in the agro based fields, low investment and high returns etc. to improve the farmer's financial status. Runa Mafi also is going to support improvise the state farmers status. The state is covered with Red and Black soils which are very supporting to cultivate Rice, Maize, Groundnut, and Sugarcane. The major horticulture crops are Chilli, Onion, Turmeric, Mango, Guava, Papaya, Pomegranate, and Tamarind etc. The state is also producing the large amount of poultry and animals meat.

**Telangana State Food Processing Society (TSFPS):** New Government has established Telangana State. Food Processing Society (TSFPS) to promote Food Processing industries in Telangana State. The FP industries are process to the raw materials like Cereals, Pulses, Oilseeds, Fruits and Vegetables, Milk related, Poultry and Meat related and Fish produces. Under TSFPS, the Government providing grant-in-aid up to 50 percent of the total project cost and other incentives to set up the processing units across the state.

The society is also providing grants for the preservation infrastructure and cold chains. Telangana Government has established Major Food Parks in the major areas of the State. They are (1) Smart Agro Mega Food Park Pvt. Ltd, in Nizamabad District; (2) Raagamayuri Agrovet Pvt. Ltd in Mahabubnagar District; (3) TSIIC Food Park in Khammam District; Basavashakti Mega Food Park Pvt. Ltd, in Medak District. The MSME's sector investors are having good scope to invest here. The districts such as erstwhile Nizamabad, erstwhile Karimnagar and erstwhile Warangal are largely dependent on agriculture and are in need of industrial development.

6.2 **Scope for Mineral based Industries:** As per the Survey of India, Telangana with varied geological basis has rich and wide variety of minerals suitable for specific mineral industries. The State is a house for various minerals specifically Coal, Iron Ore, Limestone, Dolomite, Manganese, Quartz, Feldspar, Stowing Sand, Laterite, Clays, Yellow Ochre, Barytes, Uranium, Black and Colour Granites, Limestone Slabs, Fullers Earth, Marble, Road Metal/Building Stone/Ballast, Gravel/Earth and Ordinary Sand.

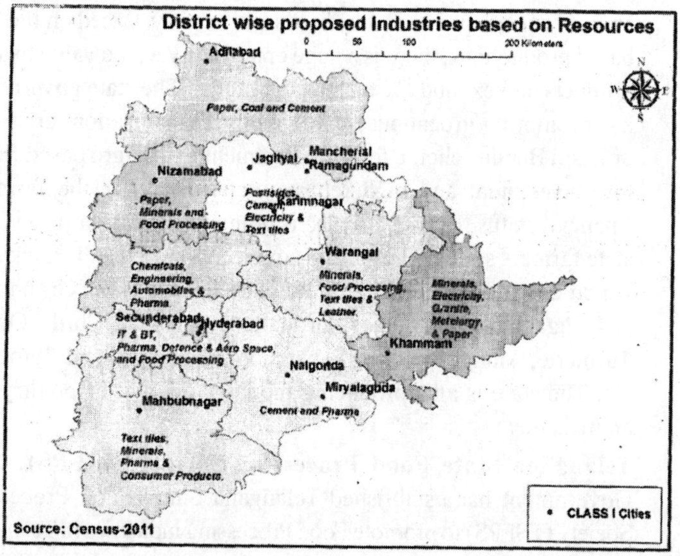


*Fig. Districtwise proposed Indusries, based on Resoures -2011.*

The following analysis has done based on the Commissionerate of Industries and Directorate of Mines & Geology Departments data. The both department have done exercise and mapped district-wise agriculture crops and minerals availability. These two departments are given information on potentiality of the agro and mineral based industries. The MSME's and other industries have better opportunity or scope to establish the industrial units at the Industrial parks or appropriate places across the Telangana State. The following discussion is going on the scope of the agro and food based and mineral based industries across the each new district of the Telangana State.

**Adilabad District:** Adilabad district has scope for the establishment of Agro based industries like Modern Rice Mill and Rice flakes in Utnoor, Mini Modern Rice Mill in Ichoda, Bazarhathnoor; Dall Mill in Narnoor, Inderavelly, Gudihathnur, Ichoda; Edible Oil Expellers in Narnoor, Gadhiguda, Sirikonda, Inderavelly, Neradigonda, Jainath mandals; The bread bakery industry also suitable in the Utnoor, Adilabad, Ichoda and Boath mandals and Ice Creams related industries are need in Narnoor, Inderavelly, Boath, Jainath, Bela, Gudihathnoor and Neradigonda mandals. Cold Storage in Adilabad, Ichoda, Gudihathnur and Cattle feed/Poultry Feed at Adilabad and Utnoor.

In Adilabad district, conduction related industrial units have better scope. The manganese ore related industries are required.

**Bhadradri district:** Rice, Cotton, Maize, and Chillies are major crops. Nurseries and Horticulture units have scope to establish at Aswaraopet, Bhadrachalam and Dammapeta region. Palm, Cashew processing units at Awaraopet and Dammapeta region in Bhadradri District. There is very huge scope for setup of mini industrial parks areas in Manuguru, Yellandu, Bhadrachalam, Palvancha, Burgampahad, Kothagudem areas. Forest based such as Tamarind processing, Honey processing, Beedi leaf, vippa, Extracts from the Medicinal plants and Agro based industries like Cotton Ginning, Rice mills, Dal mills; Food and Fruit processing units are suitable to establish in the Bhadradri district.

Bhadradri district has rich in minerals like Coal, Copper, Graphite, Quartz, Lime Stone, Marble, Chromite, and Barytes. The Mineral related industrial units have good opportunities in Kothagudem district.

**Hyderabad District:** The Hyderabad City also major marketing Centre like Secunderabad (Monda), Madannapet, Bharat Nagar, Gaddiannaram, and Gudimalkapur etc. Fish Markets are located in Secunderabad, Begumbazar, Puranapul, Mangalghat, M.J. Market etc. for outlet for the farmers to sell their produce. Other area is also having good scope for any business across the city.

In Hyderabad district, there is a demand for various minerals and ores is met from the raw materials being supplied from other district, since no quarrying is done within the city limits.

**Jagitial District:** In the district, Paddy, Maize, Cotton, Pulses, Soyabean and Turmeric related food processing units are required here. The State Government has been identified Industrial Parks in Dharmapuri Pegadapalli and Velgatur Mandals and Sthambampalli is also identified for industrial purpose in Jagitial district.

Colour Granite, Stone Metal, Ordinary Sand and Multi Colour Granites are available in the Jagitial district. The main activity of minerals is found in Jagitial, Raikal, Sarangapur, Beerpur, Dharmapuri, Buggaram, Pegadapally, Gollapally, Mallyal, Kodimyal, Velgatoor, Korutla, Metpally, Mallapur, Ibrahimpatnam, Medipally, and Kathalapur Mandals. In Jagithyal, Pegadapally, Gollapally, Malyal Mandals Granite quarry leases are located. Around Velgatoor, Buggaram, Kodimyal, Korutla some Stone and Metal quarry leases and stone crushers are located.

**Jayashankar District:** Paddy related industries are suitable in Eturunagaram, Bhupalapali; Maize related processing unit's having scope to invest in Bhupalapalli, Mulugu. Cotton industries are required in Bhupalapalli and Mahdevpur areas. Pulses like Red gram, Green gram, Black gram and Chilli processing units are needed at Bhupalapalli and Mahadevpur mandals.

Coal is available in Mulug, Ghanpur and Bhupalpally mandals. Laterite, Dolomite, Colour Granite, and Iron-ore is available in Mulugu mandal. Sand is available in Eturnagaram and Mangapet mandals. These areas are having scope to establish industrial units.

**Jogulamba District:** Major crops are Cotton, Groundnut, Castor, Chillies and Maize, Onion and Red gram. There is need to establish processing units. The Horticulture crops like Mango, Citrus, Guava and Papaya and Silk sarees related investment has good scope in Gadwal district. Raaga Mayuri Agrovet Private Limited is establishing mega Food Park in Jogulamba district.

In Jogulamba district, there is a scope to invest on Solar Park in Gattu mandal. The State Government has proposed solar park.

**Kamareddy District:** In Kamareddy district, there is a good scope for establishment of industrial park along the national highway towards Hyderabad City. Other agro based industries like Modern Rice mills, Seed processing, Vegetable Oil Refinery, Maize Starch, Mini Dhal mills, Oil mills, Spice powders, Bakeries, Ice cream, Confectionery, Chilly and Masala powder, Vermicelli, Veg-Noodles, Biscuits and cookies, Tissue Culture, Pickles, Papads, Groundnut, Chikkie, Cattle Feed Poutry Feed etc. have good opportunity to establish in the district. Readymade garments have scope in Kamareddy, Bhiknoor and Nizamsagar

The Kamareddy district is not rich in minerals. Poor quality iron ore and few places as laterite and ferrogenous quartzites are available. Alumina is available in Gurjakunta of Bhiknoor Mandal and Karedpally in Tadwai Mandal. White calcareous Kaolinised earth is found near Tippapur, Bhiknoor and Kupriyal. Granites of various quartzes and Deccan trap rocks is available in the district. Quartz and Feldspar, Laterite and Stone Metal related industrial units have scope in the district.

**Karimnagar District:** Mango, Baneshan, Dasheri, Himayath Banana, Grand naine, Papaya related units in required in the Karimnagar district. Taiwan Red lady, Tomato, Bhendi, Ridgegourd, Bittergourd, Green Chilli, Leafy Vegetables, Red Chilli, Turmeric are major crops and having good chance to establish related industries. Rice Mills, Seed Processing Spinning mill, Cotton seed oil, Mini Dall Mills, Cotton ginning and pressing, Chicken processing, Maize flakes, Poultry and Cattle feed, Bread and Biscuits, Ice Blocks Bio fertilizers, Pickles, Mango processing, Rice and Corn flakes related industries have good scope to establish here. Bommakal village of Karimnagar Mandal is also under acquisition for establishment of Industrial Parks.

Karimnagar district has mineral resource such as Granite of various colours and sand. These types of mineral related industries have better scope across the district.

**Khammam District:** Agriculture or Horticulture in Chillies related industries have good scope to establish in all 21 mandals of the Khammam district. Manufacturing, Handicraft Terracotta related MSME's are required in Singareni, Konijerla, Khammam (R), Sathupally, Vemsoor mandals.

Khammam district has vast Granite deposits at Khammam Urban, Khammam rural, Mudigonda, Thirumalayapalem and Raghunadhapalem which areas are having good scope to establish industrial units.

**Kumuram Bheem district:** The district have predominantly, black 'cotton' soil and red soil. There is a scope to setup units related to tamarind seeds, traditional bamboo and commercial bamboo based units and extraction units from medicinal plants. Cotton, paddy, red gram, Jowar, and Soya bean and horticulture crops giving good chance to get more benefits. Kumuram Bheem district has potential to be pulses hub of South India. The district has scope to establish milk chilling centres, and dairy units, and also having scope for breeding buffalos, sheep and goats. Due to plenty of water facilities, fisheries related industries need here.

Komarambheem Asifabad district has lime stone deposits at Rebbena, Dehagoan; Thiryani, Rebbena has good coal mines and Rebbena, Asifabad have white clay. The Jainoor, Kagaznagar have Road Metal and building Stone minerals which have scope to establish industrial units like cement, ceramic units and limestone based units, pickle jar making, and decorative tiles.

**Mahbubnagar District:** In Mahbubnagar district, major crops are Paddy, Jowar, Bajra and Raagi and Cotton, Groundnut, Castor, Chillies and Maize, Pulse (Red-gram), Mango, Citrus, Guava and Papaya. The above mentioned crops or fruits related industries have opportunities to establish at Mahbubnagar, Jadcherla, Badepally, Nawabpet, Balanagar, Addakal, and Midjil Mandals.

The Mahabubnagar district has rich minerals like Quartz, Feldspar, Limestone, Barytes, Semiprecious Stones. The Quartz available in Balanagar, Midjil mandals and limestone is available in Narayanpet Mandal which are giving best opportunities to establish industries.

**Mancherial District:** Paddy is the main crop in the district. Mini Rice Mills need at Luxettipet, Bellampally, Bheemini, Kannepally; Flour Mill have scope at Jannaram, Mandamarri and Dandepalli. The Mango Products, fruit processing pickles and pulp juices industries have good scope at Dandepalli, Bellampally, Jaipur, Kotapalli, Nennel. Cold Storages need at Mancherial, Bellampally, Nennel, and Chennur. Cattle/Poultry feed units required at Luxettipet, Jannaram. Readymade doors have better opportunities in Mancherial, Bellampally, and Chennur. Readymade garments by Women entrepreneurs good chance at Luxettipet, Mancherial, Bellampally, Mandamarri, Chennur, Jannaram. Dall Mill has scope at Jannaram, Luxettipet, Mancherial, Bellampally, and Tandur mandals.

Mancherial district is very rich in mineral deposits like Lime Stone, White Clay, Coal Quartz, Laterite, Stone and Metal, Iron Ore, and Sand. All minerals have better scope for the establishment of the industrial unit in Mancherial district.

**Medak District:** Narsapur is suitable to establish MSM entrepreneurs like Cold Storage hubs, Seed Processing Units, Super Speciality hospital, Bio-mass power generation plants. The Medak district is also proving lot of opportunities in the sectors of construction, hospital, hotal, educational, socio-economic development needs.

Madak district has rich minerals like Quartz, Feldspar, Building Stone, Road metal and Granite which are occur in the several mandals like

Ramanthapur, Asthalapur, Masaipet villages in Yeldurthy mandal; Ramayampet mandal; Lingareddypally, Allapur, and Ghanpur Villages in Toopran mandal.

**Medchal District:** Food Processing and Cold Storage Industries have good chance at Medchal, Uppal areas. Packaging Material need at Kapra and Medchal; Electrical and Electronics sectors have good scope at Kapra. Textile/Ready Made Garments are required in Medchal, and Shamirpet mandals. Biotech products have scope in Shamirpet. Dairy Products have scope in Keesara, Ghatkesar, Shamirpet, Medipally, and Medchal Mandals. Seed processing units have better chance at Medchal mandal. There is a place for establishment industries at Shamirpet, Balanagar, Kukatpalli, Gajularamaram, Mallapur, Maoulali, Kushaiguda, Cherlapalli, Nacharam, Uppal, and Medchal.

Major minerals of the Medchal district are Quartz and Feldspars which are need more industrial units here.

**Nagarkurnool District:** In the district, cropping area has been increasing with availability of water from mission Kakatiya scheme and MGKLI scheme. Due to this many agro based industries can be set up like Cotton Ginning mills and spinning mills, Rice Mills, Ground Nut Decorticators, Poultry and cattle feed units. The district has also good scope for fisheries sector. Due to high number of Sheep's, need many industries at Nagarkurnool, Tadoor, Bijinepally, Telkapally, Peddakottapally, Kollapur, Kodair, and Pentlavelly.

In Nagarkurnool district, Quartz and Feldspar have good industrial scope at Vangoor and Veldanda mandal. Granite industrial units have better opportunities in Telkapally mandal.

**Nalgonda District:** Rice, Jowar, Maize, Bajra, Red gram, Green gram Groundnut, Chillies, Cotton, Castor, Sugarcane are major crops in the district. Fishery related scope has in Peddaedevulapalli, Nalgonda and Miryalguda Towns. Rice Mill Cluster need at Miryalguda; Poultry grit Cluster required at Damarcherla. Pharma, Incubation centre, and testing labs also have scope for the investment in the Nalgonda district. Sweet orange, Acid Lime & Mango etc. Cotton and Ginning pressing units need here. Power Looms, Solar Power Projects, Chemical Industries, Cold storage and Ice plants, Seed processing units, Dal Mills, Groundnut Decorticating, Neem Cake, Milk Chilling and Milk Products, Poultry Farms, Meat processing, Fruits, Ripening Chambers, Agricultural Implements and Fertiliser units have better scope across the district.

The major mineral such as Limestone Slabs, Uranium, Gold, Diamond, Road Metal, Quartz, Feldspar, Black and Colour Granite, and Ordinary Sand available in Nalgonda district which are having good scope to establish the industrial units. Stone Cutting and Polishing at industrial cluster is existed at Adavidevulapally mandal.

**Nirmal District:** Paddy, Maize, Turmeric, Chilly, Cotton, Soya bean, fisheries related industries have good scope in Nirmal district. Textile industry have scope due to Cotton. Modern Rice mills have scope in Kaddam, Khanapur, Nirmal, Laxmanchanda, Dilawarpur and Lokeshwaram. Paraboiled Rice Mills required at Nirmal and Khanapur, Dall Mills, Cotton Ginning and Pressing units required at Bhainsa. Seed Processing Units need at Nirmal and Khanapur. Readymade Garments have good scope at Nirmal, Fuel Briquettes need at Nirmal and Bhainsa. Banded Cotton Industry has good scope at Bhainsa and Cold Storage need at the Nirmal and Bhainsa mandals. Stone Crusher need at Nirmal, Bhainsa, and Dilawarpur. Paper Plates have good scope in the Nirmal, Bhainsa, Khanapur, and Kaddam mandals. Fly ash Bricks need at Nirmal, Khanapur, and Kaddam. Tin Sheet Units required at Nirmal. Agricultural Implements required at Khanapur, Mudhol mandals. Bread and Bakery have better opportunities in Nirmal, Khanapur, and Bhainsa mandals. Soya products have scope for industries at Nirmal.

Nirmal district, Building Stone and Road Metals industrial units are required in Nirmal, Soan, Bhainsa, and Thanoor mandals. Quartz related industries need in Mudhole mandal. Stone crushing industries are located at Nirmal, Soan, Dilwarpur, Bhainsa and Thanoor mandals, and Quartz Powder unit located in Dilwarpur mandal.

**Nizamabad District:** Major crops in the district are Rice, jour crops like Jowar, Maize, Red gram, Green gram, Black gram and Bengal gram. There is scope for agro based Small Scale industries like Modern Rice mills, Seed processing, Vegetable Oil Refinery, Maize Starch, Mini Dhal mills, Oil mills, Spice powders, Bakeries, Ice cream, Confectionary, Chilly and Masala powder, Vermicelli, Veg-Noodles, Biscuits and cookies, Tissue Culture, Pickles, Papads, Groundnut, Chikkiee, Cattle Feed Poultry Feed etc. Agriculture modern machines, Readymade garments, Cloth weaving, School uniforms, Hosiery, Screen Printing on cloth sarees, Spinning Mills are having good scope to establish industries across the district.

Road Metal, Laterite, Quartz, Colour Granite, Ordinary Sand, Steel and Aluminium furniture, Automobile repair workshops, and Aluminium Utensils have best scope to establish industrial units in Nizamabad district.

## Table: District-wise Mineral Resources and Scope for Mineral Based Industries

| *District* | *Mineral Resources* | *Scope For Mineral Based Industries* |
|---|---|---|
| Adilabad | Limestone, Manganese Ore, Laterite, Stone & Road Metal, Ordinary Sand. | Establishment of Cement and Ferro Alloy Industries |
| Bhadradri | Coal, Copper & Lead, Garnet, Quartz, Feldspar, Road Metal, Marble, Ordinary Sand | Suitable locaton to setup coal based thermal power plants Sponge-Iron Units |
| Jagtial | Colour Granite, Stone Metal, Odinary Sand. | Establishment of Granite cutting and Polishing Units. |
| Jangaon | Granite, Gravel, Road Metal. | Granite cutting and polishing units, Manufactured Sand units and Stone crushing units. |
| Jayashankar | Iron Ore, Coal Laterite, Colour Granite, Road Metal, Ordinary Sand | Establishment of Power plants based on Coal Fly ash bricks, Hydrated lime units, sponge Iron Plants. |
| Mulugu | Iron Ore, Coal, Laterite, Dolomite, Road Metal, Gravel, Morrum, Ordinary Earth, Sand | Stone Crushing Units, Chemical Industries |
| Jogulamha | Colour & Black Granite, Road Metal, Laterite, Dolomite, Ordinary Sand. | Establishment of Road Metal crushing units. |
| Kamareddy | Quartz, Feldspar, Laterite, Road Metal, Sand. | Mineral based ancillary units like fly ash bricks and blocks, Cement Mosaic tiles, white Cement, Granite cutting and polishing Units, Ceramics and chemical industry have good scope for growth |
| Karimnagar | Colour & Black Granite, Stone Metal, Laterite, Ordinary Sand | Establishment of Granite Cutting and Polishing units. |
| Khammam | Garnet, Chromite, Marble, Mica, Dolomite, Corundum, Barytes, Quartz & feldspar, Colour & Bloack Granite, Road Metal, Ordinary Sand. | Sponge Iron units, thermal plants, Coal Washery units, Steel Plant, granite cutting and polishing units, Glass and Allied units, and Stone crushing units. |
| Kommam Bheem | Limestone, White Clay, Lateriate, stone Metal. | Establishment of ceramic industry and lime industry |
| Mahabubabad | Iron Ore, Barytes, Block Granite, Stone Metal, Laterite, Stowing Sand, Marble. | Establishment of Granite cutting and polishing Units |
| Mahabubnagar | Quartz, Felspar, Colour & Black Granite, Road Metal, Ordinary sand | Suitale for establishment of manufacture Sand units, Glass industries and Stone crushing units. |
| Narayanpet | Quartz, Feldspar, Road Metal, Gravel, Morrum, Ordinary Earth. | Pulverizing Units, Glass Industry, Stone Crushing Units etc. |
| Mancherial | Limestone, Coal, Stowing Sand, White Clay, granite, Stone Metal, Ordinary Sand. | Establishment of more number of Power plants near to the places of Coal availability fetches to overcome of power deficit for the State and scope for units of Cement Industry, Sponge Iron Units. |
| Medak | Quartz, Feldspar, Road Metal, Colour Granite, Ordinary Sand. | Suitable for establishment of manufacturer Sand units, Glass industries & Stone crushing units. |
| Molchal | Road Metal, Black & Colour Granite, Quartz, Feldspar, Amethyst. | Establishment of manufactured and units. Granite cutting and polishing units, Stone crushing units. |
| Nagarkurnool | Stone Metal, Quartz, Feldspar, Black Granite, Ordinary Sand. | Establishment of Quartz and Feldspar pulverizing units, Road Metal Crushing Units. |
| Nalgonda | Limestone Slabs, Uranium, Gold, Diamond, Road Metal, Quartz, Feldspar, Black & Colour Granite, Ordinary Sand. | Establishment of Uranium refining unit, Cement manufacturing units, glass and Ferro Silicon Industries, Granite cutting and polishing units, Stone curshing units. |

*Conted...*

| | | |
|---|---|---|
| Nirmal | Quartz, Road Metal. | Establishment of Road Metal crusher units. |
| Nizamabad | Colour Granite, Quartz, Road Metal, Ordinary Sand Gravel | Establishment of Road Metal crushing units and Granite Cutting and Polishing Units. |
| Peddapalli | Limestone, Laterite, Coal, Stowing Sand, Colour Granite, Road Metal. | Suitable location to setup Coal based thermal power plants Sponge-Iron Units |
| Rajanna | Colour Granite, Road Metal, Quartz. | Establishment of Granite Cutting and Polishing units. |
| Rangareddy | Road Metal, Laterite, quartz and Feldspar, Black Granite, Fullers Earth. | Establishment of manufactured sand units, Granite cutting and polishing units, Stone crushing units, Quartz and Feldspar pulverizing units. |
| Sangareddy | Quartz and Feldspar, Granite, Road Metal, Ordinary Sand. | Establishment of Granite cutting and polishing units, Ferro Silicon industries, manufacture of Glass, sand units. |
| Siddipet | Colour Granite, Road Metal, Quartz, Ordinary Sand. | Suitable for establishment of manufacture and units, Glass industries and Stone crushing units. |
| Suryapet | Limestone, Limestone Slabs, Road Metal, Black and Colour Granite, Ordinary Sand. | Establishing of Cement manufacturing units, Limestone cutting and polishing units, Stone crushing units. |
| Vikarabad | Limestone, Laterite, Quartz, Feldspar, Fulers Earth, Limestone Slabs, Road, Metal, Black Granite, Ordinary Sand. | Establishment of Cement manufacturing units, Limestone cutting and polishing units, Pulverizing units. |
| Wanaparthy | Road Metal, quartz, Feldspar, black Granite, Ordinary Sand. | Establishment of Quartz and Feldspar pulverizing units, manufacturing sand units. |
| Warangal-R | Laterite, Black and Colour Granite, Stone Metal, Ordinary Sand. | Establishment of Granite cutting and polishing units. |
| Warangal-U | Quartz, Black and Colour Granite, Road Metal, Iron Ore. | Establishment of Granite cutting and polishing units. |
| Yadadri | Road Metal, Colour Granite, Ordinary Sand. | Establishment of Manufactured Sand units, Granite cutting and polishing units and Stone units, Granite cutting and polishing units and Stone crushing units. |

*Source:* The Directorate of Mines & Geology Department, Telangana State, 2020.

**Peddapalli District:** Due to Shri Ram Sagar Project, Paddy, Maize, Cotton and chilly and Mango, Tomato, Onion and spices like turmeric and chillies etc. are growing. Based on the Agro Resources there is huge requirement to establish the industries in Peddapalli district. Green gram, Soya Bean and other food crops are turmeric, Ginger are the spices related industrial units need here. Seed Processing unit in Peddapalli and Manthani mandals. Cotton Ginning Mill in Manthani and Kalva Srirampur mandal, Cotton Seed Oil in Peddapalli mandal, Feed Mixing Plant in Eligaid and Dharmaram mandal.

Peddapalli district has coal deposits in Godavarikhani, Ramagundam, Ramagiri, Kamanpur and Manthani mandals and lime stone in Takalapalli village in Anthergaon mandal. Granite has good scope to establish units at Sultanabad, Odela and Dharmaram mandals.

**Rangareddy:** Major crops in the district are Paddy, Jowar, Bajra, and Raagi, Cotton, Groundnut, Castor, Chillies and Maize and Mango, Grape,

Guava, Pomegranate and Papaya. Along with above mentioned crops, fisheries are also having good scope for development of industries in areas of Budwel, Puppalaguda, Gandipet, Nanakramguda, Miyapur, Himayatsagar, Kismathpura, and Rajendranagar (Premavathipeta). Madapur, Manikonda, Raidurg, Khanapet, Maheshwaram, Kongarakalan, Ibrahimpatnam, Tummalur, Ibrahimpatnam. Kothur, Mannkhal, Nadergul, Adibatla are also having scope for the industrial parks.

Rangareddy has Quartz, Feldspar, Stone metal, Black granite, Laterite and Colour granite etc. The minerals is giving good scope to establish the industrial units at Abullampet, Amangal, Chevella, Talakondapally etc.

**Siddipet District:** Rice, Jowar, Maize, Red gram, Green gram, ground nut, Cotton, Sunflower, and chillies are major crops. Government is proposed clusters in Siddipet District. They are like Seed processing Cluster at Gajwel. Rice mill, Gen Engineering, Cotton Ginning, Seed Processing, Ceramic types of MSME units are existed and have scope very high in Siddipet, Dubbaka Miridoddi, Nangunoor, and Chinnakodur mandals.

Siddipet district has very less Mineral Deposits like Colour Granite, Stone Metal, Quartz, and Ordinary Sand.

**Sircilla:** Major crops in district are Rice, Maize, Red gram and Cotton. Government has proposed Industrial Park at Peddur village of Sircilla mandal and Namapur village of Mustabad mandal for establishment of Industrial Parks. Major Textile Park is also proposed at Baddenapally villages in the Thangallapally mandal. Sircilla is a major textile zone having 30000 power looms in decentralized manner creating employment to the 14000 workers either directly or indirectly. There is Textile Park in the Sircilla with modern (1600) rapiers looms provinding employment to (2000) workers. There is a good scope for Agro-based industries like seed processing units, Parboiled rice mills, Rice mills and cotton ginning units and spinning mills industries.

Rajanna district have mineral resources like Granite of various colours and there is a lot of scope to establish the granite cutting and polishing units in Boinpally, Ellanthakunta and Vemulawada mandals.

**Wanaparthy District:** Principal food grain crops are Paddy, Jowar, Bajra and Raagi, and Cotton, Groundnut, Castor, Chillies and Maize; Major Pulse crop is Red-gram; Principal, Horticulture crops are Mango, Citrus, Guava and Papaya. There is a scope for Popular Silk sarees at Kothakota and Tippadampally. The district has scope to establish Rice Mills, Ground Nut Decorticators, Poultry and cattle feed units. Potential Area of Parboiled Rice

Mills in Pangal, Weepangandla, Wanaparthy; Ground Nut Decorticators; Oil Expeller Units in Chinnambavi, Pangal, Gopalpet. Fish Processing Units need at Atmakur, Wanaparthy. Milk Chilling and Dairy Products have scope in Wanaparthy. Solar Power Plants at Peddamandadi, Pebbair, Ghanpur. Fisheries related industries also having scope in the district.

The Wanaparthy district has scope for establishing solar power plants, Bio diesel units, Mineral based units and especially or start-up industries. The district does not have Industrial Park. Very minor minerals are available in the district. They are Stone and Metal, black granite, Sand, Fullers Earth and Limestone slabs etc. occurs at Kothakota, Pangal mandals. Quartz, Feldspar, Limestone and Laterite occur in Pangal and Wanaparthy mandals which are need to establish industries.

**Warangal Rural:** Paddy, Maize, Red Gram, Black Gram, Bengal Gram, Groundnut, Cotton are the major crops. The district has industrial potentiality such as Rice Mills, Mini Dal Mills, Spices Powders, Spinning mill, Cotton seed oil, Cold Storages. Cotton ginning at Nekkonda and Pressing, Chicken processing, Maize flakes, Poultry and Cattle feed, Bread and Biscuits, Ice Blocks, Bio fertilizers, Pickles, Mango processing, Rice and Corn flakes, Sweet related industries have scope for Industries. Cold storages are required at Reddypalem, Mogilicherla. The district has a scope for establishment of cold storages, and Godowns in Gorrekunta nearby Enumamula Market yard.

In Warangal Rural also have minerals like Granite, Laterite, Dolomite, Iron-ore, and Stone Metal etc. and vast deposits of granites are available in the district.

**Warangal Urban:** The major crops of the district are Paddy, Maize, Red Gram, Green Gram, Groundnut, Chillies, Cotton Lint and Tobacco. The second largest city in the Telangana State has good scope for Textile Park at Madikonda, Cotton Ginning and Seed Pressing, Cotton Seed Oil, Cold Storages (Kothapet, Enumamula) and Spices (Enumamula). The City is also having vast scope for the developing of the IT and Bio Technology sector related industries.

Warangal Urban district has vast lands to establish the Industrial Development Areas (IDA) in Warangal, Dharmasagar, Hanamkonda, and Jangaon.

**Yadadri Bhuvanagiri:** The major crops of the district are Paddy, Maize, Cotton, Pulses, and fruits or vegetables. The district is located very near to the Hyderabad City. Based on the Government rules, some of the industries (orange and red category) are located in the city area need to shift Outer Ring Road area. Hyderabad to Warangal industrial corridor (passing through the district) will become the main centre to establish the industries. Spiritually, the Yadagirigutta temples is one of the major tourist places which is giving scope to invest in the tourism sector. Other industries like Cold-Storage/Godowns, paper products also have scope to establish here.

The Granite Industries ae required at Elkathurthy Mandal. Yadadri district have scope to establish to the industries in Granite, quartz, Feldspar, Dolorite etc.

6.3 **Problems in MSME's:** MSME sector is facing lots of problems such as getting funds, inadequate support from banking sector, lacking behind in adoption of new technology, scarcity of skilled or trained labour force, heavy competition in the market, low level marketing skills, and not availability of infrastructure facilities etc. In Telangana State, the new government has forced above issues and trying to resolve all the issues through the initiative programmes.

7. **Summery and Recommendation:** In India, MSME's are important and dynamic factor for the development of the economy and only source to fulfil and create employment in the rural India. It is also significant contribution to generate more employment; attract young people to settle as an entrepreneur, women empowerment. Establishment of MSME's are required very low investment and having good potentiality in the rural areas. There is a need of awareness about the Government schemes or incentives to utilise the benefits. It is also required proper monitoring mechanism to take appropriate decisions which are needed to present MSME's situation.

Telangana, earlier Hyderabad centric development was observed but now, new state government has focuses across the State to develop the industrial parks or corridor which is reducing regional imbalances, assuring more income and wealth. MSME secor is also helping in industrialisation of rural and backward areas TS-iPass is playing key role to attract the investments across the State. TS-IDEA and TS-PRIDE schemes are focuses and created special provisions for the MSME sector. The State focuses on the SEZ across the districts and allotting adequate number of small plots in the Industrial parks for the MEMEs. For the upliftment of the Micro units, the state developed sheds and also giving special fund for addressing initial sickness. The technology transfer and modernisation to the MSME sector and reimbursement of land conversion charges for the units in own land etc. incentives providing the Government. Based on the local environment, the State Commissioner of Industries has prepared district-wise scope for the establishment of the industries in the Mandal level. North and Central Telangana have good potentiality to establish agro based industries. Mission Kakatiya Scheme helped to production in the state, especially in erstwhile Mahbubnagar district.

The State has rich mineral resources to have scope to establish the industries. Blue Limestone Slab (Shahbad Stone) is available in Vikarabad. Gneissic Granite is available in Nizamabad district and Dolerite dykes are available in erstwhile Khammam, Warangal, Nalgonda and Mahbubnagar districts. Vast deposits of Coal and is being mined by Singareni Collieries in Godavari River basin districts. Medium grade Iron Ore deposits existed in Bayyaram Resere Forest and Float Iron Ore deposits in Mahabubadad district. Low grade scattered Iron Ore deposits in erstwhile Karimnagar, Adilabad, and Warangal districts. Uranium deposits in Nalgonda district. Manganese Ore is available in Adilabad district. Vast limestone deposits being mined by Cement Industries in erstwhile Nalgonda, Ranga Reddy, Karimnagar, and Adilabad Districts.

## References


1. D. Nagayya (2006); Development of Small and Medium Enterprises in Andhra Pradesh. Fifty years of Andhra Pradesh 1956-2006 book.
2. Dr. Parupally Anjaneyulu (Author)-PhD thesis-2015; Dynamics of Development in Telangana Region Using GIS Application.
3. Dr. S. Vijay Kumar; Role of Micro, Small & Medium Enterprises (MSMEs) in the Rural Development of India-A Way Forward.
4. G. Alivelu (2013-) Industrial Development in Andhra Pradesh Inter-Regional Disparities in Post-Reform Period?-CESS, Hyderabad.
5. G. Alivelu & D. P. Priyadarshi Joshi (2017)-Productivity Growth in Organized Manufacturing in Telangana, - CESS, Hyderabad.
6. *https://ipass.telangana-gov.in*
7. *https://www.financialexpress. com.*
8. Industrial policy framework for State of Telangana (2014)
9. Ministry of msme.gov.in
10. Socio Economic Outlook 2015, Government of Telangana, Planning Department
11. Statistical Abstract of Telangana State-2017
12. Telangana State budget report, 2020-21
13 Telangana State portal
14. The Directorate of Mines & Geology Department, Telangana State.
15. https://www.tsfps. Org/opportunities-in-ts.html
16. Vinary Kumar (2017), An Analysis of Growth of MSMEs in India and Their contribution in Employment and GDP of the Country.

# 9

# Identification of Potential Landfill Sites in the GVMC Area Using Multicriteria Evaluation Method

***Yenda, Padmini ; Killana Dileep and Bendalam, Sridhar***

## Abstract

*Today's world, Solid Waste Management (SWM) is a major global environment issue that leads to the environmental and health risk problems by intensifying the pollution activities and groundwater contamination. In the developing nations, Urban Solid Waste Management is considered as one of the most serious environmental problems for the municipal authorities. The enhancing waste generation rates stress on all the infrastructural, natural and budgetary resources with adverse impacts on the human health and environment due to the unscientific and improper solid waste dumping. Leachate generation and gas are the inevitable consequences of the solid waste disposal practice in landfills. The improper solid waste disposal in the urban economic center of Andhra Pradesh, Visakhapatnam would result in the environmental deterioration and negative aesthetic value for this tourist destination. The suitable disposal site selection should adhere to the government safety norms and ensure there would be no risk to involve to the environment or people. The different types of parameters involvement, a suitable location for the waste disposal is very complicated type, time consuming and expenditure involved. The Remote Sensing and GIS techniques in connection with the satellite imagery can build more accurate information based on many parameter's criteria to take the right decision for the solid waste disposal sites. The Multi Criteria Evaluation of Weighted Overlay analysis according to Analytical Hierarchy Process was performed for determining an appropriate solid waste disposal in the GVMC environs.*

***Key Terms:*** *Solid Waste Management, GIS, Multi Criteria, Analytical Hierarchy Process (AHP), Weightage Overlay Analysis.*

## Introduction

In today's world one of the major increasing problems faced is the Solid Waste Management. In cities, the natural outcomes of the human activities are the solid waste materials. Most of our cities and municipalities in a nation like India; Government's major concern is to the health problems associated with the improper waste disposal. The urbanisation, rapid population growth decreases the non-renewable resources and disposal of toxic waste and waste matter haphazardly are some of the major environmental issues posing menaces to the human beings existence. The most common associated problems with the improper solid waste management include the transmission of diseases, odour nuisance, water and air pollution, fire hazards, aesthetic nuisance and economic losses. Disposal of waste is a significant part of the solid waste management system that requires much care to avoid environmental pollution. Some sort of waste disposal system is prevailed in only major cities. In this study, an attempt was made on identifying a suitable solid waste disposal sites in Greater Visakha Municipal Corporation (GVMC), Andhra Pradesh.

The process of solid waste disposal management mainly consists of collection, processing recycling and disposing. In present situations, disposal of waste in most cities is done in the simple form of landfill disposing. Yet finding a good waste disposal site is of difficult task since land is a scarce resource. An increasing cost, environmental awareness enhancing, political and community opposition, public health concerns have made choosing the suitable land for landfills quite difficult task.

A disposal site must consider all the socio-economic, land use and environmental factors within the city as well as people safety. GIS and analyze the suitable site selection for urban waste disposal considering all the criteria (Multi Criteria analysis) which will help local governing body as a part of e-governance. The use of GIS in the selection process will enhance the accuracy and reduce the time.

Landfill site is a complex process involving the social, technical and environmental parameters as well as the regulations of government that requires the processing on spatial data in massive amounts. In a more generalised manner, the waste management issues should be confronted that means the new strategies need to be designed while considering the variable and diverse urban models. Besides, the new landfills site selection for municipal solid waste disposal is a great concern for the urban government as old landfill sites are being filled-up and new sites demand is enhancing. The recent technological development have introduced the Geographic Information Systems (GIS) as an innovative tool in landfill process. GIS is a digital database management which is ideal for advances site selection studies as it can effectively store, retrieve, analyze and display the information according to the user-defined criteria. The multi criteria decision techniques which help for the decision-maker to set the priorities and make the best decision by reducing the complex evaluations to a pair-wise comparisons series. This technique can be used together with GIS in arrival at the optimal solutions for the waste disposal site selection process.

## Study Area

Visakhapatnam, most popularly well-known name is Vizag is a fast developing port and smart city in India. There have been significant activities of migration into the city limits due to the rapid account of the industrialisation, urbanisation and extension of the municipal corporation limits. The study area under the investigation lies between the 83°5'0" to 83°25'0" East Longitude and 17°32'0" to 17°54'0". The GVMC urban area is divided into eight zones including the Anakapalli and Bhimili municipalities.

Vizag city is situated at an altitude of 24 meters above the mean sea level (MSL) with normal annual rainfall of 1180 mm. The city is presently ranking as the first largest urban agglomeration city in the Andhra Pradesh. In the Swachh Survekshan Survey of 2018, the Visakhapatnam city ranked as the 7$^{th}$ cleanest city in India. As per the 2017 statistics, around 2.01 Crore tourists are being attracted to the Vizag smart city. The city became the Indian Navy's Eastern Naval Command Headquarters. Rapid Industrialisation was experiencing with the major industries growth and IT sector development was also enhancing in Bhimili regions.

## Aim and Objectives

The aim of this study is to understand the present problems of waste disposal in GVMC and suggest best possible site for waste disposal sites using GIS and Remote Sensing techniques. The study area objectives are as follows:

- Examination of various factors affecting the site selection for GVMC solid waste disposal.

- Selection of suitable sites as waste disposal ground depending on the Analytical Hierarchy Process (AHP) and weightage overlay analysis tool through GIS and Remote Sensing techniques.

## Data and Software Used

- Survey of India (SOI) Toposheets – 65K O/1, 65 O/2 & O/3, 65 O/6 of scale : 1:50,000
- Sentinel-2A satellite image of GVMC study area with 10 m resolution (March, 2017)
- ASTER-DEM Data
- ARC GIS 10.3

## Methodology

For the present study area purpose, various data sources ike Toposheets, remote sensing data, geologic data, soil data, ground water level data, and surface water resources data etc. The Sentinel-2A satellite imagery data acquired on the date of Mar 29, 2017 was being used for the generation of various maps. The following are the important thematic layers under consideration for the solid waste disposal sites selection:

1. Land Use/Land Cover
2. Geology
3. Geomorphology
4. Soil
5. Slope
6. Drainage Network
7. Groundwater level
8. Streams
9. Tanks
10. Road and Railway Network

## Base Map

Using the Survey of India (SOI)Toposheets on 1:50,000 Scale the base map was prepared and updated with the assistance of satellite imagery. The information content of this map was used as a baseline data in finalising all the other physical features of maps. The features included in the base map are the major settlements, water bodies, major roads, canals and railways.

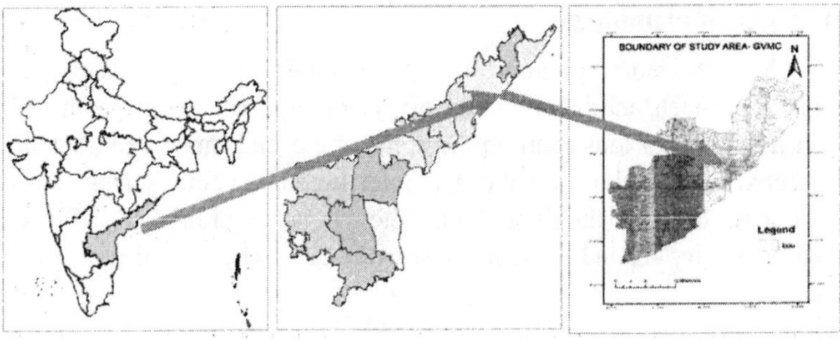


***Fig. 1. Location Map of the Study Area.***

## Land Use/Land Cover Map

The land use/land cover region patterns is an effect of both socio-economic and natural factors and their usage by humans in space and time. The spatial distribution of the various land uses/ land cover regions are interpreted based on the recent satellite data of Sentianel-2A with 10 m spatial resolution. The disposal site should not close to the built up area to avoid adversely affecting the future development and land value and to protect the human beings from environmental hazards created from dumping sites. Scrub and barren land are the most preferable for the dumping sites. Vegetation, Industries, Canals, Fallow land, Scrub land are the major land use/land cover classes in the present study area.

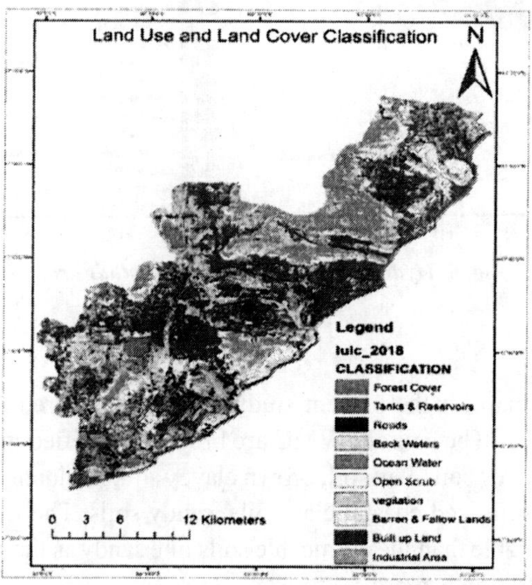


***Fig. 2. Land use Land Cover of the study area.***

## Hydrogeomorphology

The hydrogeomorphological map was prepared using the Survey of India Toposheets and Satellite imagery. Geomorphology may also help in identifying the various geomorphic units. In the study area, Pediment and dissected hills, valleys are the dominant landforms found. Denudation landforms results in the Pedi plains. The intensity and thickness of these landforms vary depending upon the structural disturbance and slope of the area.

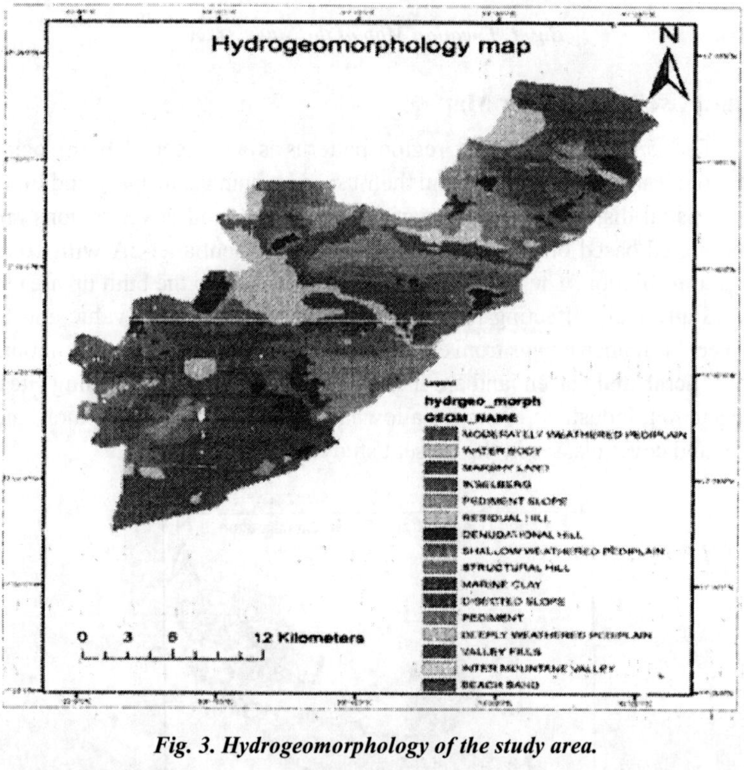


*Fig. 3. Hydrogeomorphology of the study area.*

## Soil Map

The soil map for the present study area was prepared from the Soil map Toposheets. The soil of GVMC are broadly classified into red clayey soil, brown clayey soil, clay soil, brown clayey soil, red loamy soils, brown grave loamy soils, red coastal clay soils, sandy soils. The less permeable soils are preferable than the permeable soils like sandy as the probability of leachate infiltration is more.

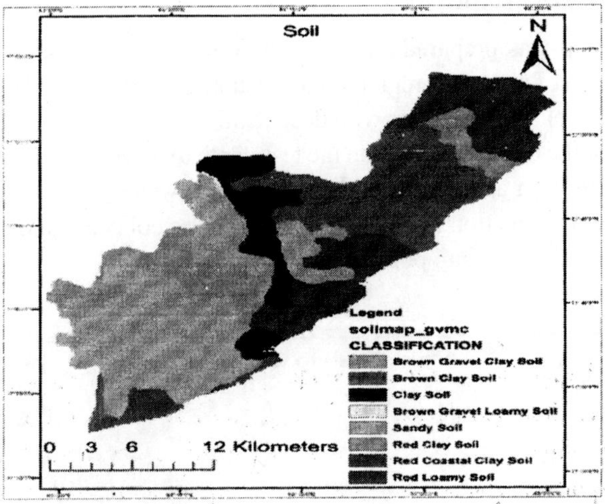


***Fig. 4. Soil of the study area.***

## Geology Map

In the ground investigation studies, the geological structures have great importance. The study area's geology has Khondalite which covers the major study area's portion. Other major geologic features observed in the study area are Charnockite, quartzite, laterite and granite gneiss. The geology map was prepared based on the geological Toposheets of the study area.

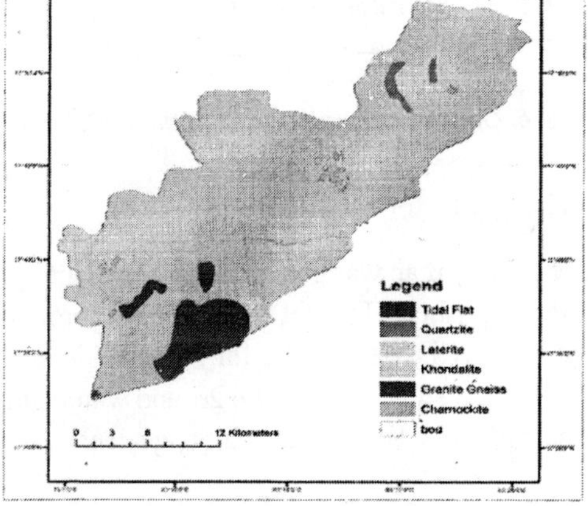


***Fig. 5. Geology of the study area.***

## Ground Water Table Map

The map was prepared based on the information obtained from the measurement of open well regions and questionnaire from the nearby people about bore wells. The regions with deep depth to water table level are most suitable for the disposal sites than the less depth to water table level regions as the infiltration and contamination of ground water is more. Using the Mobile Data Collection (MDC) app, the data was collected and converted to .csv data and then into point data.

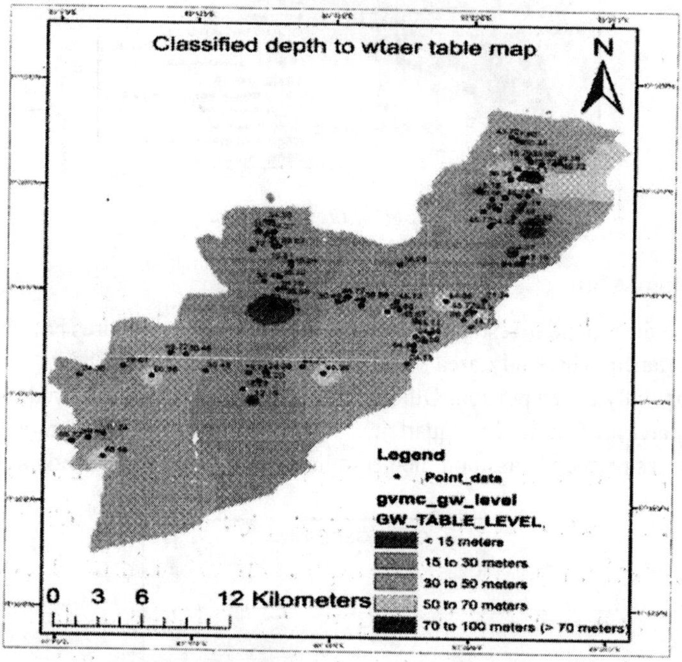


*Fig. 6. Ground water table map of the study area.*

## Drainage Density Map

The drainage density map was generated from the interpreted drainage network data in the Toposheets Data of sudy area. Generally, region having the high drainage density is not suitable for the consideration into the site for a solid waste disposal site as it feats the ground water and surface water through the leachate process. Hence a low drainage density regions is mostly preferable.

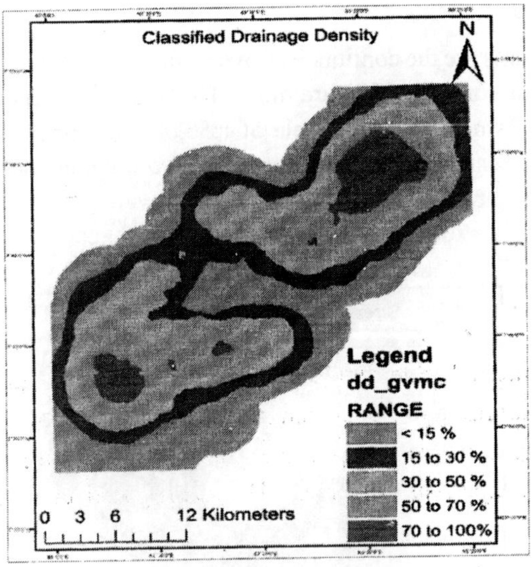


***Fig. 7. Drainage Density map of the study area.***

## Tanks Map

The tanks or water bodies play an important role as surface water resources and they are the initial feasible contamination sources. The tanks map in the study is prepared from the use of recent satellite data. The residential development in this study area made the disappearance of major tanks.

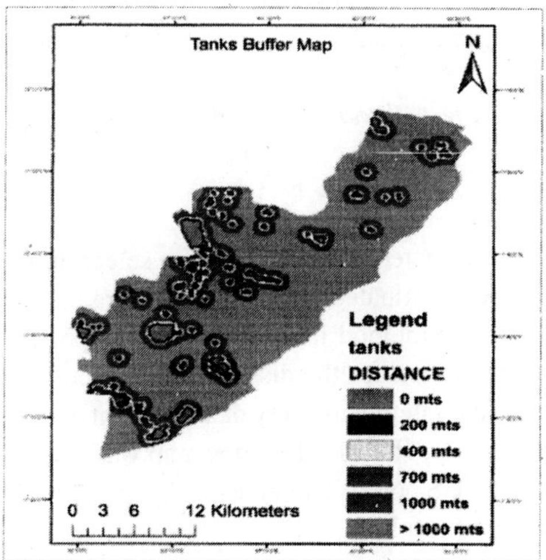


***Fig. 8. Tanks map of the study area.***

## Stream Map

The streams are the continuous flowing surface water resources where the chances of contamination are more. The map was prepared using the Toposheets of study area with scale of 1:50,000. Major river streams are found near the Marikavalasa, Gambhiram reservoir region, Meghadhri gedda reservoir and Narava gedda.

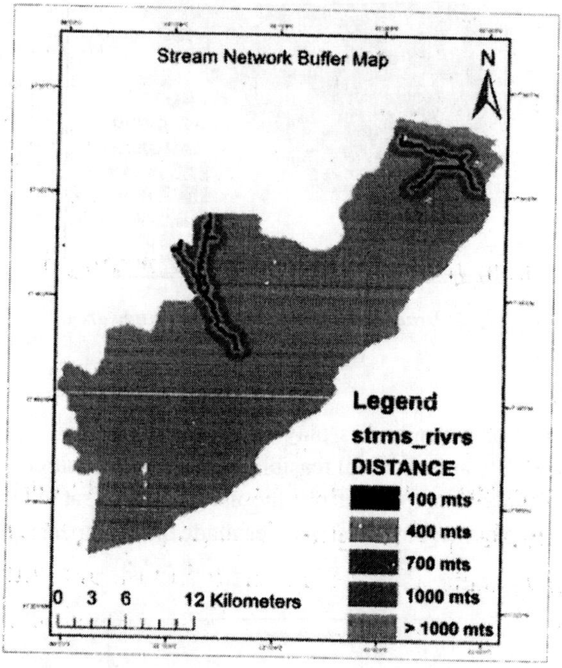


***Fig. 9. Streams map of the study area.***

## Slope Map

A significant parameter in the landfill site selection is elevation. The land morphology was evaluated using the slope grading and specified in the percentages, in the method used over here. Slope was an important parameter of consideration for the disposal site selection. The slope map was prepared using the satellite imagery data of recent data. From the digital elevation model (ASTER-DEM), the slope map was generated which was obtained from the USGS portal. The areas with high slopes are not suitable for the solid waste disposal.

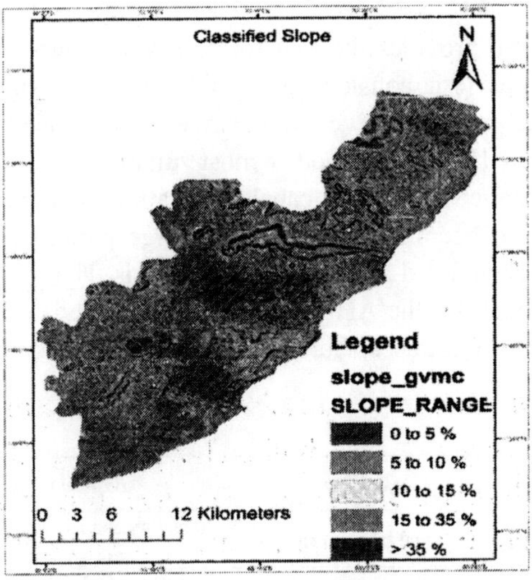


***Fig. 10. Slope map of the study area.***

## Road and Railways Network Map

Road and railway networks play a significant role in the region's overall development. These two network maps are prepared using the Survey of India (SOI) Toposheets on 1:50,000 scale. The road and railway coverage with the Toposheets are updated with the latest available data for extracting additional information on the newly developed roads.

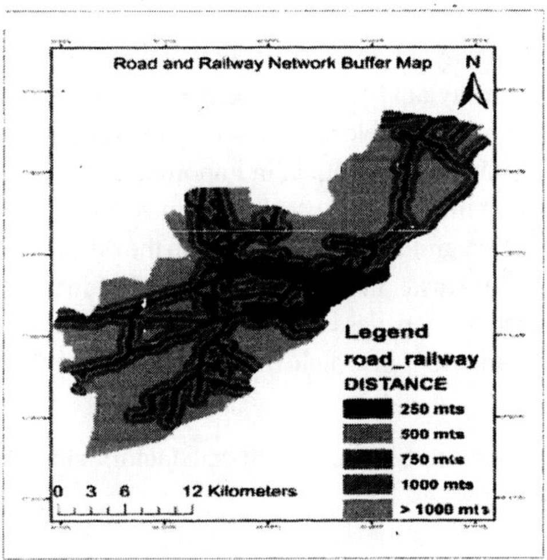


***Fig.11. Slope map of the study area.***

## Analytical Hierarchy Process

This method provides the tool for pair-wise comparison of various criteria and subcriteria considered for the selection of landfill sites. The criteria/subcriteria's relative importance is expressed in numerical value from 1 to 10. This method is most suitable when the quantitative criteria like distance from roads, canals, habitation etc. are considered. The method tends to become complex when large parameter numbers are required to be considered for any decision analysis. The sensitivity analysis results obtained from the AHP gave the consistency ratio less than 0.1 justifying the results are acceptable. One common scale (adapted from Saaty) shown below:

| *Intensity of Importance* | *Definition* | *Explanation* |
|---|---|---|
| 1 | Equal importance | Two factors contribute equally to the objective |
| 3 | Somewhat more Important | Experience and judgment slightly favour one over the other |
| 5 | Much more Important | Experience and judgment strongly favour one over the other |
| 7 | Very much more Important | Experience and judgment very strongly favour one over the other. Its importance is demonstrated in practice |
| 9 | Absolutely more Important | The evidence favouring one over the other is of the highest possible validity |
| 2,4,6,8 | Intermediate values | When compromise is needed |

**Weighted Overlay Analysis:** This tool applies one of the most used approaches for overlay analysis to solve the multi criteria problems like suitability models and site selection. Each of the criteria in the weighted overlay analysis may not be of equal in importance. It was a technique for applying a common measurement scale of values to dissimilar and diverse inputs to create an integrated analysis. Based on the different thematic layers possible location for waste disposal sites have been identified. Weightages have been assigned to each class of all the thematic maps for GIS analysis. Weights range from 1 to 5 in which 1 stands for unsuitable while 5 stands suitable.

The chosen scale is of 1 to 5 with satisfactory suitability ratings as shown in Table below:

| ***Scale*** | ***Suitability Rating*** |
|---|---|
| 1 | Poor |
| 2 | Fair |
| 3 | Good |
| 4 | Very good |
| 5 | Excellent |

## Results and Conclusions

The socio-economic and environmental problems associated with the solid waste disposal site selection are complex due to the quantity and waste material's diverse nature. Each of these generated data layers are judged with respect to the environmental, social and community impact and due weightages need were assigned before taking any decision. Remote Sensing and GIS techniques were most suitable tools to address the problems related to the spatial decisions. The highly suitable areas in the given study area constitutes 1.87 square kilometres, suitable areas of 267 square kilometres, moderately suitable areas of 283 square kilometres and not suitable areas of 17.5 square kilometres. The integration of different datasets in GIS has resulted in multi-layer display of the data, which would have otherwise been difficult to do manually using the conventional site suitability methods.

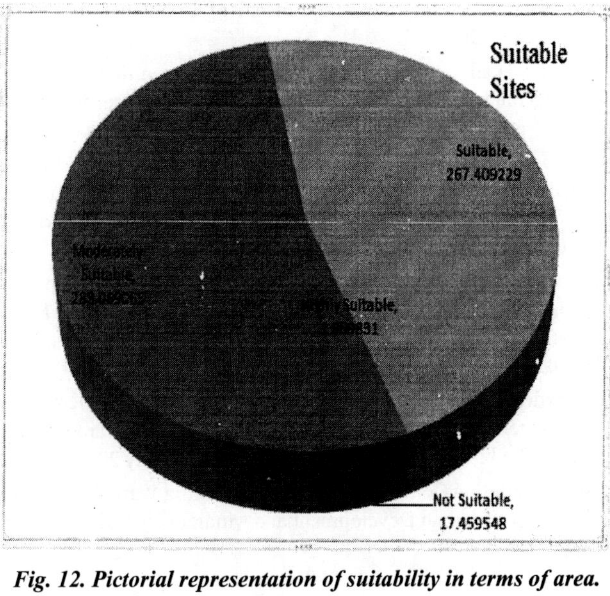


***Fig. 12. Pictorial representation of suitability in terms of area.***

## References

S. Suresh Babu, S. Sivasankar (2015). GIS and remote sensing in urban waste disposal and management: A case study of Usilampatti municipality, India. International Journal of Applied Research (IJAR)-1(9):1047-1051, June-July 2015.

Aruna, D, T. Byragi Reddy, Swamy, A.V.V.S. (2012). Selection of Potential Solid Waste Dump Sites for Kakinada City Using GIS and Remote Sensing Techniques. International Journal of Engineering Sciences Research (IJESR)-Vol 03, Issue 05, September-October 2012.

Ravindra Jaybhaye, Nitin Mundhe, Bhalachandra Dorik (2014). Site Suitability for Urban Solid Waste Disposal Using Geoinformatics: A case study of Pune Municipal Corporation, Maharashtra, India. International Journal of Advanced Remote Sensing and GIS(IJARSG), Vol 3, Issue 1. December -2014.

N. Victor Babu, P. Jagadeeswara Rao, I.V.R.K. V. Prasad. Impact of Municipal Solid Waste on Groundwater in the Environs of Greater Visakhapatnam Municipal Corporation Area, Andhra Pradesh, India, International Journal of Engineering Science Invention (IJESI), Volume 2, Issue 3, March 2013.

Karthikeya P.N. Dr. Yeshodha. L, Site Selection for Urban Solid Waste Disposal Using Remote Sensing and Open Source GIS in Krishnagiri District, Tamil Nadu. International Journal for Innovative Research in Science and Technology (IJIRST), Volume 2, Issue 10, March 2016.

Shoba, B, Dr. Rasappan, K. Application of GIS in Solid Waste Management for Coimbatore City. International Journal of Science and Research Publications (IJSRP), Volume 3, Issue 10, October 2013.

Nishanth, T, Prakash, M.N, Vijith, H. Suitable Site determination for urban solid waste disposal using GIS and Remote Sensing techniques in Kottayam Municipality, India, International Journal of Geomatics and Geosciences, Volume 1, No. 2. 2010.

Sunil Srigirisetty, Thadivalasa Jayasri, Chitti Netaji. Open dumping of Municipal Solid Waste-Impact on Ground water and soil, International Journal of Current Engineering and Scientific Research (IJCESR), Volume-4, Issue 6, 2017.

Victor Babu Neela, Solid Waste Landfill Site Selection for Greater Visakhapatnam Municipal Corporation Using Remote Sensing and GIS, International Journal of Civil, Structural, Environmental, and Infrastructure Engineering Research and Development (IJCSEIERD), Vol 3, Issue 5, Dec 2013.

Narasimha Rao, M.M., Sachikanta Nanda, Raghava Reddy, S.V., Mapping of Solid Waste Disposal Sites using MCDA in Guntur Municipal Corporation, Andhra Pradesh, International Journal of Pure and Applied Mathematics, Volume 119, No. 14, 2018.

Truptil, Lokhande, Sachin J.Mane, SandipT.Mali. Landfill Site Selection using GIS and MCDA methods: A review, International Journal of Research in Engineering, Science and Technologies (IJRESTS), Vol 3, No. 3, May 2017.

Andhra Pradesh Pollution Control Board (APPCB). Solid Waste Management Rules 2016, Ministry of Urban Development and Municipalities, Andhra Pradesh.

# D. Social Engineering (S.E.)

# 10

# Human Resource Development in the Knowledge Economy – A Global Perspective

***Prof. T. Kamaraju and Dr. N. Santosh Ranganath***

**Abstract**

*With the advent of globalisation, organisations – big or small have ceased to be local, they have become global! This has increased the workforce diversity and cultural sensitivities have emerged like never before. All this led to the development of Global Human Resource Management. Even those organisations who consider themselves immune to transactions across geographical boundaries are connected to the wider network globally. They are in one way or the other dependent upon organisations that may even not have heard about. There is interdependence between organisations in various areas and functions. The preliminary function of global Human Resource Management is that the organisation carries a local appeal in the host country despite maintaining an international feel. To exemplify, any multinational/international company would not like to be called as local, however, the same wants a domestic touch in the host country and there lies the challenge.*

***Keywods:*** *ICTs, Global information, Indian economy, Global HRM, Knowledge Economy.*

## Introduction

The revolution in information and communication technologies (ICTs) is drastically altering the way things are done in nearly every field of human activity. The competitive pressure of the global economy is compelling businesses and countries to embrace ICTs at a frenetic pace for competitive advantage, convenience, quality of life, affordability, creativity and many other factors. The advent of ICTs has resulted in dramatic changes in employment patterns, skill-sets needed and the range of opportunities for employment and economic advancement over the whole world.

In particular, an unprecedented window of opportunity has opened up for developing countries. The key to exploiting the opportunity lies in creating the kind of human resources that are needed by the global information economy. Extremely rapid and continuous change in skills needed makes the task a complex and challenging one. A huge shift occurring in white-collar jobs globally. Technology is redefining many of these jobs and making them increasingly location independent.

Tens of thousands of jobs are shifting *en masse* across the globe, thanks to innovations by IT-enabled service companies. A tidal wave of change is taking place also in employment patterns and opportunities for IT workers. The IT worker is now clearly a global resource and increasingly, the white-collar worker is fast becoming one. For highly skilled and highly paid IT workers, relocation is a possibility. But the trend is towards outsourcing and offshore activity, both for white-collar workers and, at increasingly higher levels of technical competency, for the IT worker.

## Global Scenario of IT based HRM

The global supply-demand scenario now determines salary levels. The emergence of technologically intermediated global human resource marketplace offers breathtaking opportunities and challenges for the entire Asia-Pacific region and, in particular, for the developing countries.

- The global scenario is characterised by:
- A growing market for ICT products and services;
- An explosive growth in e-commerce;
- A rising need for IT skills in all professions;
- A declining trend in enrolment for IT in developed countries; and
- A billowing gap between demand and supply of qualified human resources for IT in terms of quantity, quality and specialisation.

Information Technology has emerged as a key dominant sector of the Indian economy. Various agencies have studied the issue of developing Human Resources for the IT sector. The issue of human resources development for IT cannot be handled through a linear Cause-Effect model. In this report is analyzed the needs and constraints of various stakeholders affected by the issue through a Systems Approach. It derives viable design interventions that would balance the needs and constraints. It is also attempt to map the knowledge and skill components for different educational streams against taxonomy of IT careers.

It is recognized the constraints in terms of instructional material and faculty. The limited funds available for the education sector have to be judiciously balanced between conventional brick and mortar infrastructure and providing an e-learning environment. We bring out the interconnectedness in the roles of Government, Academia, Industry and Professional bodies. Although we would have liked to tackle the issue of IT education in its entirety, we have focused on Software for the simple reason that we have a lesser understanding about the other components, notably Hardware and Networks. The design solutions contained in the paper need a wide discussion and eventual consensus among educationists, planners and industry if India's potential position as an IT superpower is to be realised.

## Growth of IT Industries

India is also one of the BRICs countries (Brazil, Russia, India, and China), and is in the midst of rapid economic growth spurred by liberalisation of its economy and growth in IT-related industries, giving the country a rapidly increasing presence in international society. According to one estimate, India is expected to become the world's third largest economy by around 2032. According to a 2019 report that studied 100 emerging companies located in fast-growing regions including the BRICs, Indian companies already account for 21 of these 100 companies, and seven of these are classified as "companies that have developed technological capabilities into innovation in the global economy". As these reports suggest, India's potential is already recognized by the world.

Unlike Japan, where the declining birthrate is a major problem, in India, young people under the age of 25, who will play a key role in the next generation, account for 50 percent of the country's total population of 1.1 billion. In addition to an abundant workforce, India's competitive superiority can also be attributed to the fact that it is the world's largest democratic country, its people have a high level of English proficiency, and labour wages are relatively low. However, the most important factor may be India's social system, which continuously produces human resources with high potential.

India's rapid growth is supported by IT-BPO (IT and Business Process Outsourcing), centering on software. In this industry, hardware-related business accounts for a mere 20 percent of the whole, while the entire remainder represents the contribution of software and service-related businesses. India has grown to be a major global player in the software business. The entire market of the IT industry has achieved growth.

In particular, software development and services excluding hardware have grown by more than 30 percent annually, of which about 80 percent is exported, thereby becoming India's largest export industry. Exports in 2016 were mostly to English speaking countries, with 67 percent to United States and 25 percent to Europe (of which 15 percent was to the UK). Only 1.5 percent was to Japan. In the business area of software development and services excluding hardware, the direct labour force with a high level of expertise. Although it is also necessary to consider the supporting labour force in addition to the direct labour force, it is possible to calculate that only 0.2 percent or less of India's population is creating 5.4 percent of GDP.

## Human Resources Supply System

The rapid growth of India is supported by highly educated human resources with engineering backgrounds. In India, universities and colleges that offer the academic degree of Diploma are classified as institutions of higher education. The number of colleges has also increased similarly to universities, to 16,000. This was more than 40 times greater than the number of universities in previous year. The aggregate enrollment in institutions of higher education, including both universities and colleges, is more than 10 million.

Limited to engineering (but excluding science), it is forecast that more than 530,000 students will graduate, and of that number, approximately 300,000 will be IT engineers with majors in computer science, electrical/ electronic engineering, and telecommunications. Compared to other countries which are candidate offshore IT development sites, India supplies 2.5 times more human resources with engineering background than 2$^{nd}$ ranking China. Particularly outstanding human resources are supplied by the country's leading universities, which include the Indian Institute of Science (IISc), Indian Institute of Technology (IIT), and Indian Institute of Information Technology (IIIT). However, these institutions graduate only 10,000 students each year. In addition, numerous colleges and professional schools specialise in IT. From this, it can be understood that the supply of human resources that supports India's rapid growth comes mostly from colleges and professional schools specialised in IT.

A study of the compatibility of human resources between institutions of higher education and industry reported that the number of human resources with the skills to be effective immediately upon entering an IT company is limited to 25 percent of new graduates from universities with technology backgrounds and about 10 percent of graduates from colleges. If no measures are taken, a shortage of 500,000 persons out of total demand of 2.3 million in IT-BPO-related business is forecast in 2025. The problems associated with this shortage of human resources may have a ripple effect on the whole range of industries based on IT, and an impact on bioinformatics, which relies heavily on IT, is also conceivable. Quantitatively, the number of human resources that are immediately effective seems quite large.

However, India believes that even this number will be insufficient. This suggests that India has a higher awareness of the critical nature of the shortage of human resources than Japan. One reason for such concern can be found in the background strategy of transforming India from the conventional outsourcing of the past to knowledge-based outsourcing. India is attempting to transform itself into a knowledge-based society through the accumulation of the world's most advanced knowledge. From this viewpoint, it is obvious that the shortage of human resources may be a formidable barrier not only to sustained economic growth, but also to increasing the country's international competitiveness.

## HRM in the Knowledge Economy

The nature and characteristics of work in the knowledge economy herald new opportunities for HRM. To maximize benefit from knowledge assets, a fourfold contribution from HRM is proposed. In the knowledge economy, HRM must:

- Provide expertise in understanding and defining firm-level strategic knowledge capabilities;
- Develop and manage knowledge workers by leveraging the knowing-learning-doing nexus;
- Build knowledge value as an organisation as well as an individual asset; and
- Minimize the organisation's knowledge risk associated with loss of requisite capability and knowledge.

Knowledge creation, use, sharing and retention have always been important. What is new is the significant shift towards a systematic and strategic approach to managing the primary assets of the knowledge economy: people, knowledge processes, and knowledge products. Globally, knowledge has become the most important factor in economic development and knowledge assets are considered essential for economic growth, competitive advantage, human development and quality of human life. Research conducted by the OECD has found that the quality of workers' skills and knowledge has a significant impact on the economic and social future of developed nations such as Australia. Four key points distinguish the knowledge economy:

1. **Knowledge is recognized as important to organisations** and is acknowledged as critical to organisation success. Globalisation, rapid change, and competition in a global market of increasingly sophisticated consumers have led organisations to seek a sustainable advantage that distinguishes them in their business environments.
2. **Relationships** amongst employees are more complex. New types of business-to-business relationships require everyone to develop skills that emphasise interdependence, communication, and the ability to build and maintain strong work relationships. Virtualisation has changed the ways that humans interact, and the need for physical contact has been reduced or in some cases eliminated.
3. **Information and communication technology** is embedded in most human interactions and business transactions. People are more 'technologically savvy' than at any other time in history. Fundamental IT skills are requisite for all employees but in addition, the speed with which employees can learn new software and technology is critical.
4. **Time span of discretion.** Speed has become the key to competitiveness, but paradoxically, people need to plan over a longer time span. There is a stronger need for efficiency, analytic thinking, and planning skills. Taken together, these characteristics change the landscape in which HRM operates and herald the opportunity for new contributions. Further impetus for a revised role is provided by knowledge-related changes at the firm level.

## e-HRD

In the course of prevailing trends like globalisation, customer orientation and specialisation, most of the companies place emphasis on recruitment, sustainment and evolution of qualified employees. The companies are aware of the fact that human resources have changed more and more from a cost factor to success factor.

Electronic Human Resource Development (e-HRD) is a web based tool to automate and support HR process. The implementation of e-HRD is an opportunity to delegate the data entry to the employees. E-HRD facilitates the usage of HR marketplaces and offers more self service to the employees. E-HRD is a collection of many different technologies. At first the growing attention of companies on the factor knowledge is mainly driven by the evolution of information technology. Information systems like e-HRD solutions –that network information enable companies to get a consistent concept for their knowledge management. In this sense Knowledge Management is always a collection of different techniques. A variety of these techniques is used in companies to acquire knowledge, to organise knowledge and to make knowledge transparent.

One of these mentioned techniques is Knowledge Discovery in Database (KDD) respective Data Mining as a step of the KDD-process.

e-HRD offers the opportunity to automate administrative HR-work and to optimize value creating HR-activities. Three levels of development can be distinguished:

1. Web-presence HR,
2. Web-enabled HR, and
3. Web-energized HR.

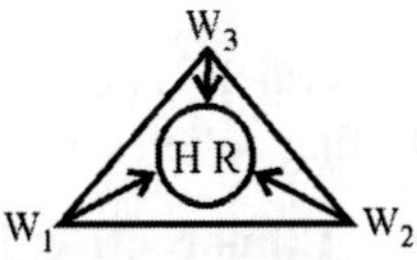

**Fig.** 10.13 w.s

$$HR \rightarrow (w_1 + w_2 + w_3)$$

The first level means that parts of the e-HRD-solution are present. Web-enabled means that all parts of the e-HRD-solution are present and can be accessed online. The third level describes the e-HRD-solution that is fully implemented, can be accessed online and is used intensively by the employees. The desire level and the pace of implementation for HR-solutions are specific for each company. At Daimler Chrysler AG, Plant Worth the e-HRD-solution is on level two at the moment and is to reach level three where it is intensively used by the HR-workers and the employees.

As weak definition e-HRD shall be known in the following as an integrated optimisation of HR-prices consequently using web-based technology for all facets of HR-work. Amongst other facets e-learning in the field of continuing education, employee-self-service (ESS) in the field of HR-administration and the utilisation of the intra and extranet in the field of recruitment belong to the main fields of e-HRD that are supported by the e-HRD system.

The main benefits of e-HRD are an increase of quality and pace, because the existing administrative processes were slow and inefficient condition upon mainly paper based processes, e.g. the tendance of standing data and the payroll. The direct access of the network enabled employee avoids double entries for example, at the tendance of standing data, travel expense accounting and applications for leave. With e-recruitment the company gets an additional possibility besides the normal application by paper to recruit people over the web in an online application process.

## Global HRD and the Staffing Policy

Here also the role is no different i.e. hiring individuals with requisite skills to do a particular job. The challenge here is developing tools to promote a corporate culture that is almost the same everywhere except that the local sensitivities are taken care of. Also, the deciding upon the top management or key positions gets very tricky. Whether to choose a local from the host country for a key position or deploy one from the headquarters assumes importance; and finally whether or not to have a uniform hiring policy globally remains a big challenge.

Nevertheless an organisation can choose to hire according to any of the staffing policies mentioned below:

- **Ethnocentric:** Here the Key management positions are filled by the parent country individuals.
- **Polycentric:** In polycentric staffing policy the host country nationals manage subsidiaries whereas the headquarter positions are held by the parent company nationals.
- **Geocentric:** In this staffing policy the best and the most competent individuals hold key positions irrespective of the nationalities.

Geocentric staffing policy it seems is the best when it comes to Global HRM. The human resources are deployed productively and it also helps build a strong cultural and informal management network. The flip side is that human resources become a bit expensive when hired on a geocentric basis. Besides the national immigration policies may limit implementation.

Global HRM therefore, is a very challenging front in HRM. If one is able to strike the right chord in designing structures and controls, the job is half done. Subsidiaries are held together by global HRM, different subsidiaries can function operate coherently only when it is enabled by efficient structures and controls.

We may therefore, enumerate the **objectives of global HRD as follows:**

1. Create a local appeal without compromising upon the global identity.
2. Generating awareness of cross cultural sensitivities among managers globally and hiring of staff across geographic boundaries.
3. Training upon cultures and sensitivities of the host country.

The **strategic role of Human Resources Management** in such a scenario is to ensure that HRM policies are in tandem with and in support of the firm's strategy, structure and controls. Specifically, when we talk of structures and controls the following become worth mentioning in the context of Global HRM.

- **Decision Making:** There is a certain degree of centralisation of operating decision making. Compare this to the International strategy, the core competencies are centralised and the rest are decentralised.
- **Co-ordination:** A high degree of coordination is required in the wake of the cross-cultural sensitivities. There is in addition also a high need for cultural control.
- **Integrating Mechanisms:** Many integrating mechanisms operate simultaneously.

## Transforming HRD in the Knowledge Economy

The idea that people and the knowledge they possess is the organisation's most valuable asset is not new. The shift in the terminology from over 20 years ago from 'Personnel Management' to 'Human Resources Management' signalled what some claimed was a metamorphosis for the profession. This altered the conceptualisation and practice of HR from a series of ad hoc functions, and evolved it into its role of corporate strategist. The transition was a significant one for the profession of HRM, because it was different from personnel management: it promised strategic contribution through integrated activities that confirmed employees as assets to be nurtured and developed.

Today, the central role of individual and organisational capabilities is significantly amplified with the advent of the knowledge economy. Commanding a central role in realising value from knowledge assets is proposed as the new strategic role for HRM. What is the nature of the transition proposed for HRM? How does this translate to the functional areas of HRM? The areas represent the elements of HRM that offer the greatest opportunity to acquire, build and retain organisational capability.

Knowledge management present HRM with the opportunity to become pivotal to the strategic management of the organisation and a catalyst for knowledge creation and building value. This involves more than just re-labeling Human Resources – it is a fundamental paradigmatic shift for HRM and senior management. The transformation begins with viewing HRM through a 'knowledge lens' and repositioning the functions in relation to strategic knowledge capabilities. Managing knowledge workers, building value from knowledge, and assessing knowledge risk are also new requirements of HRM in the knowledge economy. We propose that HRM must respond to the key challenges presented by the knowledge economy and command a central position in realising value from knowledge assets as a strategic role for HRM.

## Conclusion

Human resources are the key to the process of economic development. Any approach to develop human resources for development through science and technology should aim at the utilisation of these resources for more productive activity. It should also facilitate the fullest possible development of skills and knowledge of the labour force relevant to such activity. Information Technology has emerged as a key dominant sector of the Indian economy. Various agencies have studied the issue of developing Human Resources for the IT sector. The issue of human resources development for IT cannot be handled through a linear Cause –Effect model. The rapid growth of India is supported by highly educated human resources with engineering backgrounds. In India, universities and colleges that offer the academic degree of Diploma are classified as institutions of higher education.

Electronic Human Resource Development (e-HRD) is a web based tool to automate and support HR process. The implementation of e-HRD is an opportunity to delegate the data entry to the employees. E-HRD facilitates the usage of HR marketplaces and offers more self service to the employees. e-HRD is a collection of many different technologies. At first the growing attention of companies on the factor knowledge is mainly driven by the evolution of information technology.

## References

Ashok Jain *et al*, *Diffusion of Innovation*, JSIR, 1991, New Delhi.

Ayres. R. and Zuscovitch E. 'Technology and Information: Chain Reactions and Sustainable growth', *Technovation*, Vol. 10(3) May, 1990.

Brian, C. Twiss, *Managing Technological Innovations*, Longman, London 1974.

Burbach, R., & Royle, T. (2010). Talent on demand?: Talent management in the German and Irish subsidiaries of a US multinational corporation. Personnel Review, 39(4), 414-431.

Chen, J., & Eldrige, D. (2010). Are "standardized performance appraisal practices" really preferred? A case study of China. Chinese Management Studies, 4(3), 244-257.

Dalton, K., & Druker, J. (2012). Transferring HR concepts and practices within multi-national corporations in Romania: The management experience. European Management Journal, 30(6), 588-602.

Elron, E., & Viga-Gadot, E. (2006). Influence and political processess in cyberspace. The case of global virtual teams. International Journal of Cross Cultural Management, 6(3), 295-317.

Langrish, John. *The Importance of Design in Technology Transfer*, Paper Manchester Polytechnic, UK, 1987.

Pearson, A. W. 'Innovation strategy' *Technovation,* Vol. 10(3) May, 1990.

Rajan, Y.S. *Introduction of Technologies: The Management of Innovation Cycle,* August 1990, TIFAC, New Delhi.

Santosh Ranganath N., (2010). "FDI and India's Economic Growth: The New Paradigm", Mangalmay Journal of Management & Technology", Greater Noida, Volume: 4, Number: 1, January – June, ISSN: 0973-7251, pp. 40-49.

Santosh Ranganath N., (2013). "Impact of Knowledge Management in e-HRM Practices", International Journal of Innovative Research and Practices, Vol. I, No. 3, March, ISSN: 2321-2926, pp. 30-37.

Santosh Ranganath N., (2013). "The Effect of Techno-entrepreneurship on Indian Economy", International Journal of Innovative Research and Practices, Vol. 1, No. 8, August, ISSN: 2321-2926, pp.28-37.

Santosh Ranganath N. (2013). "Knowledge Management Approach for Effective Business Operations", International Journal of Management Focus, Vol. 3, Issue 4, Oct-Dec, ISSN: 2250-2971, pp. 43-46.

Santosh Ranganath N., (2011). "Knowledge Management in Organisations – A Business Intelligence Technique", Rai Management Journal, New Delhi, Vol. VIII, Issue II, December, ISSN: 0975-4326, pp. 139-147.

# 11

# Self Help Groups – The Mechanism for Social and Women Empowerment

## Introduction

Sri Narendra Modiji, Hon'ble Prime Minister of India in his address in 2017 on the occasion of the $68^{th}$ Independence Day, expressed his cherished dream of emancipation of the poor and youth through employable skills of global standards and called for every Indian citizen to strive to achieve this. Quoting the sloka "***San gachchdvam, sam vadadvam, sam vo manansi, jaanatham***" which succinctly translates to capture the spirit of social mobilisation "**We walk together, we move together, we think together**", he added that 'we resolve together and together we take the country forward'. A look at all the rural and urban human resources development initiatives in India today shows considerable focus on bringing together the community, based on common need or opportunity to develop strong grassroots level institutions. While such collectives of the community or section therein, like farmers other occupation or social based collectives like Resident Welfare Associations are in existence since long and have to their credit many accomplishments, the collectivisation of the poor for achievement of many financial, material and more importantly, societal goals has been landslide successes in the contemporary times.

The establishment of community level architecture in terms of groups and federations, are activities that have come to stay and account for sustainability of many initiatives. The current chapter deals in some details with the advent and development of Self Help Groups and rural and urban poverty alleviation with a brief analysis of their status vis-à-vis few institutional parameters like management styles, social audit, peer influence, etc. and performance parameters like, indebtedness, internal and external loaning and recovery performance.

Social mobilisation is a mechanism that is aimed at bringing both human and non-human resources together into the building of groups and federations usually also termed as the development of community infrastructure or development of Social Capital, to achieve sustainable development. The primary objective of social mobilisation and institution building is to have strong institutions at community level where people can organise themselves to take action collectively by developing their own plan and strategy rather than being imposed from outside. Social mobilisation thus aims **to engage people's participation and achieving** a specific development goal through self-reliant efforts. It involves all relevant segments of society, decision and policy-makers, opinion leaders, bureaucrats and technocrats, professional groups, religious associations, commerce and industry, communities and individuals. It is a planned decentralised process that seeks to facilitate change for development through a range of players engaged in interrelated and complimentary efforts particularly in addressing the felt needs of the people **embracing the critical principle of community involvement and seeks to empower individuals and groups for action.**

## Rationale for the Development of Community Infrastructure

A study of the performance of social development programmes by an independent SAARC committee[1] has revealed that there are three important factors that impact the performance of any programme which stand to explain almost every phenomenon related to development:

- Excessive dependence on the government curtailed people's initiatives.
- Obsessive preoccupation with capital accumulation almost invariably resulted in neglecting the capacity of the poor.
- Concentration on industrialisation/modernisation creates wide gaps in the continuum due to poor understanding and discontinuous actions related to the two.

The report has also come with seminal findings that had a bearing on all subsequent urban and rural poverty alleviation initiatives. The learnings are as follows:

- Where poor participate as subjects and not as objects, it is possible to generate growth, human development and equity.

- Poor have contributed to growth and human development under varying socio-political circumstances.
- Building organisations of the poor is an essential pre-requisite of poverty alleviation.
- Empowerment of the poor/women is the means to poverty reduction.
- There is a strong need for sensitive support mechanism in terms of a dedicated structure supporting the established unit of the government with the right autonomy.
- Participation of the poor translates in the most common parlance to participatory monitoring and evaluation.

The firm conviction that the success of any programme is measured by the level of participation of the community or user group has resulted in incorporation of community centeredness of every development perspective. This is especially true in the area of accessing amenities and services made available through the local body, where community involvement at all stages of initiative from planning to post-project period results in effective utilisation of the related provisions by all sections of the community especially the poor, to improve their quality of life.

## Defining Community

The traditional definition of community was limited to denoting a social group other than family, sufficiently large so that its members habitually entertain the shared concern for the welfare of its inhabitants. The definition of community also took into its ambit the network of relationships – various caste, class, religious and socially exclusive groups, providers of goods, facilities and the users of these services – by which the community is bound. The characteristic here is the inter-relatedness of the various institutions (like religion, commerce, etc.) that binds them into a network.

With globalisation and technology growth however, the concept of Community is also undergoing a radical change with the introduction of internet and social media applications. This has widened the concept of community location, proximity and geography and now the concept of virtual community is in vogue thanks to the social networks like Facebook, etc. The significant point here is that as opposed to the traditional view, which places a lot of importance on face-to-face interaction, there is now global concept of networking and interaction which typifies a community and face to face interaction is not a necessity. However, in order to accelerate the pace and improve the quality of virtually any initiative, community participation may be considered an important factor. Community participation in this context involves the members of the community in planning, implementing and monitoring of infrastructure development and social welfare activities. Community participation in this sense denotes the process in which the community assumes responsibility for its own welfare. The members constituting the community come to know their own situation better and are motivated to solve their common problems.

## Social Mobilisation and Institution Building – Certain Insights

The *Social Mobilisation* – process that engages and motivates a wide range of partners and allies at national and local level to raise awareness of and demand for a particular development objective through face-to-face dialogue. Leadership, organising capacity, communication chennels, assessment, problem solving, are some of the common resources that need to be embedded into social mobilisation in any sector. An important factor is that **the collectives operate** in an overall societal context and become integral parts of the societal network. The stakeholders include other non-targeted citizens, service providers, individuals and institutions that represents the bureaucratic, political and economic realms of the community. The activity of bringing together of all these stakeholders in a society on a common frame of understanding with convergence of concern and focus on the achievement of any objective **is the success** of Social Mobilisation. The **solidarity of all stakeholders** particularly government and non-governmental organisations is also equally critical for the attainment of any change oriented development goal which calls for journey among partners and results in the successful transformation of developing goals into societal action. Therefore, social mobilisation may be viewed as the process of enlisting the participation of all stakeholders for accomplishment of a common goal.

**The primary target** will be **the poor families,** who will be organised and their capacities will be enhanced in a range of areas to enable them to identify their needs, plan the set of activities to address these needs, prioritize the needs and target for phase-wise implementation, fix responsibility and participate in implementation, management and post-project ownership including O&M. The process of social mobilisation begins with awareness campaign. A community becomes mobilised when a particular group of people becomes aware of **shared concern or common need** and decides together the course of action for shared benefits. Social Mobilisation is looked at as "the primary step of community development as it allows people to think and understand their situation and to organise and initiate action for their recovery with their own initiative and creativity". Through mobilisation, people can organise themselves to take action collectively by developing their own plan and strategy for recovery rather than being imposed from outside. Social mobilisation is founded firmly on the view of the community as not merely a group of individuals but a complex network of inter-relationships and transactions that define the community in totality and places it vis-'a-vis other communities to which it is connected geographically, or at higher levels of existence and movement. Social mobilisation as an approach, then, attempts to understand various patterns of inter-relationships, the collectives involved and hand-hold these collectives of actors to realign their activities to make them more beneficial to themselves and the other collectives.

Social mobilisation is normally built on four pillars: **community engagement, defining the need, choice/decision and action.** However, there are four Meta – issues that may commonly arise in the process which needs to be kept in mind by the project implementers for ensuring success.

(1) **Community investment** – In a society, both the rich and poor may live together and though the process of social mobilisation involves the society as a whole, investing more in understanding and supporting specific communities rather than whole population helps better for its success. Thus, the process of social mobilisation begins with identifying particular communities of common interest as the target for common good rather than involving the whole society. However, though the problem pertains to a particular group or community, understanding the broad panoply of challenging issues has to be understood by the whole society to ensure convergence of various stakeholders.

(2) **Whole person** – The individual is facing a constellation of needs, each of which is competing for his attention but the priority need may vary on daily basis and are likely to be food, shelter, safety, among others than the problem of unemployment. Therefore, looking at the whole persons and his needs, need to be addressed as a whole person. The NULM have rightly identified three major vulnerabilities among the urban poor. (1) Occupational vulnerabilities, (2) residential vulnerability and (3) social vulnerability.

The Govt. of India as part of urban poverty alleviation have launched numerous other programmes like Rajiv Awas Yojana to address residential vulnerabilities, Rajiv Rinn Yojana to facilitate the poor to own their own homes by getting subsidy on the housing loans, Prime Minister's Jan Dhan Yojana as part of financial inclusion, Sarva Siksha Abhiyan, JBY, RSBY, total sanitation programme, etc. to be converged and addressed holistically. The NULM is one such converged set of initiatives not only to provide placement linked employment skills but also facilitated advocacy and convergence of various other social welfare development programmes. Thus, the whole person need to understand not only from the perspective of the problem but also understanding the impact on persons. For an example providing placement linked employable skills to a person is the agenda. But such placement has certain connotations on various issues like his place of stay, family, travel to the place of work, children's education, health issues, etc. As such, a whole person approach is to be taken in the process of social mobilisation.

(3) **Flexibility** – Every social development programme requires domain knowledge. The community consists of different castes, creed, religions, regions, desires, challenges, etc. Having a rigid approach with such multidimensional community may straightjacket the scope. Though the Govt. of India issued guidelines it also gave opportunity to the states and urban local bodies to formulate their own suitable and viable plans with required flexibility with a view to increase the scope of NULM and to optimise the coverage. Another aspect, flexibility also differs from state to state and city to city. Socio-economic and political factors play a vital role in identifying the beneficiaries, building community level institutions, arranging bank linkage, organising capacity building programmes, etc. The quote "different strokes for different folks" holds good in this situation also. Therefore, flexibility is an essential component in grassroot approach of community centric governance.

**Small is ideal** – The National Urban Livelihood Mission envisions to build three tier structures of community institutions, one at the national level, second, state level and third, in the city level. It is pertinent to mention here a mega city/metropolitan city may have larger jurisdiction with a varied socio-economic and political ethos. Especially in the Indian context, such differences may be found within a smaller spread. In this context, it is very important to suitably modify or tailor the implementation details and operationalise some of the generic aspects in the guidelines to suit he specific community in question. In livelihoods for example, the choice of certain products given for livelihood options which are given in general, may have varying degrees of success in terms of marketability within the vicinity making it necessary to make more relevant choices. The maxim 'small is beautiful' may well be suited here. The advantage of adopting such a strategy of smaller, community relevant choices, is that the risk of 'spreading too thin' where smaller innovations get compromised in the huge spread of the initiative will be avoided, while the scope of building best practices and catalyzing on community-centric action will be augmented. Such an approach will also encourage innovations.

**The Participation Continuum:** As shwon in the diagram continuum, participation has different levels: Passively receiving benefits of a programme e.g.: health services or eduction; by contribution – land, labour or money for the programme; assuming in the programme; involving in monitoring and evaluation and; actually deciding on the programme, mobilising the resources and implementing it.

In terms of the types of participation, it can be progressively incremental as follows:

- As contributive – contribution of labou r, cash or materials in pre-determined programmes
- As an organisation – creation of structures to facilitate participation
- As empowerment – developing power to make choices or having control over the programmes

From the above, the type of community participation envisioned in the implementation of NULM, is to develop an organisation that facilitates participation through a host of ways including capacity building and long-term hand-holding to upgrade the level of participation of each of the individual members within the group and member groups in the federation.

Second, the ultimate aim of participation is empowerment where deeper change in the Knowledge, Attitude and Practice (KAP) levels of the individual (members or groups in a federation) to make choices and effectively have control over and manage programmes results in growing self-sufficiency and self-actualisation of the members.

## The 7 Steps of Community Participation

As seen in the above paragraphs Community Participation is a process where the progress depends on the sureness of the preceding steps. A broad example, the way in which the team introduces itself to the community has a strong bearing on the expectations, level of leadership, level of participation which together determine the future direction that the community will take in its development and emancipation.

It might be stated that except for the need for clarity on the part of the facilitator there are no set rules on the steps to be followed for community participation. However, in an effort to present a broad outline for effective process, the following seven steps have been identified as being crucial:

***Step 1:** Introductory/preliminary workshop with all stakeholders at LUB level.*

This workshop will be with the influencers of the community, such as council members, municipal functionaries, CSOs, NHG representatives and other stakeholders. This being the first step, the agenda should be carefully drawn out. Some of the important issues discussed in the preliminary meeting are, objective and scope of activity/sub-activity, extent of Community involvement, roles of each stakeholder, Nittygritty of activity (e.g. issues like house ownership monthly income during survey; community representation during Micro-planning), eliciting deliverables of activity, etc.

***Step 2:** Building rapport after entry into Slum*

Team members should meet important persons – Councilor, AWW, school HM / Teachers / MPHWs /Municipal functionaries / Bank Reps / Prominent Local Leaders / Elders. The members of the team should ensure that they meet the aforementioned in *their* houses – Spend considerable time – Eat / drink whatever is offered (avoid being treated as a guest).

***Step 3:** Understanding the target area*

This is accomplished by taking up the participatory method called Transect walk in the slum along with prominent / knowledgeable persons. This helps those involved to gain firsthand knowledge on age of slum and history, approach roads, basic services, Govt. infrastructure, housing / lifestyles / livelihoods pattern. The transect walk may be followed up with the employment of other methods like resource mapping, preparation of Venn diagram to get the people's access to services, regularity of availing services and a host of socio-economic factor obtaining in the community.

***Step 4:*** *Household mapping*

This step involves triangulation of the information gathered during transect walks. This is akin to the social mapping employed in participatory appraisal methods. This activity is carried out in the presence of a sizeable number of residents. This also involves gathering family information including education, occupation, disability status, etc. This can be further triangulated by way of survey and/or reconciliation with existing records.

***Step 5:*** *Ongoing meetings with the community*

There is need to have provision for regular interactions with the community as stakeholders, at different phases of the implementation. This helps to keep the community to stand on a common platform and arrive at a common frame of reference with reference to the information and taking on responsibilities. Regular interactions also help in constant review of the activities underway and in taking up course correction if required. These interactions also help in straightening out any problems and dynamics and facilitate community audit.

***Step 6:*** *Situational Analysis and Needs Assessment*

In this step the team conducts a situational analysis with various groups within the target community in an effort to understand the situations obtaining in the area including the pattern of occupation, migration, occurrence of diseases, as well as the different dimensions of poverty, coverage under SHG system, coverage under skill trainings and a host of other such information. An important exercise that needs to be conducted which will enable the organisers is to take up a needs assessment i.e., the kind of support the community feels it needs to overcome poverty. These needs could further be prioritised with common consent.

***Step 7:*** *Debriefing session with the community*

In this step the team of organisers will sum up the entire feedback based on the activities taken up from Step I through 6 and present the same to the community and get their acceptance of the major findings. This document will serve like a draft Community development Plan which can be a useful reference for any development activity. This set of steps will ensure that the initial entry point activities are accepted and secondly that the ground is set for taking up other activities. The most important accomplishment that can be attributed to this approach is that the sense of ownership of the activities is felt within the community rather than their feeling that the inputs are external to them.

## Building Community Level Structures (SHGs)

### Origin of groups in the rural and urban sectors – role of pioneer institutions

In India, Self Help Groups or SHGs represent an unique approach to financial intermediation. The approach combines access to low-cost financial services with a process of self-management and development for the women who are SHG members. SHGs are formed and supported usually by NGOs and (now, increasingly) by Government agencies. Linked not only to banks but also to wider development programmes, SHGs are seen to confer many benefits, both economic and social. SHGs enable women to grow their savings and to access the credit which banks are increasingly willing to lend. SHGs can also be community platforms from which women become active in village affairs, stand for local election or take action to address social or community issues (the abuse of women, alcohol, the dowry system, schools, and water supply).

SHGs are formed by NGOs, Government agencies or Banks – the three types of 'Self Help Promoting Agencies' or SHPAs. While the NGO promoted SHGs are probably the oldest, financial activities may not be a part of operations which could be theme based like integrated agriculture and allied activities, watershed management, integrated women and child development, etc. Success of this model has prompted the government to adopt this as an approach in all the development schemes. Some examples of this are the DWCRA and DWCUA groups, user groups, T&C Groups, women's groups, etc. where saving and credit was considered as the start of the empowerment of the women within the groups. The Bank promoted groups were the ones exclusively designed for financial activities (Rashtriya Mahila Kosh for example) and for group entrepreneurship activities. The current groups are those that have a combination of financial and non-financial activities, where capacity building skill development and individual and group activities are encouraged on the basis of group strength. These are effectively used by banks to extend various types of support in the form of micro-credit, loans for taking up small enterprises, etc.

National Urban Livelihoods Mission (NULM) has placed tremendous importance on the community mobilisation and the nurturing of SHGs and federations through various programme provisions in designing its package. The National Urban Livelihoods Mission (NULM) has given paramount importance to social mobilisation as the essential steps in programme implementation and has placed community capacity building and further strengthening through various strategies like financial inclusion, employment generation and promotion for self-employment, as precursors to its other components.

## Models of Groups Based on Scope and Function

The SHGs can be formed for any common cause or development activity. Normally it is found that initially though the groups are formed for a specific activity, gradually they diversify and take up more than one development activity in the area. SHGs practicing saving and credit along with other activities have been more successful and sustainable generally. The various types of possible groups are: (i) Saving and Credit Groups, (ii) Social Forestry Groups, (iii) Water Users' Groups, (iv) Watershed Development Groups, (v) Farmers' Interest Groups, etc.

## SHGs Defined

In its broadest sense a Self Help Group may be defined as 'A development group for the poor and marginalised categories of society recognised by the government, not requiring any formal registration and built with the purpose of building the functional capacity of the poor and marginalised in the areas of employment and income generation with the members are responsible for their own future'.

## SHG Membership and other Norms

Since the group is taken as the smallest unit of social change and empowerment, set criteria have to be followed for enrolling members. There are criteria that make women eligible for membership in groups. More important however, are the criteria that make women ineligible for membership in groups and consequently federations. Having ineligible incumbents in a group can prove to be counterproductive and in the long run work for the large-scale divisions and ultimate dissolution of the group initiatives.

### *Norms for the Formation of Self Help Groups*

With groups being the most basic unit in the institutional building process, considerable care needs to be taken for its formation. The groups once formed are given various types of inputs both for their beneficial participation in the group including their roles as members, groups leaders or sub-committee members and for their individual capacity building or empowerment. Given the significance of the right member being in the group, many methods are deployed to ensure that they truly understand the philosophy behind the SHG formation and the rights and privileges of the members and the protocol to be followed as group members.

The essential steps followed in group formation are identification of members that have commonness of need, purpose and a willingness to congregate to discuss and identify possibilities of effective address of issues. Contiguity of location almost always remains as the non-negotiable in this process – same village, same ward, or lane are usually taken as matters pertaining to contiguity.

In the NULM, the method suggested for the formation of groups is to start with the area or section within an area that is most responsive to the philosophy of group formation and gradually scale out to other areas in the outreach mode. This allows enlisting the participation of the organised members to reach out to other groups in a peer outreach method.

**Structure of SHGs**

SHGs are constituted by 10 to 20 women or men coming together to improve their life through common activities like savings, internal thrift and credit, first from their own savings and later with support from banks etc. A SHG is ideally formed without the need for registration but rather held together, as it were, with the thrift activity in order to differentiate it from loose groups as per the NULM document, the mandate is for 70 percent of the members to be poor to qualify for funding. With respect to the gender composition, the document states female membership as the ideal, with possibility of groups of disabled to also have male members. The document also specifically recommends bringing all the urban poor families into the SHG fold but qualifies it by stating that in the selection of poor, preference under NULM will be given to areas where the poor are concentrated.

**SHG Management – Some non-negotiable**

In order to build efficacy into the functioning of groups for development and poverty alleviation, there are some non-negotiable relating to the structure and functioning of groups. For example, an ideal group is one that is comprised of members sharing a common social and economic background as well as conforms to the understanding that the group is effective in identifying and addressing common problems that beset them. Common minimum set of norms across groups also helps in maintaining uniformity in structure and functioning for example, 10 to 20 members as the ideal size, preference of women under normal circumstances with inclusion of men only in exceptional situations like disability as found in the NULM guidelines mentioned above. The norms are for the following dimensions:

Membership

Group savings

Meetings (regular and special)

Management of group bank account and group finances including loans repayments, etc.

Record maintenance of records relating to meetings, financial behaviour like deciding on loans group pass book, etc.

Disqualification of members and issues attracting their termination as members

Based on best practices in group management the NULM has proposed the five golden principles referred to as the Pancha Sutras of group, i.e., pertaining to savings etc. as the foundation of good groups. These principles are: Regular Savings; Regular Meetings; Regular Accounting and maintenance of books of account; Regular Repayments, and; Adherence to rules and regulations of the SHG.

## SHGs under SJSRY and their Transition into the Livelihoods Sector

Formation of groups and federations has been the focus under UPA since the SJSRY and has gained momentum after the revamping of the SJSRY. Here under the Urban Community Development Network (UCDN) formation of NHGs, NHCs and the CDS under the CDS structure bringing the premise that 'SJSRY shall rest on the foundation of community development and empowerment' into being. Apart from the CDS structure, Thrift & Credit Groups that had their own savings and engaged in internal lending and repayments were also in vogue, further proliferating their financial ambit to include loans from external financial institutions for strengthening the groups' income generating activities.

It must be mentioned here that the above specifically implies the change in the nomenclature with reference to existing groups and further the inclusion of thrift and credit activity, to be able to optimally utilise the provisions under NULM. It would be useful to give a brief glimpse of the nomenclature utilised by some of the states in the implementation of the SJSRY vis-á-vis the nomenclature under NULM, in the table.

Under NULM, the document specifies that Thrift and Credit would be encouraged in all the groups and federations. It specifies that T&C groups and SHGs will continue to function whereas the NHGs and NHCs will be encouraged to take up Thrift and Credit activities, in keeping with the focus on financial inclusion under the programme and the taking up of minimum financial practices as a precursor to the financial empowerment of the poor for poverty reduction. With this, the structures can gradually transit into the NULM structure specified above.

***Comparison of Nomenclature of Community Structures***

| Andhra Pradesh | CDS Structure under UCDN | Kerala | NULM |
|---|---|---|---|
| Town Level Federation (TLF) | Community Development Society (CDS) | Community Development Society (CDS) | City Level Federation (CLF) |
| | | Area Development Society | |
| Slum Level Federation | Neighbourhood Committee (NHC) | | Area Level Federation |
| Self Help Group (SHG) | Neighbourhood Group (NHG) | Neighbourhood Group (NHG) | Self Help Group (SHG) |

## Building Community Level Structures (Federations)

### Federation structure and its formation with representatives of respective SHSs

Federations can be defined as formal organisations formed at the slum level in which 10-25 SHGs are clustered within that slum, with representation of at least two members from each SHG. In the NULM, the boundaries of the "Area" are not pre-determined and the document gives the prerogative to the ULB to decide on the number of members SHGs that can go into one Area-Level Federation.

The Area Level Federation performs the functions that include; monitoring of SHGs, providing support needed to maintain good book keeping records, providing the documentation needed for linkages with banks, implementing various programmes, the provision of risk mitigation through insurance agencies, promoting community health, nutrition and sanitation, providing training to enhance the conceptual clarity and management skills of SHG members, resolving conflicts that arise within SHGs, providing the essential monitoring needed to reduce default rates and the facilitation of additional services such as marketing and social development. In addition to the above services, the creation newer SHGs and expansion of their operational area to include all poor families, and identify and make available informed, motivated and skilled members for offering various services within and outside their boundaries based on the need.

## Legal Process of Registration

The ALF should be registered either as a Society or an Association in accordance with the prevalent law in the state. The registration of the Federation limits or expands the scope of its activities therefore, care should be taken to ensure the registration in such a manner that the scope of its activities are optimized. Registration of the federation can be done as a Society or as an association. Under the Societies Act also the ALF can be registered as a Society or as a cooperative or Literary Scientific and Charitable Societies Act, the Act under which it is registered play an ALF should be registered as a society/an association under relevant law of the State. Model bye-laws for ALFs are at Annexure II. However, these are only indicative and ALFs should be encouraged making their own bye-laws.

## Structure of SHG Federations

At the level of the ward or slum level federation, the membership consists of 15 to 20 SHGs. In slums which are larger and consequently there are more number of SHGs more than one SLF is also formed. The membership of the SLF is constituted by the two leaders of each SHG. The SLF will elect from among them an Executive Committee (EC) and Office Bearers (OB). Apart from the EC and the OB there is also the nomination of Sub-Committees, each for various functional areas like Health, Nutrition, Sanitation and Hygiene Promotion, Disability Welfare, monitoring and review, etc. These members are selected based on their interest in the area and willingness to work for dealing with these areas and related programmes within their jurisdiction. At the Town level, the membership consists of the EC and the OB of the member SLFs. Thus, there is a robust system of membership at various levels of the SHG and Federations. It should be mentioned that there are set criteria on the basis of which the readiness of the SHGs in the area is gauged for their federation at the Slum and Town levels.

## Representation in SHG Federations

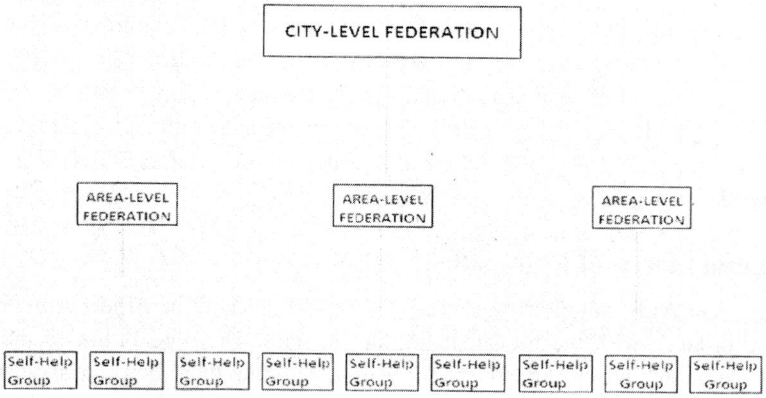


Each SHG is represented by two leaders often called as President and Secretary or Leader 1 and Leader 2. Usually the most accepted woman in the entire group they are the catalysts of the SHG in the first place. These two representatives are the ones holding bank accounts and monitoring the smooth functioning of the group as seen in the embedded figure.

**Membership of Area Level Federation:** An Area Level Federation (ALF) may be formed with 10 to 20 SHGs covering an area of a ward or slum or such other geographical unit with a minimum of two members (nominated representatives) per SHG. However, the Urban Local Body (ULB) may decide the number of SHGs in a federation as per the local conditions. An ALF should be registered as a society/an association under the relevant law of the State.

Model bye-laws for ALFs are at Annexure II. However, these are only indicative and ALFs should be encourages to make their own bye-laws.

## Responsibilities of an ALF

(1) Facilitate bank linkages for member SHGs i.e. opening of their accounts and helping them getting loans;

(2) Providing hand-holding support in the development of loan proposals by member SHGs;

(3) Capacity building of new SHGs as well as existing member SHGs for their successful functioning;

(4) Facilitate member SHGs' access to benefits under NULM as well as access to social assistance benefits under various government programmes;

(5) Support the formation of new SHGs and monitor and evaluate functioning of its member SHGs (An indicative checklist for a functional SHG is at **Annexure III**);

(6) Resolve issues raised by member SHGs in accessing credit from banks;

(7) Raise issues of importance at the level of the City-Level Federations (CLFs);

(8) Regularly report to the ULB about the SHG's functioning.

The ALFs will come together to form a City-Level Federation (CLF). It is expected that each city will have at least one CLF. The CLFs should be registered as societies/association under the relevant law of the State. All ALFs in a city should be represented at the CLF. Bigger cities may have more than one CLF based on the size and population. The CLF is expected to work with ALFs, member SHGs, city administration and financial institutions to ensure social and economic empowerment of the urban poor.

**Responsibilities of a CLF:**

(1) To represent the needs of the urban poor at various levels;

(2) Advocacy with the ULBs and state governments for pro-poor planning, master plans, vendor planning, etc.;

(3) To facilitate access of member ALFs' and member SHGs' to banking services;

(4) New group formation and support;

(5) To identify specific training and capacity building needs of its member ALFs;

(6) Work closely with the respective ULB to facilitate identification of beneficiaries for various government programmes;

(7) Facilitate marketing of SHG produce/products.

## Thrift & Credit – the Binding Factor of SHGs

According to Mohammad Yunus, Nobel Laureate, "Credit link is the birthright of every poor man." In an interesting episode that set the precedent for the setting up of the Grameen Bank in Bangladesh, involving his interaction with a 22 years-old petty vendor by name Sofia, the harsh reality of the credit needs of a poor individual and the lack of a mechanism to offer that, dawned on the doyen. The credit needs of a poor individual are very small (Sofia needed only $27 to make her debt-free) which formal institutions like banks find too miniscule to offer. This forces them to take loans from sources that offer unreasonable rates of interest. The Grameen

Bank model facilitated by Dr. Yunus, which is run by the poor women, is now replicated by many women-based institutions in the country.

The implementation of urban poverty alleviation in India in its transition from the infrastructural model to the community participation models have come to the conclusion that along with collectivisation of poor communities, lending them access to micro-credit needs accounts for concrete growth of the poor to improve their quality of life. In order to instill financial discipline into the groups and encourage group based financial activity, starting with internal lending from the group's own savings over a minimum period of six months, to accessing bank support for micro-credit needs.

## Thrift & Credit in Groups, the Need and Advantages

The need for Thrift & Credit among groups for their financial empowerment and their mainstreaming cannot be over emphasised. As observed by the Hon'ble Prime Minister in his speech to the national on the occasion of the initiation of the Prime Minister's Jan Dhan Yojana (PMJDY), access to finance spells freedom from many shackles and fetters that bind the poor in any country and relegate them to the position of 'untouchables', and the responsibility rests on the shoulders of the government and public institutions like banks etc, to create that access. However, in keeping with the idiom that all action originates from the precincts of the home, self-generated thrift is where the whole issue of financial discipline starts. Thrift activity in a group implies both mutual trust between fellow members and a sense of accountability towards them. This is important especially in the absence of the need for a formal registration, it is this activity that holds the group together. From a business point of view, the group that has some amount of corpus, can meet the minimum requirement in order to approach financial institutions for credit support.

Credit needs of the poor and the need for facilitating bank linkages based on group strength. The credit need of the urban poor range from ensuring food security, education, health exigencies, to higher level needs that include setting up or expansion of individual livelihoods activities. Many times the need for such loans that surface in the lives of the urban poor very often, and the inability to meet the requirements of formal institutions like banks force them to fall into the hands of private money lenders who are quick to support but charge upto five times the interest charged by banks and are extortionist in their approach for recoveries. So a unique need that is often expressed by the urban poor is that they would like a one-time loan which they can use to pay off the private money lenders and be content with paying lesser amount by way of interest (debt-swapping).

For such members becoming members of the SHG would allow them to capitalise on group strength, duly dovetailed by their own savings and the experience gained by internal credit, to access banks for small sized loans. Further the positive steps taken by the banking institution to support groups gives them an added reason to become group members.

**Basic pre-requisites of the SHGs for accessing micro-credit**

As per the NULM, there are certain pre-requisites for SHGs in terms of the number, the membership norms and the like. These need to be fulfilled by the group to be eligible for accessing benefit under NULM including micro-credit from banks. These pertain to the following:

Group membership 10 to 20 members

Thrift and credit to be regular and with sufficient corpus

Inclusion of urban poor to the tune of at least 70 percent

Concentration of urban poor should be high

Availability of Specific norms for the following:

1. Norms for membership
2. Norms for group savings including the amount, date of deposit with the group
3. Role of every office bearer in the SHG
4. Norms for conduct of group meetings including the number of times the group meets, and the convening of special meetings
5. Management of savings of group including maximum amount of loans to SHG members, the interest rate, repayment details, and basic criteria to grant a loan
6. Management of the SHG group bank account
7. Maintenance of various records including minutes of meetings, member passbooks, savings and loan register and group pass book
8. Withdrawal of membership, disqualification of membership, change in the rules and regulations and dissolution of the SHG
9. Norms for imposition of fines/penalties on group members and amount of penalty for: [a] not attending the meetings, [b] irregular savings and [c] non-repayment of loan on time, etc.

10. Norms governing the access to higher need based loans to groups and federations for various needs
11. Groups become eligible to access once the quantum of their credit needs become higher than the existing corpus complete with the revolving fund. In such a case some additional requirements may come up as follows:
12. In case the loan is required by only few of the SHG members then declaration by the other members of the group agreeing to stand by the other members for availing the loan as well take responsibility for the repayment of the loan.

## SHG Members Profile

Historically it can be seen that the development of

The socio and economic conditions of sample respondents are studied by analyzing the respondent's position with respect to literacy level, income level, family income, occupation, borrowings, residential accommodation, consumption expenditure, assets and liabilities. Further, the relationship between impact of the programme and social background of the respondents like caste, age and marital status is also analysed.

### The development of Self Help Groups – the journey

*Economic support is one of the primary areas of lack faced by the poor in the community in both rural and urban areas.* Poverty and ill-health are very closely intertwined. Poverty breeds ill health. And it works both ways – Ill-health perpetuates poverty. This is the root of the poverty cycle.

Economic backwardness is one of the main characteristics of rural and urban poverty. Together with ill health and lack of access to information on poverty alleviation it forms a vicious cycle that is perpetual and incremental in impact. *Finance interventions provide small-scale credit and other financial services to poor households and very small, informal businesses. They provide a mechanism for poor people to smooth the effects of income shocks on consumption, find safe and affordable repositories for their savings, take advantage of profitable investment opportunities and insure against risk.*

"*Experience worldwide shows that when microfinance services reach women, the benefits are particularly sustainable. Savings rates are higher; group life is more intensive; repayment rates are remarkable; enterprise growth and graduation are stronger; and there are measurable improvements in child nutrition and education, family health and household sanitation, shelter and general welfare.*

"Self-help groups (SHGs) were piloted initially by NGOs in India in the mid-1980s, in order to provide financial services to poor people, notable among which was MYRADA. What started as a pilot programme has now become a movement for social empowerment – particularly for rural poor women. The number of SHGs linked to banks has increased from about 500 in the early 1990s to more than 1.6 million in 2006."

The journey of SHGs from nascent stages in the mid 1980s to the present structure, is an eventful yet interesting one. Over the decades, SHGs have moved from strength to strength, with varied levels of participation along the way. This process of growth has built for practitioners as well as for the SHG members themselves, tremendous learnings which have paved the way for considerable improvement in the programme package. Starting from situation based collectives of agriculture based women, over the decades SHGs have grown to become centres of decision-making and familial and societal changes.

Self Help groups first emerged in MYRADA (Mysore Resettlement And Development Agency) in the year 1985 when the women, faced with the situation of returning the loan amount they had borrowed from the NGO promoted cooperatives opted to return the amount directly to the NGO rather than to the cooperative as they had reached a stage of mismanagement. MYRADA suggested the women to form groups and start pay back to themselves. On its part the NGO started training the women on organisation of meetings and books of accounts and minutes as well as sensitizing them on the importance of trust and need to transcend considerations of religion, caste and creed but build on the commonness of need and opportunity and also spatial proximity.

With the above beginnings in 1985, till the year 2000-01 when the SHG strategy was included in the Annual Plan by the Government of India, the inputs to the women for their empowerment saw different dimensions – from NABARD, RBI, national and trans national NGOs and multinational agencies like IFAD.

The ensuing 20-year period saw a quick paced growth of the SHGs also referred to as Self-Help Affinity Groups (SAGs) as also supportive mechanisms in terms of provisions offered to groups and federations by government and financial and non-financial institutions. These can be classified into three broad phases, namely.

(a) Increasing support to SHGs by NGOs and financial institutions (1987 to 1992)
(b) SHG Bank Linkage programme (1992 and ongoing)
(c) Empowerment of SHGs and their proliferation to other areas

These three phases will be discussed briefly in the following paragraphs:

## Support to SHGs

During this period NABARD focussed on supporting NGO initiatives to promote SHGs and following up their potential for growth and performance. The first financial support was to the tune of ₹ I million given to MYRADA as a grant against their proposal to enable the NGO to identify SHGs (then more popularly known as SAGs) build their capacity and march their savings after a period of 3 to 6 months. Based on the very positive feedback from the initiative, NABARD scaled up the project to identify similar NGOs and support them with similar grants the multiplier effect of this initiative largely coupled with the advocacy of the NABARD. Top and sernior level funcationaries, the RBI accepted the SHG strategy as an alternate credit model.

NABARD (1992) issued guidelines to provide the framework for a strategy that would allow banks to lend directly to SHGs. Based on these initial experiences, the SHG-Bank Linkage Programme was launched in 1992 (this second phase is described in Section III). Since then – and on the basis of its extensive network of officers – NABARD has promoted and monitored the SHG programme, provided funds for capacity building and innovation, and helped change policy to create enabling environment.

## The SHG Bank Linkage Programme

This programme started in 1992 as a two-year pilot project with the objective to link 500 SHGs, initiated by NABARD and not involving SHGs promoted by them since 1987. Slow to pick up initially, the activity gained footage from 1999. It received unstinted support from RBI, the Central and several State Governments prominent among which have been the Southern States of Andhra Pradesh, Tamil Nadu, Karnataka as well as Maharashtra, with thousands of NGOs, the banking sectors and several multinational agencies like IFAD became its torchbearers and supporters.

According to several reliable reports notably from NABARD state that as of March 200 there were about three million SHGs in India of which 1.6 million were linked to bank.

- **Poor family Vs others**

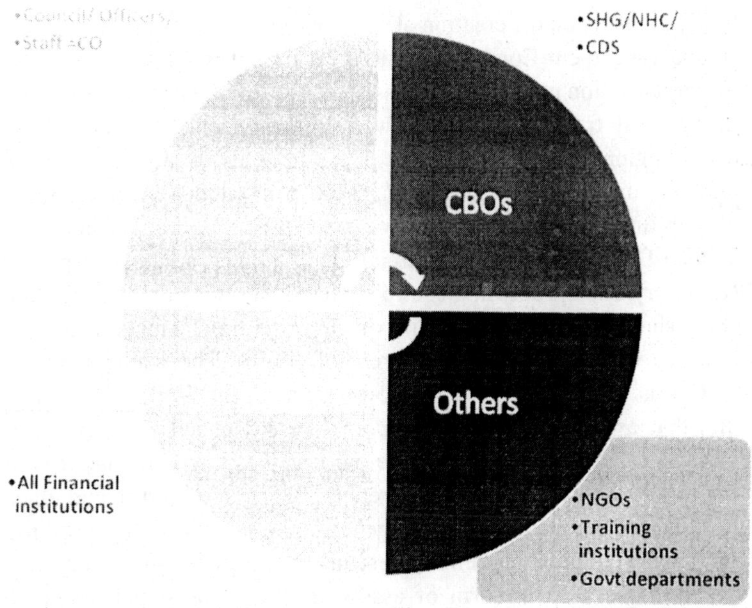


**SM & ID - Best Practices**
*Fig. SM & ID – Best Practices.*

## Introduction

Though documenting analysis of best practices in poverty reduction has certain constrains there is a tremendous and even overwhelming choices of practices and experiences available as part of socio-economic development strategy. But they differ in terms of their experiences from state to state and country to country and naturally the best practices are generally skewed by the self interests of the agency or group in identifying or selecting such practices. Despite such constrains, some of the examples are cited for the purpose of understanding as to how the poverty reduction programmes are implemented through the community participation. Most of the best practices of poverty alleviation emphasises the role of women's groups through a range of focus on poverty reduction. The other point is about information and transparency in decision making which are accessible to the poor communities to realise their full developmental potential. The community participation and their partners acceptability in the local community than their outside parties is also another biggest challenge. The sustainability part is most important which are ensured initially focusing on the creation of social capital. The case of Bangladesh Rural Advancement Committee (BRAC) which was set up in 1972 as a relief organisation to provide and assistance to resettle refugees returning to Bangladesh from India after the war of Independence. Though it had a modest beginning, it is stated that it has now 26000 regular staff and 34000 part time teachers establishing 34000 schools and the provision of micro credit loans to 3.5 million women which is familiarly known as Grameen Bank. It runs a commercial bank, a diary, a hatchery, poultry feed factory, seed processing centre's internet service provides, clothing and cat shops and a university apart from providing healthcare at about 90 clinics with more than 2000 prenatal clinics. The whole model of BRAC was social mobilisation. However, a recent World Bank study found that extreme poverty among borrowers dropped 18 percent over seven years but it has also become evident that micro finance cannot substitute for growth. Some of the reports like Imran Martin, and others states that though micro credit can benefit only those with the capability cannot help all others. Therefore, those in extreme poverty will need more cost intensive help in form of assets and skill training to generate sustainable returns from borrowed money.

## Goward Kalinga in Philippines

This is another successful story of building communities and neighbourhoods for construction of houses and improvement providing livelihoods, healthcare, and other priority areas. The houses are kept affordable for the poor through self help by the poor, voluntary inputs from large number of volunteers, donations by individuals, cooperation with local governments. This organisation have been successfully running since their prime objective is to enhance the responsibility of the poor in their own slum/squatter communities through values formation and community development and to encourage the rich and well to do to contribute towards the betterment of the poor. It has large number of achievements like building about five lakh housing units in 5000 communities in five years in 2002 and recently announced a target of 70 lakh housing units in 7000 communities in seven years. However, it is a big question and a challenge regarding the faith driven programme to look whether it will remain succinctly cohesive and cooperative to look after the common facilities and how the income levels of the poor residents be improved furthermore.

### Thailand Fishland Development Project

The objective of this programme is to increase fish production for local consumption to provide a stimulus for local employment and to alleviate non nutrition and poverty, they have selected ponds, tanks, etc. to foster the training of local professional to increase the supply of fish and provide technical advice. This project achieved establishment of 10000 ponds throughout the country in schools and all these ponds reflect the countries credible performance in developing its fisheries to meet the needs of its population. This is a village based fish production and achieved through social cohesiveness and community cooperation and convergence of other stakeholders. The participating schools have been benefited from the direct benefits of fish consumption and improved water supply and academic skills inculcated positive work and life values among the end. Thus, this is one of the good practice in school based adaptive learning in community driven learning in poverty alleviation. It is also a good model for non-formal elements that can be transferred relatively easily to other learning situations to avail the opportunity.

Sarvodaya Shramadhana Movement in Sri Lanka

Social Governance Programme in Kirgistan

Yadfone association mangrove restoration in Thailand

Agakhan rural support programme in Pakistan

Self employed women's association (SEWA) in India

Dairy cooperatives in India

Community hill forestry in Nepal

Kecamatan Development Project in Indonesia

These are some of the internationally acknowledged best practices how the community mobilisation ensure success in poverty alleviation and social development.

## Development of CBOs under NULM-study of best practices from AP, Kerala, Gujarat; Developing a sustainable strategy for community empowerment

### UPA Programme-Mission Mode Approach

This initiative of creating mission mode approach is the culmination of reforms in the urban sector, ushered in by the 74th Constitutional

Amendment. The current chapter is a case study of mission mode approach of Andhra Pradesh state which has recently bagged the national award for social mobilisation. The history of MEPMA goes back to initiatives that are taken for poverty alleviation under the scheme of Andhra Pradesh Urban Services for the Poor (APUSP) which out of its third component was focusing on the strengthening of civil society as part of urban poverty alleviation. It is pertinent to mention here that the other two components, namely Municipal Reforms and Urban Infrastructure Development have been successfully implemented in the state of Andhra Pradesh as they become part and parcel of Municipal Administration Department with certain accountability and transparency in view of allocation of state funds while the third component is running under the central government funds being allocated as plan grant. However, the state of Andhra Pradesh have successfully implemented most of its urban poverty alleviation which are discussed as part of reforms for the other states while reforms to be introduced within the MEPMA for its further strengthening and enhanced productivity.

## Urban Reforms Facilitating Mission Mode Approach

The Urban Poverty Alleviation initiatives in India have to a large measure targeted the emancipation of women along with infrastructural development. While the projects in themselves were wholesome, the poverty alleviation strategy missed out on the essential aspects of urban poverty. Urban poverty has three aspects, namely lack of formal means of livelihood, lack of security for residence, and other social insecurities, that come with the other two in addition to the lack of social security, micro-credit, etc. However, it is staggering to note that only a miniscule percentage of these initiatives actually targeted the creation of livelihood opportunities for the poor.

Till the ninth plan period, the urban initiatives were subsumed within the overall ambit of other programme implementation. Thus, the specific needs of the urban poor were largely ignored. Similarly, the informal sector has also been largely ignored. Huge hours of work, with incommensurate wages, lack of any security like for accidents, etc., inhuman conditions and their need to be available at all times forces them to stay close to work-places, thereby by default settling in slums. While pointing to the high development of cities in comparison to village development as responsible for the influx of migrants to cities, efforts at village development was given focus. However, this has not taken into account the development of urban migrants already settled in the cities.

Extending credit for the urban poor has also been a contentious issue where first, while micro-credit was not available through banks, higher level of credit which was not the poor man's priority, required collateral security. Due to this twin disadvantage, the urban poor had to settle for transaction with other middlemen and the recent mushrooming micro-finance institutions, willing to pay higher rates of interest in return for non-competitive and timely credit supply.

The subsequent FYPs recognized these lacunae in quickening community partnership and the sole onus for this resting with the municipalities, have gone in for radically different strategy that vests the local government with the freedom to bring in community especially the poor within- to play an express part in the design, putting in place, their judicious utilisation and post-project self management.

The JnNURM and the NULM, of the Ministry of Urban Development and the Ministry for Urban Poverty Alleviation sought to implement urban reforms in a specific and decisive manner. Further revamped in 2009, the NULM gave the much needed focus on livelihoods and skills development and the development of individual and group-based self and wage employment. Further with the fillip given by the call of Inclusive Development in the 11$^{th}$ and 12$^{th}$ Five Year Plan, inclusion of these elements gave high level of freedom to the states in their implementation. Few successful models came up in states especially in the South which reiterated the successful elements in the poverty alleviation programmes. Many of the strategy applied for implementation had to do with re-vamping itself into the Mission Mode in order to effectively implement its programmes. Such was the case while some states continued to implement the programme within the framework of the state itself. Thus, one finds that within the country, there are both the mission mode and the state structure mode for the implementation of urban poverty alleviation programmes.

The 74$^{th}$ Constitutional Amendment Act 1992 is one of the landmark initiatives designed to decentralise urban governance that gave constitutional recognition to urban local bodies. The Act which requires state governments to amend their municipal laws in order to empower ULBs with the powers necessary to enable them to function as institutions of self governance have specified the list of local functions in the Twelfth Schedule which are wide in their scope and content to vest them with the powers to function as self governing institutions. The implementation of the Act by the states is further a mandatory reform to be carried out at state level under JnNURM. In the face of lack of financial backup and need to seek state approval for either enhancement of existing taxes or levying new tax, the inbuilt thrust of the JnNURM reforms is to improve urban governance and tighten up their revenue generation by improving urban governance and service delivery mechanisms.

The 74$^{th}$ Amendment was an overall approach to eliminate poverty. It was also a very large step in democratic decentralisation. It gave more power to the local bodies to participate in the development process and conducted direct elections for seats in municipalities via the State Election Commissioner appointed by the Governor. One-third of the seats were reserved for women. This amendment act included urban poverty alleviation plans, plans for slum improvement and up-gradation as a legitimate municipal function. An Urban Poverty Eradication (UPE) Cell was set up in each town headed by a trained Town Project Officer under the concerned Urban Local Body (ULB). A Finance Commission was constituted at the state level to review the municipal finances every five years.

## Institutional Framework for Implementation

In the implementation of reforms in the Urban Poverty Alleviation sector, proper back-up in the form of a robust institutional arrangement is crucial. The setting up of a dedicated structure and mechanism reflects the willingness of the state to give enhanced focus on urban poverty alleviation, and as it were, accelerates the process of involving the community especially the user groups in the implementation process which leads to their systemic empowerment (i.e., from the basic level of creating the awareness and demand, through the process of rising to take up the responsibilities that it entails).

This has been adequately exemplified in the implementation of Kudumbasree (Kerala), MEPMA (Andhra Pradesh) and UMMEED (Gujarat) models of urban poverty alleviation which have earned national acclaim for themselves, some elements of which have also been incorporated into the latest version of the UPA programme, namely, the National Urban Livelihoods Mission.

However, there are many administrative reforms at the administrative level that are not only desirable but imperative, in order to make the institutional setting viable. In the absence of an adequate administrative reform set to go with the institutional mechanism, the poverty initiative will not only be just a short-lived success, but in its reactive form, will also face the danger of presenting with many unintended results as side-effects, many times which are undesirable.

## Mission Mode Approach vs. State Level Committees

While some state have adopted mission mode approach with a view to attack poverty on a high priority basis some others have appointed state level committees for the purpose. However, each one of them has its own merits and demerits in addressing the poverty in urban areas. Therefore, our attempt is to look at the relative advantage of each state approach adopted in the implementation of urban poverty issues. The following table explains the state/district/ULB level arrangements made in the southern states for the implementation of activities under NULM.

**Table 11.1 UPA Institutional Framework of Southern States: A Comparison**

| *Sl.No.* | *State/Implementing Agency* | *State level* | *District Level* | *ULB level* |
|---|---|---|---|---|
| 1. | **Andhra Pradesh**<br>Mission for Elimination of Poverty in Municipal Area (MEPMA) | Governing Body Executive Committee and State Mission-MEPMA/SUDA | District Project Management Unit (DPMU)/DUDA Coordination Monitoring Committee At District Urban Development Agency (DUDA)/ District Project Monitoring Unit (DPMU) | UPA Cell Co-ordination and Monitoring Committee at ULB Level/ Circle Level in Mission Cities of Hyderabad, Vijayawada and Visakhapatnam |
| 2. | **Kerala**<br>Kerala State Poverty Eradication Mission (KUDUMBASHREE) | Governing Body Executive Committee The State Mission | District Mission | Community Development Society (Area Development Society (ADS) Neighbourhood Group |
| 3. | **Karnataka**<br>State Level Committee | State Level Committee UPA Cell | District Level Committee UPA Cell | Commissioner (Corporation) UPA Cell |
| 4. | **Tamil Nadu**<br>State Urban Development Agency (SUDA) | Governing Body Executive Committee State Urban Development Agency (SUDA) UPA Unit | Governing Body Executive Committee District Urban Development Agency (DUDA) Project Implementation Unit (PIU) | Town Urban Poverty Eradication Cell (TUPEC) |
| 5. | **Puducherry**<br>Puducherry Urban Development Agency (PUDA) | Governing Body Puducherry Urban Development Agency (PUDA) | Municipal Commissioner | |

## Conclusions

(1) It is concluded that the Mission Mode Approach may be a good strategy for solving the Urban Poverty.

(2) It is further examined that individual states have to design their own approaches besides G.O.I, to solve Urban Poverty.

# 12

# Ph.D. Thesis
# Financial Inclusion: Inclusive Banking Initiatives and Practices – A Study with Reference to Andhra Bank

***Dr S. Tarakeswara Rao***

**Abstract**

*Financial inclusion is emerging as a new paradigm of economic growth that plays major role in driving away the poverty from the country. It refers to delivery of banking services to masses including privileged and disvantaged people at an affordable terms and conditions. Financial inclusion is important priority of the country in terms of economic growth and advances of society. It enables to reduce the gap between rich and poor population. In the current scenario financial institutions are the robust pillars of progress, economic growth and development of the economy. When and where all citizens are participated in financial system, the economy and system will become very strong. In this regard the research article was focuses on customer perceptions towards inclusive banking practices.*

***Keywords:*** *Inclusive banking, financial inclusion, public sector banks.*

## Introduction

Financial inclusion may be defined as the process of ensuring access to financial services and timely and adequate credit where needed by vulnerable groups such as weaker sections and low income groups at an affordable cost. Financial Inclusion, broadly defined, refers to universal access to a wide range of financial services at a reasonable cost. These include not only banking products but also other financial services such as insurance and equity products. The essence of financial inclusion is to ensure delivery of financial services which include bank accounts for savings and transactional purposes, low cost credit for productive, personal and other purposes, financial advisory services, insurance facilities (life and nonlife) etc.

## Inclusive Banking

Inclusive banking is an important tool to achieve the financial inclusion. Of all the financial inclusion products, banking products play key role in the development of economy. Having a bank account and access to the financial products like deposit, loan and other services from the bank is unavoidable for every household. Hence, there is a need of inclusion of each and every household in the country in the formal financial system by opening of account in the bank.

Indian economy continues to suffer from the problems of poverty, sectoral divergences in growth and employment opportunities and a poor progress of various socio-economic indicators despite of higher economic growth in recent past. Attaining the objective of hundred percent financial inclusion is today one of the biggest challenges for Indian formal banking system. Greater financial inclusion shall be a catalyst for accelerating the pace of economic growth with equity. Achieving financial inclusion through formal banking system is a herculean task. Unavailability of adequate financial services like credit, insurances and remittances to majority population at an affordable cost is a major hurdle for the growth of financial sectors.

Financial inclusion can create win-win environment for both customer and financial institution in an economy. It enables customer to avail various kinds of financial products for productive purposes. It also helps customers in availing micro remittance facilities and micro credit at an affordable cost. The Government also can use the bank accounts of people for providing various social security services for the vulnerable section of society. Thus, financial inclusion with inclusive banking can be considered as pre-requisite to achieve inclusive growth which would further helps to achieve sustainable economic growth.

**Financial Inclusion Initiatives:**

1. Advised all banks to open Basic Saving Bank Deposit (BSBD) accounts with minimum common facilities such as no minimum balance, deposit and withdrawal of cash at bank branch and ATMs,

receipt/credit of money through electronic payment channels, facility of providing ATM card.

2. Relaxed and simplified KYC norms to facilitate easy opening of bank accounts, especially for small accounts with balances not exceeding ₹ 50,000 and aggregate credit in the accounts not exceeding one lakh a year. Further, banks are advised not to insist on introduction for opening bank account of customers. In addition, banks are allowed to use Aadhar Card as a proof of both identity and address.
3. Simplified Branch Authorisation Policy, to address the issue of uneven spread bank branches, domestic SCBs are permitted to freely open branches in Tier 2 to Tier 6 centers with population of less than 1 lakh under general permission, subject to reporting.
4. Compulsory Requirement of Opening Branches in Un-banked Villages, banks are directed to allocate at least 25 percent of the total number of branches to be opened during the year in unbanked (Tier 5 and Tier 6) rural centers.
5. Opening of intermediate brick and mortar structure, for effective cash management, documentation, redressal of customer grievances and close supervision of BC operations, banks have been advised to open intermediate structures between the present base branch and BC locations.
6. Public and private sector banks had been advised to submit board approved three year Financial Inclusion Plan (FIP) starting from April 2010. These policies aim at keeping self-set targets in respect of rural brick and mortar branches opened, BCs employed, coverage of un-banked villages with population above 2000 and as well as below 2000, BSBD accounts opened, KCCs, GCCs issued and others. RBI has been monitoring these plans on a monthly basis.
7. Banks have been advised that their FIPs should be disaggregated and percolated down up to the branch level. This would ensure the involvement of all stakeholders in the financial inclusion efforts.

## Need for the Study

The progress of financial exclusion in India is found to be higher as compared with many developed and some of the major emerging economies. The wide extent of financial exclusion in India is visible in the form of high population per bank branch and low proportion of the population have access to basic financial services like savings accounts, credit facilities and credit and debit cards. According to an estimate by the World Bank, the credit requirement of the poorer sections in India was placed at around ₹ 50,000 crore per annum in 2002. Against this requirement the credit outstanding of the poorer sections with the formal banking sector is stated to be ₹ 5,000 crore or 10 percent of the total demand.

The RBI has observed that out of 6,00,000 habitations in the country, only about 6 percent have a commercial bank branch. Also only about 55 percent of the population across the country has bank account (savings), and this ratio is much lower in the North-Eastern states. India has significantly low level of financial penetration compared with OECD (Organisation for Economic Co-operation and Development) countries. Even though there are so many initiations have been taken by the Government and the RBI, the financial inclusion process is not up to the mark. Thus, there is a need to study the inclusive policies, initiations and practices of the banks in India in general and of the public sector banks in particular.

## Objectives of the Study

**The main objectives of the research study are :**

1. To explain the rationale and dimensions of the practices and initiatives of financial inclusion by the Indian Banking System with the objective focus of inclusive banking.
2. To provide a review of the policy emphasis of the Reserve Bank of India and the initiatives of the Government of India in the direction of promoting realising the edifices of financial inclusion.
3. To examine the efficacy of inclusive banking strategies of public sector banks with special reference to Andhra Bank with a customer perception focus.
4. To suggest policy recommendations for efficacious inclusive banking.

## Hypothesis of the Study

For the purpose of the present research study following hypothesis are tested:

$H_1$ Inclusive banking despite the policy propagation and emphasis over the years could not progress much in number.

$H_2$ On the part of the banking system and the banking personnel the inclusive banking is more pervasive in terms of target realisation rather than objective realisation.

$H_3$ Financial inclusion could be more achieved no doubt through inclusive banking practices but the basic underlying objective of promoting savings and income generative activities could not be hatched.

**Methodology of the study:** The methodology adopted for the research study includes a detailed analysis of secondary data related to inclusive banking performances of Andhra Bank and a study of primary data on the views and opinions of a select sample group of Andhra Bank Customers. The survey of primary data is made taking a sample the customers on Random cum Convenience sample basis selected from the zones of Visakhapatnam and Kakinada covering four districts such as Srikakulam, Vijayanagaram, Visakhapatnam and East Godavari in Andhra Pradesh State.

## Review of Literature:

**Deepti K.C. (2014)** state that micro-finance has been recognised as an important tool in connecting the unbanked population to mainstream finance. The clearance of the draft document of the Micro-Finance Institutions (Development and regulation) bill by the Union Cabinet is an indication of the Government's faith in the sector. The RBI and NABARD have supported the propagation of micro-finance considerably through the SHG-bank linkage programme (SBLP) and have designed incentives to support Micro-Finance Institutions (MFIs) in forming Joint Liability Groups (JLGs). Commercial banks are incentivised to lend to MFIs by placing MFIs under Priority Sector Lending (PSL). PSL requirements mandate banks to ensure 40.00 of their aggregate.

**Dr. Gurusharan Singh Kainth (2014)** observed that there is a large overlap between poverty and permanent financial exclusion. Both poverty and financial exclusion result in a reduction of choices which affects social interaction and leads to reduced participation in society. Full financial inclusion, therefore is a state in which all people who can use them have access to a full suite of quality financial services, provided at affordable prices, in a convenient manner and with dignity for the clients.

**According to G. Padmanabhan (2013)** Technology plays a vital and crucial role in financial inclusion, a sustainable banking theme very relevant to a country like India that has a large unbanked population. Internet and mobile technologies are in the direction of reaching out to the populace starved of bankng services as well

## Customer Perceptions on Inclusive Banking Practices – An Analysis

In the broad conceptual framework of inclusive growth originated during the eleventh five year plan focus in India, the Financial Inclusion has been emphasised significantly in view of the pervasive touch of the financial sector and system throughout the breath and length of the economy in the financial system of the country, the banking sector stands pivotal and predominant. Therefore, for realising the objectives of the financial inclusion, an inevitable emphasis on the mechanism of inclusive banking need not to be reiterated. The Indian Banking system consists of the forerunning and front line public sector banking besides the private sector, foreign and cooperative banking. Because the financial inclusion is the prime concern and policy priority of the government, minimizing exclusion and maximizing inclusion is the task that rests on the shoulders of the Public Sector Banks (PSBs) mostly. The Andhra Bank is the doyen of Public Sector in the country with a wide branch and customer ways in the country. The selection of Andhra Bank for a specific study of the Policies and Practice of financial inclusion in rural areas is basically with this rationale behind. For the sake of convenience and comprehensive empirical presentation, the study is focused on the Visakhapatnam and Kakinada zones of the Andhra Bank in the state of Andhra Pradesh.

**Table 17.1 Possession of Bank Account by the household**

| *Response* | *No. of households* | | | | | | | | |
|---|---|---|---|---|---|---|---|---|---|
| | *Srikakulam* | | *VZM* | | *VSKP* | | *East Godavari* | | *Total* |
| *Yes* | 550 | 22.95 | 672 | 28.05 | 560 | 23.37 | 614 | 25.63 | 2396 |
| | (62.79) | | 60.76 | | 55.45 | | 61.71 | | 60.10 |
| *No* | 326 | 20.49 | 434 | 27.28 | 450 | 28.28 | 381 | 23.95 | 1591 |
| | 37.21 | | 39.24 | | 44.5 | | 38.29 | | 39.9 |
| *Total* | 876 | 21.97 | 1106 | 27.74 | 1010 | 25.33 | 995 | 24.96 | 3987 |
| | 100.0 | | 100 | | 100.0 | | 100.0 | | |

1. Figures in lower brackets indicate percentages to respective vertical totals.
2. Figures in side brackets indicate percentages to horizontal tools.

**Table 17.2 Chi-square Test**

| ***Results*** | |
|---|---|
| Critical Value | 7.814728 |
| Chi-square test statistic | 13.03253 |
| p-Value | 0.004567 |
| **Reject the null hypothesis** | |

The select Visakhapatnam and Kakinada zones covers four districts, namely Srikakulam, Vijayanagaram, Visakhapatnam and East Godavari. For an inquisitive study of the banking inclusive practices, policies and their efficacy, the sample of the customers are chosen from the stated districts under the said zones of the Andhra Bank. The sample of customers for eliciting the perceptions and opinions on inclusive banking practices of the Andhra Bank is a convenience sampling on random basis and consists of 1684 customers picked equally from all the four districts at the rate of 241 from each district. The structured schedule is canvassed by the researcher and his team of assistants personally to elicit the multidimensional customer perceptions on the inclusive banking practices of the PSB giant the Andhra Bank.

**Reasons for not having bank account:** Financial exclusion and banking exclusion is widely prevalent in country like India, which is traditional, rural based and poverty stricken. No doubt, since the economic reforms and the sailing of the economy for more than two decades in the globalised and privatised environment, it is a socio-economic expectation that the economy should experience a transformation in the direction of increasing financial inclusion and inclusive banking. It is evident from the fact that is observed from the analysis of the data in Table 1 that 60.10 percent of the total households (3987) were touched for eliciting the information regarding the possession of bank account, positively asserted that they possess the bank account. Still it is disappointing for the policy makers to note that nearly 40 percent (1591) of the households reported not possessing any bank account. The reasons reported for the observed phenomenon of not having the bank account are varied.

Table 2 presents the elicited reasons for not having the bank accounts by the households. It can be seen from the table ethat 27.78 percent of the households reported that the basic reason for not having a bank account is that their earnings are adequate only to live hand to mouth. It is followed by the reason of absence of bank branch in their vicinity. It is reported by 22.25 percent. 15.78 percent of the households stated that they do not feel the need for the bank account and it is followed by 9.11 percent reported the fear of communication as the reasons for that 8.93 percent of the households reported that they tried to but refused by the bank to open the account and it is followed by 7.79 percent who reflected that they lack of knowledge to operate the bank account.

**Table 17.2 Reasons for not having bank accounts**

| *S.No.* | *Reason* | *No. of Respondents* | *Percentage* |
|---|---|---|---|
| **1.** | Earning adequate only hand to mouth | 442 | 27.78 |
| **2.** | Absence of bank branch in the vicinity | 354 | 22.25 |
| **3.** | Afraid of communication process | 145 | 9.11 |
| **4.** | Felt no need | 251 | 15.78 |
| **5.** | Tried but refused by the bank | 142 | 8.93 |
| **6.** | Fear of rejection by the bank | 62 | 3.90 |
| **7.** | Lack of knowledge to operate the bank account | 124 | 7.79 |
| **8.** | Banking is more time taking | 24 | 1.51 |
| **9.** | Indifference of the bankers accepting small amounts | 47 | 2.95 |
| | **Total** | **1591** | **100.00** |

The analysis clearly shows that among the reasons for banking exclusions, as reported by the majority of the households (442) include the earning of the household only adequate to live hand to mouth, absence of bank branches in the vicinity, feeling of no need, fear of communication with bank officials refused by the bank to open the account and lack of knowledge to operate the bank account.

**Occupational Profile of the respondents:** The occupational profile of the respondents presented in Table 3. It can be seen from the table that in the entire zones under review, a dominant proportion of 50.53 percent of the respondents are farmers. It is also the case with respect to the constituent districts i.e., Srikakulam District (60.33%), Vijayanagaram District (47.03%). Visakhapatnam District (48.69%) and East Godavari District (46.08%). The other predominant occupational segment of the respondents is land labourers (20.06%) in the two zones followed by 22.57 percent in Srikakulam District, 22.92 percent in Vijayanagaram District, 25.89 percent in Visakhapatnam District and 22.57 percent in East Godavari District. The other following occupational segments among the select respondents include students (10.63%), those in business (8.67%) and employment (4.45%). The analysis of the occupational composition of the sample of respondents in the select Andhra Bank zones consists of the formers and the labourers on land which unitedly constitute 75.59 percent. The job holders constitute only 4.45 percent and the students stand with 10.63 percent. There is a significant difference between the rows and non-significant among columns. The occupation of the respondents within the district is different. Farmers and land labourers are more number in the respondents. This occupational profile is more or less same in all four districts of two zones.

**Table 17.3 Occupational Profile of the Respondents**

| *No. of households* | | | | | | | | | |
|---|---|---|---|---|---|---|---|---|---|
| ***Occupation*** | ***Srikakulam*** | | ***VZM*** | | ***VSKP*** | | ***East Godavari*** | | ***Total*** |
| ***Students*** | 18 | 10.06 | 45 | 25.14 | 54 | 30.17 | 62 | 34.64 | 179 |
| | 4.28 | | 10.69 | | 12.83 | | 14.73 | | 10.63 |
| ***Farmer*** | 254 | 29.85 | 198 | 23.27 | 205 | 24.09 | 194 | 22.80 | 851 |
| | 60.33 | | 47.03 | | 48.69 | | 46.08 | | 50.53 |
| ***Job*** | 18 | 24.00 | 24 | 32.00 | 19 | 25.33 | 14 | 18.67 | 75 |
| | 4.28 | | 5.70 | | 4.51 | | 3.33 | | 4.45 |
| ***Business*** | 34 | 23.39 | 28 | 19.18 | 29 | 19.86 | 55 | 37.67 | 146 |
| | 8.08 | | 6.65 | | 6.89 | | 13.1 | | 8.67 |
| ***Land*** | 95 | 22.51 | 123 | 29.15 | 109 | 25.83 | 95 | 22.51 | 422 |
| ***Labourer*** | 22.57 | | 29.22 | | 25.89 | | 22.57 | | 25.06 |
| ***Other*** | 2 | 18.18 | 3 | 27.27 | 5 | 45.45 | 1 | 9.09 | 11 |
| | 0.48 | | 0.71 | | 1.19 | | 0.24 | | 0.65 |
| ***Total*** | 421 | 25.00 | 421 | 25.00 | 421 | 25.00 | 421 | 25.00 | 1684 |
| | 100.0 | | 100.0 | | 100.0 | | 100.0 | | |

**ANOVA: Two-Factor without Replication**

| ***Source of variation*** | **SS** | **Df** | **MS** | **F** | **p-value** | **F crit** |
|---|---|---|---|---|---|---|
| ***Rows*** | 122186.3 | 5 | 24437.27 | 81.36715 | 0.00 | 2.901295 |
| ***Columns*** | 0 | 3 | 0 | 0 | 1 | 3.287382 |
| ***Error*** | 4505 | 15 | 300.3333 | | | |
| ***Total*** | 126691.3 | 23 | | | | |

**Table Value: 2.90 Calculated Value: 81.36 Significant at 5% level**

## Income Level of the Respondents

The annual income level of the respondents is presented for the analysis in Table 4. A look into the table clearly shows that the respondents with the income level between ₹ 50,000 to ₹ 1,00,000 constitute to a dominant segment followed by those with an annual income level below ₹ 50,000. It is evident from the fact that 49.05 percent of the total respondents are in the income between ₹ 50,000 to ₹ 1,00,000. In the individual district of the zones, the proportion of the respondents in this income level between ₹ 50,000 to ₹ 1,00,000 ranged between 35.87 per cent (East Godavari District) to 5986 percent (Srikakulam District). Further those with income level below ₹ 50,000 constitute 37.83 percent of the total respondents in the zones where as among the districts in the zones, the proportion of respondents under this annual income level ranged between 27.79 percent (Srikakulam District) to 47.74 percent (East Godavari District). Thus, a majority of the respondents (86.88%) of the select zones of the Andhra Bank fall under the annual income below ₹ 1,00,000 and those with annual income level above ₹ 1,00,000 constitute 13.12 percent.

**Table 4 Annual Income Level of the Respondents**

| *Annual Income* | *No. of households* | | | | | | | | *Total* |
|---|---|---|---|---|---|---|---|---|---|
| | **Srikakulam** | | **VZM** | | **VSKP** | | **East Godavari** | | |
| ***Below* ₹ 50,000** | 117 | 18.37 | 156 | 24.49 | 163 | 25.59 | 201 | 31.55 | 637 |
| | 27.29 | | 37.05 | | 38.72 | | 47.74 | | 37.83 |
| ₹ 50,000 to ₹ 1,00,000 | 252 | 30.51 | 213 | 25.79 | 210 | 25.42 | 151 | 18.28 | 826 |
| | 59.86 | | 50.59 | | 49.88 | | 35.87 | | 49.05 |
| Above ₹ 50,000 | 52 | 23.53 | 52 | 23.53 | 48 | 21.72 | 69 | 31.22 | 221 |
| | 12.35 | | 12.53 | | 11.40 | | 16.39 | | 13.21 |
| **Total** | 421 | 25.00 | 421 | 25.00 | 421 | 25.00 | 421 | 25.00 | 1684 |
| | 100.0 | | 100.0 | | 100.0 | | 100.0 | | 100.0 |

**Type of bank account of the respondents:** In banking practices a variety of bank accounts are offered and operative for the customers. These include savings and current accounts besides the recurring and fixed deposit accounts in addition to loan accounts. To make clear, the incidence of the type of bank accounts held by the customers in the inclusive stream, an analysis of the type of bank accounts holds by the customers is presented in the Table 5. As evident from the table at the zones level the savings accounts assume a greater proportion (29.33%) followed by the loan accounts (28.74%) and the fixed deposit accounts (24.94%). Similar is the scenario among the constituent districts of the two zones. Moreover the savings, loan and fixed deposit accounts put together assumed a share of 83.01 percent at the zones level. And at the level of the constituent districts of the zones, the share of this ratio is 83.84 percent, 88.12 percent, 79.57 percent and 80.52 percent in Srikakulam, Vijayanagaram, Visakhapatnam and East Godavari Districts. There is a significant difference between the rows and non-significant among columns. Type of bank accounts is different in nature. Most of the accounts are loan accounts and savings accounts. This scenario is visible in all the four districts of the zones under the research study.

**Table 17.5 5 Types of Bank Account held by the Respondents.**

| *Types of bank account* | *No. of households* | | | | | | | | *Total* |
|---|---|---|---|---|---|---|---|---|---|
| | *Srikakulam* | | *VZM* | | *VSKP* | | *East Godavari* | | |
| ***Saving A/c*** | 116 | 23.48 | 126 | 25.51 | 138 | 27.94 | 114 | 23.08 | 494 |
| | 27.55 | | 29.93 | | 32.78 | | 27.08 | | 29.93 |
| ***Current A/c*** | 9 | 16.67 | 11 | 20.37 | 18 | 33.33 | 16 | 29.63 | 54 |
| | 2.14 | | 2.61 | | 4.28 | | 3.80 | | 3.21 |
| ***Recurring Deposit A/c*** | 42 | 23.60 | 26 | 14.61 | 54 | 30.34 | 56 | 31.46 | 178 |
| | 9.98 | | 6.18 | | 12.83 | | 13.30 | | 10.57 |
| ***Fixed Deposit A/c*** | 91 | 21.67 | 111 | 26.43 | 89 | 21.19 | 129 | 30.71 | 420 |
| | 21.62 | | 26.37 | | 21.14 | | 30.64 | | 24.94 |
| ***Loan A/c*** | 146 | 30.17 | 134 | 27.69 | 108 | 22.31 | 96 | 19.83 | 484 |
| | 34.68 | | 31.83 | | 25.65 | | 22.80 | | |
| ***Any Other*** | 17 | 31.48 | 13 | 24.07 | 14 | 25.93 | 10 | 18.52 | 28.74 |
| | 4.04 | | 3.09 | | 3.33 | | 2.38 | | |
| ***Total*** | 421 | 25.00 | 421 | 25.00 | 421 | 25.00 | 421 | 25.00 | 1684 |
| | 100.0 | | 100.0 | | 100.0 | | 100.0 | | 100.0 |

**17.6 Anova: Two-Factor Without Replication**

| *Source of Variation* | *SS* | *Df* | *MS* | *F* | *p-value* | *F crit* |
|---|---|---|---|---|---|---|
| *Rows* | 476845.5 | 5 | 95369.1 | 44.94377 | 0.00 | 2.901295 |
| *Columns* | 60.5 | 3 | 20.16667 | 0.09335 | 0.962556 | 3.287382 |
| *Error* | 3240.5 | 15 | 216.0333 | | | |
| *Total* | 480146.5 | 23 | | | | |

**Table Value: 2.91 Calculated Value: 441.45 Significant at 5% level**

**Regularity in Account Operation of the respondents:** Financial Inclusion has become the watch word for the Government, RBI and also all the players in the Financial System especially the bankers. After all the main philosophy behind Financial Inclusion or Inclusive Banking practices is to spread. The banking habit is to the unbanked and also to sustain the habit of banking among the rural unbanked segments of the society. For realising this philosophy through Inclusive banking efforts, the regularity and frequency of operations of the bank account for the purpose of savings is important. The data analysed evidences that the majority of 54.99 percent of the respondents reported not operating their bank account regularly for the purpose of savings and the other end 45.01 percent affirmed positively in this regard.

**Frequency of saving in the bank account of the respondents:** It is not just opening bank account but it is inculcates the habit of savings, frequency of savings and sustaining the habit of savings that counts and contributes in realising the prime objective of Inclusive Banking. In this direction to know the frequency of savings in the bank account by the customer is assessed through customer perception are analysed. It could be seen from the analysis that the total zones of Andhra Bank under review, the sizable proportion of 33.34 percent of those opened the account reflected affirming that they could not save money. The similar trend could be observed in the case of all the four constituent district of the zones. It is evident from the fact that 35.15 percent, 36.58 percent, 28.50 percent and 33.49 percent of the customer respondents in the respective districts of Srikakulam, Vijayanagaram, Visakhapatnam and East Godavari reiterated saying that they could not save. 28.03 percent of the customer respondents stated that they save money as and when surplus balance is in hand. A proportion of 26.60 percent each in Srikakulam and Vijayanagaram Districts, 25.18 percent in Visakhapatnam District and 33.73 percent in East Godavari District also opined the same.

**Assess to Insurance Policy:** Micro Insurance in an area of emphasis under the SHG phenomenon and Inclusive Philosophy. In this regard the reflections of the customer respondents, with respect to their access to insurance products by the bank, are elicited and analyzed. It is to the sense of one and all that the insurance products generally include the Life Insurance, Health Insurance, Accidental Insurance and Livestock Insurance. A bird's eye view of the table brings out the glaring observation that a majority of the customer respondents (71.67%) reported not having any insurance. It is also the case with the four constituent districts of the zones. It is evident from the fact that 71.97 percent, 70.07 percent, 74.11 percent and 70.55 percent in the respective districts of Srikakulam, Vijayanagaram, Visakhapatnam and East Godavari state having no access to any Insurance. But it could be noted that a fair proportion of 22.51 percent of the respondents reported as having access to Life Insurance. And among the constituent districts, the proportion of respondents having access to life insurance ranged between 21.14 percent (Srikakulam District to 23.99 percent (Vijayanagaram District). The other products of insurance assumed a very little access. There is a significant difference between the rows i.e., the respondents access to different insurance facilities is significantly different. The same reponse is observed in the constituent districts.

## Summary

The inclusive growth as a strategy of economic development received attention owing to a rising concern that the benefits of economic growth have not been equitably shared. Growth is inclusive when it creates economic opportunities along with ensuring equal access to them. Apart from addressing the issue of inequality, the inclusive growth may also make the poverty reduction efforts more effective by explicitly creating productive economic opportunities for the poor and vulnerable sections of the society. The inclusive growth by encompassing the hitherto excluded population can bring in several other benefits as well to the economy.

India has the highest number of households (145 million) excluded from banking. There is only one bank branch per 14,000 people. Of the 6 lakhs villages in India, rural branches of SCBs including RRBs number is 33,495. Only a little less than 20 percent of the population has any kind of life insurance and 9.6 percent of the population has non-life insurance coverage. Just 18 percent of the population has non-life insurance coverage. Just 18.00 percent had debit cards and less than 2 percent had credit cards.

## Recommendations

1. It is observed that the newly entered public sector banks and private sector banks are enthusiastic to collect deposits but reluctant to advance loans. Hence, RBI should direct them to start their branches in any one of the unbanked villages instead of opening branches in district headquarters. They can make use of the services of BCs or use mobile banking in rural area where it is not possible to open bank branches.
2. For inclusive banking and for achieving the objectives of financial inclusion of rural poor and unreached sections of the population are the target market. It is observed that proper communication and awareness drive are widely absent in the banking efforts for inclusion. Therefore, awareness of banking concept in rural areas should be redefined for rural population. It can be visualised by using different communication methods like play lets burrakathas, puppet shows, folk songs and short films etc., which will be appreciated by the rural folk. Further banks have to conduct awareness campus in rural areas to inculcate the habit of thrift among the poor. The same may be of useful in the areas where urban poor are residing.

3. In view of the observation that the business correspondents mechanism is not facilitating the access of the account even through the smart card by the account holder. It is suggested that the bank braches have to develop such facility that account holder can access his account from both bank branch as well as from BC. Transaction should be made possible from both BC and branch through same smart card, which is given to BC should be made accessible at any place have good network connectivity within the village. This will enable BCs to get internet connection anytime in day and transaction can be possible anytime without interruption.
4. The priority sector advances to total deposits of private sector banks is gradually declining and hence proper monitoring by RBI is required in directing the banks to use the locally mobilised deposits for local development in order to motivate the local people to come more under the umbrella of banking.
5. The public sector banks as lead bank should organise loan melas in rural areas to create awareness about the various deposits schemes, interest rates on deposits and loans. Banks should devise suitable schemes taking into account the needs of the area. Financial Literacy-cum-credit counselling centre has to play a lead role in credit counselling aspect. They have to create awareness about use of formal finance than taking loans from local money lenders at high rates.
6. Financial inclusion is the road which India needs to travel towards becoming a global player. An inclusive growth will act as a source of empowerment and allow people to participate more effectively in the economic and social process. Banks that have global ambitions must meet local aspirations.
7. It could be observed that, though technology is a great enabler, financial services to the poor could not be provided and the poor remain financial exclude in spite of Inclusive Banking initiations. It is reported and personally observed that, though there is technology interface in Financial Inclusoin efforts of banks, technology with a human touch and friendly technology interface are highly absent.
8. The banks should also consider giving no frills accounts to those interested by leaving the application forms at grocery stores (pacharikottu) general stores, pan shops, bigger shops and super markets. People should know it is available at these places by putting small boards and hoards exactly like how the mobile

recharging is possible at small places also and it is known to people also as it is visible at the entrance of the shop.

## References


1. Aditya Puri (2011). Revolutionizing Banking Through Financial Inclusion & Literacy: The HDFC Bank way.
2. AFI survey. The AFI survey report on financial inclusion policy in developing countries 2010.
3. Agarwal, H.C. (2006). *Banking Law and Practice.* Agra, Swan Publications.
4. Alpesh Shah. Indian banking 2020: Making the Decade's Promise come true September, 2010.
5. Collins, D.Morduch, I. Rutherford & S. And Ruthven (2009). *Portfolios of the Poor.* New Jersey, Princeton University Press.
6. Dr. Gupta, S.P. (1997). *Statistical Methods.* New Delhi, Sultan Chand & Sons.,
7. K. C. Shekhar Lakeshmy Shekar (2010). *Banking Theory and Pratice, nineteenth edition.* Page No. 375, Vikas publishing house.
8. M.L. Jhingan. (2011). *Money, Banking, International trade and Public Finance* *7th* addition Page No. 616, Vrinda Publications (p) Ltd.
9. Patnaik, U.C. & Patnaik Manoj (2005). *Profitability in Public Sector Banks.* New Delhi, Sonali Publications.
10. Ranganadhachary, A.V. and Paul, R. R. (2005). *Banking and Financial System,* Ludhiana, Kalyani Publications.
11. S. N. Maheswari & S.K. Maheswari. *Banking Law and Practice,* Page No. 1-33, Ludhiana, Kalyani Publications.
12. Sancheti, D.C. & Kapoor V.K. (2013). *Business Statistics,*New Delhi, Sultan Chand & Sons.
13. Srivastava, R.M. & Divya Nigam (2001). *Management of Indian Financial Institutions,* Mumbai, Himalaya Publishing House.

# E. Analysis (A)

# 13

# Analysis

## Introduction

The 'analysis' relating to Research in Commerce and Management: A Survey 2021, has been presented in this chapter. The analysis has been carried-out from the First chapter to 17th chapter. The main thrust has been given to the research direction from the background studies as well as earlier studies and inclusive of the 17th Chapter. Six broad areas have been identified and recognized for the entire research activity and the present title is "Research in Commerce and Management, A Survey: 2021", they are :

(A) Business Environment this sub-field has been identified with an introduction and later on, the changing patterns of business environment through an excellent paper has been author by G. Tulasi Rao and *et al*. sub-field have been presented here under.

(A) Business organisation includes the research relating to

(3) Trade by Life Insurance Corporation of India: The internal and external trade link patterns have been presented including global business.

(4) Banking operations by the Indian Bank has been presented not only the internal banking operations but also the external and abroad (foreign) banking operations, of the government of India organisation.

(5) Fifth chapter deals with commercial operations by New India Assurance Company Limited: Mumbai. Though this is one and only one organisation which has undertaken the non-life insurance in particular in India. It has covered many uncovered areas and has its impact upon human life also.

(6) The Sixth chapter have been authored by Karuna and Hanumantha Rao, "E-Commerce in India", particularly the growth and development in this sphere.

Chapter 7, deals with the theme of International trade, which has been presented by Dr. A Venkata Rayadu, facilitate the reader to enable to understand the business patterns and environment too!

Third broad field has been entitled as C-Industry and management (Environment). Professor. Ramakrishna *et. al* have presented thematically the status and structure of MSME in Telangana State, India in the 8th Chapter.

In the 9th Chapter, Smt. Y. Padmini et. al have presented broadly, "Solid waste management (SWM) and its identification and extent through R.S. & GIS Technologies".

The Fourth broad sub-field has been recognized as Social Engineering (SE). In the 10th chapter, T. Kama Raju et. al have presented the most-potential paper entitled, Human Resource Management in the knolwdge Economy : A Global perspective and have identified the preliminary function of the global Human Resource Management is that the organisation carries a local appeal in the host country despite maintaining an international feeling and exemplify, any multinational/international company would not like to be called as local, however the same wants a domestic touch in the host country and there lies the challenge.

Under the same sub-field, G. Ernest Leslie, has presented an exemplary paper, "Self help Groups- The mechanim for social and women empowerment" and attempted to look at the relative advantage of each status approach adopted in the implementation of the urban poverty issues and etc. Further it has been explained the State/district/ULB level arrangements that were made in the southern states for the implementation of activities under NULM. The author further opined that the very operation of self help groups and they are much depend upon the mechanism, stresses for social and women empowerment exclusively.

Finally, Analysis part has been presented in the 14th chapter. Summative analysis (SA), New Areas of research (NAR); ICSSR major research project proposal in 16th chapters. To enable the researcher/reader, one Ph.D. Thesis layout has been presented in 12th chapter, one belong to "Commerce" as ready reference.

In chatper, 18, conclusions have been presented covering the chapters from 1st to 17th chapter (both are inclusive). Detailed analysis has also been presented in the following pages in order to understand the process through the excellent papers from 2nd chapter to 12th chapter (both are inclusive), which is considered as an excelling academic exercise both intensive and extensive in nature.

Detailed account and assessment of potential areas of commerce have been presented. The paper one deals with an introduction to commerce and Management studies and survey.

G. Tulasi Rao, S. Tarakeswava Rao and M.P. Suri Ganesh have presented the "Impact of Covid-19 on Indian Economy: A study on new business opportunities with corona virus in India" and stated that the economy has taken a very bad experience and infrieted the untold miseries especially to the poor people of the country and there has been a significant reduction in orders and cash-flow across the sector, deep hit in the supply chain and a significant downslide effect on business. As a result, the travel and hospitality sector has suffered one of the harshest blow and airline companies are on the verge of facing bankruptcy.

**Comment:** The authors have identified the current problem in the Indian context. This study should have to be extended globally in order to identify and recognize its effect on supply chain and demand side have to be examined totally while conducting the active research in this field.

3rd 4th and 5th chapters were presented in the sub-field of B: Business organisation. Wherein, the major organisations such as the turnover of business by Life Insurance Corporation of India (LIC) with an historical perspective, this is one and only one organisation which has been exercising business (trade) with people's life, educating the party that the untold life risks have to be faced by people with enforcing and endangering situations of life in security. "The essence L.I.C. is to cover the life risks, one has to choose a good life policy to cover the future risks of the individuals and their family." The pattern of trade and the accruing funds have been scientifically planned the investments for the growth and development of L.I.C., India and the changing patterns of business has been presented in the 3rd chapter.

**Comment:** Though life coverage has been extended through its operation, still there are poor people who could not have a life coverage due to the non-availability of substantial amounts for investment by the individuals.

## Innovative Special Policy for People's Welfare

A new direction has set in by L.I.C. of India, in the areas of social security schemes. They are as follows:

(1) Converged Pradhan Mantri Jeevan Jyothi Bima Yojana (PMJJBY) and converged Anam Adami Bima Yojana (AABY) are administrered by the Ministry of Labour and Employment, Government of India. These schemes are implemented through LIC of India. Members in the age group of 18 to 50 years are provided insurance cover of ₹ 2 lakhs under converged PMJJBY for the premium of ₹ 330/- per member per annum. These members are also covered under PMSBY for Accidental and Disability Insurance for premium of ₹ 12/- per member per annum through General Insurance Company. The scheme is named as converged PMJJBY/PMSBY with an annual premium of ₹ 342/- only. Out of which 50 percent premium is contributed from GOI social security fund maintained by LIC of India.

## Scholarship Benefit

Scholarship as a free add-on benefit is also provided under converged PMJJBY and converged AABY (Anam Admi Bima Yojana (AABY). Scholarship is payable annually to a maximum of two children of the beneficiary, studying between 9th to 12th standard ₹ 100/- per month for each child as a free-Add on benefit. The scholarship component of the converged AABY/PMJJBY will be paid through national scholarship portal (NSP).

## PMJDY Scheme:

Pradhan Mantri Jan Dhan Yojana was launched on 28-8-2014 for facilitating comprehensive financial inclusion. Under this scheme, bank accounts were opened and benefits were given to the account holders. One of the benefits is providing the life insurance cover of ₹ 30,000/- on death due to any reason, only through life insurance corporation of India.

For availing the Life Insurance Coverage of ₹ 30,000/- on death arising out of any cause under this scheme, a person should be aged between 18 to 59 years and he/she should have been enrolled under PMJJDY between 15-08-2014 to 31-01-2015 and should be holder of Ru Pay card.

*The most important point we should identify in this scheme is to provide comprehensive financial inclusion and also to provide scholarships for students who are poor with merit. Social security schemes are quite important in the society to safeguard human skills and talents.

In chapter 4, an attempt has been made to present the welfare schemes, of Indian Bank. They are :

Indian Bank's role is considered as service Industry i.e. Banking Industry there are some important and special opportunities which have been provided by the Indian Bank. In chapter 4, Indian Bank's role with an historical perspective has been provided still some uncovered topics previously now covered and they are stated in the following paragraphs. They are:

(1) I. B. Smart Kid SB Account.

(2) Our services grow with your age, Indian Bank understanding the need of senior citizens, offers a bouquet of services ensuring that our care and concern for you are always high.

(3) High-powered current account super-charged business. Indian Bank's supreme current account.

(4) Soar more easily with IBS structural loan products for SME's

(5) Pure Gold, Indian Bank Gold; usher in prosperity and happiness.

(6) Indian Bank's Home Loan scheme.

(7) Financial inclusion... opening up new evenues; towards inclusive growth.. spreading services.

(8) Indian Bank – Multiplying green on the fields. Beneficiaries: Small, Marginal and other farmers, Tenant farmers and joint liability groups (JLG's).

(9) IB – Balavidya scheme

Education loan scheme

IB Jeevan Vidhya Life

Insurance cover – Our inspiring support

——— to Aspiring students.

*Visit us at: www.Indianbank.in

(10) IB Doctor plus

(11) One click Bills paid.

Fast Track banking (Ind net banking), Ind phone Banking Global ATM cum Debit card, Ind. Corp. Net Banking and Ind Mobile Banking;

and

Ind. SME Secure

Small & Medium Enterprises

The above schemes are exclusively meant for people.

For planning and execution of the schemes for their welfare.

*In chaper 5, the role of the New India Assurance in the growth and development of the nation in different fields of specialisation are presented. They are :

(1) Motor policy

(2) Med claim policy

(3) Be sure with shopkeepers policy.

(4) Be sure with floater medi claim

(5) Be sure with personal accident policy

(6) Director's and offers liability policy and

(7) Be sure with office protection shield policy etc.

**Comment**

The above schemes are exclusively useful to protect Human life in different angles and in multiple spheres. This is considered as a planning business strategy besides non-life policies (in particular medi-claim etc. senior citizens policies exclusively trade, banking and commerce are three important broad-fields of specialisation and line of operations further growth and development human being, has been providing since its inception. It is concluded that 'help us to help you' is a good logo for long-term safety with growth and it is considered as never zeroing process in the total process and perspective.

In chapter 6, Dr. Karuna and Hanumantha Rao have presented the process of E-commerce, nowadays, the E-commerce has occupied and assume prime importance in commerce with E-commerce. Physical process has little role in commerce and has done away with. For example, Amazon (on, line purchase) of goods/ordering through electronic media and it is done totally and may receive the goods at your door step.

It is opined that, "the survivial of the e-commece firms in a highly dynamic environment, becomes a challenging task when coupled with the cut throat competition prevailing in the sector".

This study attempts to explore the revolution of e-commerce in India and identifies various challenges to as well the factors responsible for the future growth and development of e-commerce.

Multiple roles are existing/present quite well in e-commerce. E-commerce is the most important function to operate, though it is expensive, with the least time factor, the ordered goods will reach to our door step, which is a major strategy in the entire commerce and management (facets) spheres.

In chapter 7, "International Trade"- has been presented by Dr. A. Venkata Rayulu. The details are related to the following aspects:

(1) Characteristics of global trade
(2) Differences from domestic trade
(3) History
(4) Theories of models
(5) Most traded export products
(6) Largest countries by total international trade
(7) Top traded commodities by value (Exports)
(8) Observances
(9) Notes
(10) References
(11) External links
(12) Data-official statistics
(13) Other data sources and other external links.

**Observations**

1. It is observed that almost 21 largest trading nations are aggregated according to the world trade organisation (WTO).
2. Volume of world merchandise exports are presented in the table format.
3. Most traded export products are presented through a graph.

**Assessment**

Most important to a researcher to undertake is as follows:

1. International Trade Pattern (and its change, over a period of time (by nationwise) may give a scope to understand the time series

data and its fluctuations. By the method of moving average, it could be detected and identified the partterns.

2. Impact of price structure upon goods export/import could be helpful to understand the marketing strategies followed by nations (continentwise).

The changing pattern (spatial structural changes) are quite important in identifing the patterns)- now the researcher arise questions such as: What?

Why? When? And where? are the four important questions to be authored by a researcher through his Ph.D. work for future researchers.

In chapter 8, Prof. S. Ramkrishna & P. Anjaneyulu have presented that according to the International Finance Corporation (IFC) total 6.5 crores MSME's firms are registered in the developing countries and it needed 5.2 trillion dollars every year. Compare to present situation it will be around 1.4 times more of the world MSME lending.

The major objectives in this paper are as follows:

(1) To analyse the industrial policy of the Telangana.

(2) To understand MSME's sector situation in the state.

(3) To discuss the scope for the establishment of MSME's across the districts.

This paper has been prepared and based on secondary data which is collected from various official websites like MSME and industrial websites, reports and newspapers/magazines/journals.

**Most Important**

1. There is every need to assess the scope of micro, small and medium scope enterprises (MSME's) in Telangana primarily and also help to understand this structure and situation. There is also a need further to undertake such studies in Andhra Pradesh for comparative study;

and

2. Resource Base and pattern of development through MSME's of different states in India. (Structural changes).

Yenda Padmini and Bendalam Sridhar have presented a good paper in Chapter 9, "Identification of potential landfill sites in the GVMC area using multicriteria evaluation method".

They have presented that, "the different types of parameters involvement, decides upon a suitable location for the waste disposal is very complicated type, time consuming and much expenditure is involved.

Methodologically deduced from the remote sensing, and GIS techniques connected with the satellite imagery could build more accurately and the information is based on many parameters criteria which enables to take the right decision for the solid waste disposal sites: the multi-criteria evaluation of weighted overlay analysis according to analytical (Hierarchy, process was performed for determining an appropriate solid waste disposal in the G.V.M.C. environs.

1. This study may help to governments major concern is to solve the health problems associated with the improper waste disposal.
2. The disposal of toxic waste and waste matter haphazardly may create major environmental issues posing menaces to human beings existence.

Contextual studies relating to environmental hazards and its impact on human health may be a good study of research for the governance to take-up administrative reforms to a maximum possible extent. It would be a multifaculty study further helps to understand the problem in toto and find a solution to the problem, is an urgent need.

The theme relating to Social Engineering/social aggregation to solve the problems of the society over a period of time is an important factor for development studies.

Professor T. Kamaraju and Santosh Ranganath have presented the paper entitled, "Human Resource Development in the knowledge Economy: A global prospective" and has increased the workforce diversity and cultural sensibilities have emerged like never before. All this led to the development of Global Human Resource Management.

Further, it has been identified that the preliminary function of global Human Resource Management is that the organisation carries a local appeal in the host country despite maintaining an international feeling. To exempify, any multinational/international company would not like to be called as local, however, the same wants a domestic touch in the host country and there lies the challenge.

**Comment**

1. It is observed from this study that the competitive pressure of the global economy is compelling business and countries to embrace ICT's.

2. The advent of ICT's has resulted in dramatic changes in employment patterns, skill-sets needed and the range of opportunities, for employment and economic advancement over the whole world.

**Need**

There is every need to study the aspects further such as :

1. "Skilled" are over shortage as a sign for unemployment.
2. Impact technology on Human Resource Management.

In chapter 11, G. Ernest Leslie has presented thematically, and lucidly the aspects, such as :

1. Capture the spirit of social mobilization and bringing together the community, based on common need or opportunity to develop strong grass-roots level institutions.
2. Social based collectives like Resident Welfare Associations are in existence since long and have to them credit many accomplishments, the collectilisation of the poor for achievement of many financial, material and impotently social goals have seen landslide successes in the contemporary times.

**Need**

There's every need to unite the lower starta (layered) population upon a platform, and encourage their skill to help other's as well as for themselves to undertake profession to enhance their merit to produce a good product needed by the society both vertically and horizontally through self help groups (SHG's) operation and mechanism.

This mechanism is aimed at bringing both human and non-human resources together into building of groups and federations and results to the development of community infrastructure or development of social capital to achieve sustainable development. This process aims to enage people's participation and achieving a specific development goal through self-reliant efforts.

This strategy may mobilise the merit of the individual/individuals to make use the same unitedly, to produce a commodity/good which is needed by the society in long way with the critical principles of community involvement and seeks to empower individuals and groups for good action.

This strategy may help for poverty alleviation and participation monitoring helps to human growth and human development over a period of time.

Human or social mobilisation may take a new direction for community development whether it is rural/urban area in an hiearchic way.

## Critical Evaluation

1. Human Resources/Natural Resources/Acquired Resources may help for the alleviation of poverty and further to upgrade and up-keep the merit of the individuals to undertake a project to fulfil their objectives and achieve development in different wings.
2. G.O.I. or State Governments may have to plan to use human resources to a maximum possible extent within a short period of time for the inclusive growth (rating jobs by G.O.I. or state may depend upon skilled development programmes and strategies for skill population, for skill development.

## Reference

*Online.New india.co.in – www.newindia. Co.in

# 14

# Summative Analysis

## Introduction

'Summative analysis' relating to the entire volume has been presented in the following paragraphs. The entire text consists of six sub-fields broadly. Business Environment, business organisation, industry and trade, organisation and management of social environment (Aggregation of different social groups into one social head) gearing up and formed as self help group; Disaster Management through GIS and RS, quantitative techniques and its applied nature in commerce and management research have been presented in order to identify and recognize as important contributory factors for the growth and development of research in commerce and management.

In Chapter 1, the volume of work deals with the identification of commerce as a social science by Indian Council of Social Science, Research, New Delhi besides presenting the content of commerce, Economics and Geography. To enable the reader particularly the non-commerce researchers to understand the commerce terminology in vogue. A viable and valuable attempt has been made to acquaint and accommodate themselves to carryout their research in the areas of multi-disciplinary and inter-disciplinary facets to meet the challenges both at local and international level. The entire chapter has been divided into four parts. They are:

Part 'A' deals with accountancy, cost accountancy, business organisation, business management, business statistics in addition to financial environment and practical auditing.

Economic and commercial geography would help to understanding the resources and also establish resource based industries in India has been resolved. Banking theory, law and practice by Maheswari and R.R. Paul has been reviewed in order to identify and recognize the concept of Banking and its influence of law and its relation. (Text book based review has been added).

Part 'B' deals with the aspects of the following themes: 1. Impact of environment on Agriculture, 2. Business environment/industrial environment, 3. Health management, 4. Human Development and 5. Social Engineering/ social groups for the formation of capital.

Part 'C' deals with the content of commerce particularly management (review of articles based on Journals and also deals with the current scenario as well as the design of the present volume and its need has been stated and finally conclusions have been presented in this volume to enable the researchers to conduct the interdisciplinary and multidisciplinary approach to a research topic (current) of them. At the end of the chapter, notes has been stated to the beginner to understand the commerce and management terminology for the non-commerce faculty members to carry out their research activity.

Chapter 2, deals with the impact of Covid-19 on Indian economy – A study on new business opportunities with corona virus in India by G. Tulasi Roa, S. Tarakeswara Rao and M.P. Suri Ganesh.

Chapter 3, deals with business environment and development B. Polisu has attempted to present the concepts such as 1. Meaning of environment, 2. Characteristics, 3. International business Environment and 4. Components of Global environment and economic Environment.

Part – B deals with trade i.e. role of Life Insurance Corporation in Human Economic development making an adequate financial cover in order to cover the enforcing and endangering life insecurity in the event of life of an individual (insured) in a family environment.

In Chapter 4, the author has presented the service industry (Banking), and the services rendered/rendering by Indian Bank in the areas of Banking industry in the given trade environment. An humble attempt has been made by the author to present the concept such as Indian Bank, its origin, growth trend and development in the economic sector with an historical perspective.

Chapter 5, deals with non-life goods insurance and the profile and progress of the new Indian Assurance Company Limited, India's premier General Insurance Company in trade/commerce) industry. The entire work is related to 1. New India Network, global and India, 2. New India Assurance's 20 point Action plan, 3. Our vision and our Mission and

4. Indian insurance. The changing patterns of its policy besides providing mediclaim, means to human (life).

In Chapter 6, E-commerce in India prospects and issues have been presented by Karuna and Hanumantha Rao. They have identified that, "with the new advancements that are taking place, people have easy access to goods and services than ever before, which is because of the concept of e-commerce/or electronic commerce.

The present chapter portrays the concept and prospects of E-commerce, its market size and growth in India and the various issues faced by the e-commerce players and government initiatives for E-commerce in the economic growth.

Industry and trade environment' is the third sub-field of this study. The major trade have been presented through the potential contributions of Dr. A Venkata Rayudu. And the 7th chapter deals with International trade, in particular the trade process of the countries (Economic goods) and their patterns are most important, idenfiable and recognizable one. This is in two fold i.e. 1. Identification and 2. Recognition. The structured trends are presented through tables and growth in order to understand the process of export and import by countrywide and goodswise. The changing patterns of International trade is the most important aspect of trade/business (commerce/and Manageability (Management).

## Comment

The art of trade may be exhibited through the patterns of its structure and the process are within the process of Management.

'Commerce' and 'Management' are nothing but two faces of a coin, which has its inter-changing link between imports and exports this is considered to be an activity which compared to the two blades of a scissors one is 'demand' and the other is 'supply' which intersects and intercepts to determine the price line. The bulk process is much depended on demand and supply of the friendly nations, globally.

In chapter 8, Prof. S. Ramakrishna and P. Anjaneyulu have presented an interesting paper through this chapter, dealing with the, "scope of the micro, small and medium scale enterprises (MSME's) in Telangana State", India. They have the keen objectives centering upon:

1. To analyse the industrial policy of Telangana.
2. To understand the MSME's sector situation in the state and also

3. To discuss the scope for the establishment of MSME's across the districts.

They opined that, "the technology transfer and modernisation to the MSME sector and reimbursement of land conversion charges for the units in own land etc. incentives providing the government".

Yend a Padmini and Bendalam Sridhar have presented an excellent paper entitled, "Identification of potential landfill-sites in the GVMC Area using multicriteria evaluation method with the multi-criteria evaluation of weighted overlay analysis according to analytical Hierarchy process was performed for determining an appropriate solid waste disposal in the GVMC environs.

It is a good paper to create more inquisitiveness and interest to a new research/reader to identify and recognize the new patterns and methodologies for evaluating the health hazards through new utilisation of technology and science.

In the sub-field of social engineering (SE), there are two important topics such as Human Resources Development (HRD) and equally important thought relating to social aggregation (SA) from the state of social disorganisation process in a environment suitable to create workability to humanforce which enforces to be united for undertaking a common business and a good activity.

In this process, Prof. T. Kama Raju and Dr. N. Santosh Ranganath have made an important and still impressive one, "Human resource Development in the knowledge Economy – A global perspective" and high-lighted that the preliminary function (PF) of global human resource management is that the organisation carries a local appealation the host-country despite maintaining an international feeling and to exemplify, any multinational/international company would not like to be called as local, however the same wants a domestic touch in the host country and there has the challenge (key contribution).

It is quite a good paper to understand the scenario in the total prevailing environment, in particular human resource/should have to be managed substantially and sustainably on scientific lines over a period of time to the maximum possible extent with minimum cost.

In Chapter 11, of this volume and related to the sub-field of social engineering theme the most interesting and important paper, "Self Help Groups – the mechanism for social and women empowerment". Through self help groups only, the social aggregation from the social disorganised state, structure and process and it is the weapon to achieve women empowerment in any society/unit/state/nation/nations in a given human environment.

G.E. Leslie has identified that, "social mobilisation is a mechanism that is aimed at bringing both human and non-human resources together into the building of groups and federations usually also termed as the development of community infrastructure or development of social capital, to achieve sustainable development" (key factor) and "addressing the felt needs of the people embracing the critical principle of community involvement and seeks to empower individuals and groups fraction" (Prime factor).

"The key factor and prime factor as stated above are quite important as well as to achieve sustainable development which is not complementary but highly competitive in the area of Social Engineering/Social Environment besides commerce and management of a state/country/countries upon the earthosphere" (Dr. Narasimha Murty).

In chapter 14, the whole process of analysis of core chapter from 2nd to 13 chapters, have been analysed with critical and necessary comments to understand the whole process within the process of good research. The sub-fields have been identified to an extent of 6, with the chapters ranged from 2nd to 12th chapter (both are inclusive). The detailed account is given in this chapter and various themes are involved in the chapters are further stated for the furtherance of research in the following paragraphs - they are:

In this first chapter, introduction has been stated and also identified the gaps of research which have been filled in with the contributions of scholars. In this chapters, at the end, the commerce terminology has been stated which facilitates the non-commerce doctorates to understand the potential content in commerce and also may facilitate to apply potential methods by applying them in the areas of "inter-displinary research" as well as "multidisciplinary research". These are considered as an art and science of research followed by technology (latest) in the 21$^{st}$ centunary research from 2$^{nd}$ chapter to 13$^{th}$ chapter, "important themes have been presented with critical evaluation and identified and found new areas of research (NAR) for the furtherance and improvement of research with innovative methodologies and its associated elements of potentiality" (Dr. Murty).

In Chapter 14.2 Summative Analysis has been presented with an historical and hierarchic manner. New areas of research (NAS) have been identified and the most important topics 80 so far not covered (uncovered) which may lead to the analytical scientific thoughts and their through research is always possible in congenial environment. This has been presented in this chapter.

I.C.S.S.R. Major Research project proposal (blueprint) has been stated in the 16th chapters.

Further, the Ph.D. Theses relating to one represents for "Commerce" has been presented to facilitate and enable the reader/researcher for the indepth understanding as well as for generating new ideas for the furtherance of knowledge for their own research in the chapters conclusions are presented in chapter 17.

## Conclusion

The most important point for any research process, one should have to understand the topic with historical perspective along with scientific and technological methodology followed by statistical validity. This process is quite righteous as well as the best method of conducting a good piece of research. 'Search' should be the prime objective associated with research for deeper understanding of problem which may yield good fruits through their contributions.

# 15

# New Areas of Research in Commerce and Management Studies

## Introduction

'Commerce' is a branch of "Economics" and "Management" is the art of human skill and is vital that is to say that Management skills are a part and parcel of Commerce and Banking. The role of a researcher has been changing from local to global level and it creates new perspectives in development. A wide spectrum of studies that have been added to Commerce and Management researches not only in India but also in the world. Secondly, interdisciplinary and Multi-disciplinary research have been encouraged since 1970. (As per the communication of Indian Council of Social Science Research, New Delhi).

The major areas which have been concerned are so far uncovered in this study and there is every need to adopt the changing methods in commerce and management studies in future. So an attempt has been made to identify and recognize New Areas of Research (NAR) and they were eventually and subsequently were documented. They are (1) Banking, (2) Infrastructural studies, (3) Agricultural Development studies, (4) Sustainable Development, (5) Health Management/Nutritional studies, (6) Human Resource Development, (7) Rural development, (8) Development studies and (9) Miscellaneous studies.

**The New Areas of Research (NAR) are presented topic-wise and they are as follows:**

1. **Banking**
    1. Role played by the State Bank of India with Special Reference to financing agriculture and small scale industries.

2. Role of money lenders in Development process – An Enquiry
3. Role of Reserve Bank of India to Develop the Indian Market, Market (using Time Series Data).
4. Indian Commercial Bank – Recent Trends in Commercial Banking
5. Nationalisation of Banks – After effects in the development process
6. Financial Sector Reforms: An Enquiry
7. National Agriculture Bank for Rural Development: A critical Appraisal of Functions of NABARD and Achievements
8. Structure and functioning of Co-operative Bank : A Case Study
9. Reserve Bank and Rural Finance with special reference to Agricultural credits
10. Co-operative Banking Service area approach for Rural Lending
11. Indian Banks Abroad: A study on the expansion of Indian Bank Abroad
12. The working of Indian Money Market: Its Structure, Process and status in Economic Development
13. Deposit Mobilisation scheme – An Enquiry Before 2000(2K) and After 2K.
14. Digitalisation in Banking – A comparative study of Private/ Public Sector Banks.

2. **Infrastructural Studies**

2.1 Infrastructural facilities in a state – A case study of Andhra Pradesh, using cost-Benefit Analysis (CBA) Methodology

2.2 Regional Framework of Informal Sector – A State level study

2.3 12[th] Five year plan, Social Sector: An Approach for Development.

3. **Agricultural Development Studies**

3.1 Trends in Agrarian structure in India – A Study (using the Cost-Benefit analysis and Time Series Data)

3.2 Water Resources Development planning for sustainable Agriculture in Telangana State, India

3.3 Regional Disparities in the level of Agricultural Modernisation in two states: Andhra Pradesh and Telangana, India

4. **Sustainable Development**

   4.1 Technical and Vocational Education and Training (TVET) system in India for Sustainable Development – A critical Appraisal

   4.2 Development of Social sector in Andhra Pradesh, A study in Inter-District Disparity

   4.3 Sustainable Development of problem Prone Areas-Flood, Drought and Disaster processes in a state/country

   4.4 Developing social sector – 1950 to 2020 : A comparative study

   4.5 Environment and Development: A case study in the Coastal Andhra Pradesh

   4.6 Environment and Development: A case study of southern Coastal Andhra Pradesh, India.

5. **Health Management/Nutritional Studies**

   5.1 A Study on Socio-Economic condition and Nutritional profile of Women workers in shrimp and Agriculture Sectors: A comparative study of two districts – East Godavari and Krishna in Andhra Pradesh

   5.2 Women Health in India: An Analysis of Healthcare Delivery in Andhra Pradesh –A Study

   5.3 Healthcare Patterns and planning

   5.4 Rural Healthcare in Tamil Nadu state, India

   5.5 Primary Healthcare: Health for All

6. **Human Resource Development**

   6.1 Inter-District Variations in the level of Human Development in Andhra Pradesh and also a comparative study of two states – Andhra Pradesh and Telangana in India

7. **Rural Development**

   7.1 Economic impact of Self Help Groups: A study of micro credit and Women Empowerment.

   7.2 Poverty Alleviations Programmes in Telangana state, India Transfer of Technology to Rural SMES in Kerala: A case study.

   7.3 Socio-Economic and Commercial Development in Andhra Pradesh. Development of BC's/Scheduled Castes/Scheduled Tribes in a state, India.

8. **Development Studies/Economics/Commerce**
   - 8.1 Changing role of Business Environmental Management Process. (A Study process in Organisation and Management)
   - 8.2 Trade, Commerce and Service industry through Govt. of India organisation such as LIC/NIA/Nationalised Banks
   - 8.3 E-Commerce in Andhra Pradesh. The Role of Amazon in the delivery process
   - 8.4 Chain Management process in Pharma Products – Delivery system.
9. **Miscellaneous studies**
   - 9.1 Corporate finance: Its Role and Development of Industrial Waste/Management
   - 9.2 Andhra Bank – Multiple function – Changing Roles
   - 9.3 NRI funds – Deposit schedule, Reutilisation and Marketing for development
   - 9.4 Role of Corporation Bank in Development sector
   - 9.5 Progress and Performance of Syndicate Bank before 2000 and After 2000 (2K)
   - 9.6 Role of Syndicate Bank in rural development sector : A case study
   - 9.7 Bank Mergers with other Banks – A Vulnerable and feasible study
   - 9.9 Rich Bank and Sick Bank: A case study of S.B.I. of S.B.H. Role of Nationalised Banks in Industrial Development
   - 9.10 Bank (Financial Institution) & Entrepreneur –An Analytical study.

# F. Research Project Proposal

# 16

# ICSSR Major Research Project Proposal Industrial Development: A case study of North Coastal Andhra Pradesh

1. **Introduction:** Development is essentially Multidimensional phenomenon, such as the level of economic development, level of industrial development, level of education, level of health services, degree of modernisation, Gender status, level of food security, level of nutrition, quality of housing, distribution of goods and services and also access to communication.

   Keeping in view of the structure and status of the Northern Coastal Andhra Pradesh, there is a need to focus the attention of the planner to plan for development in multiple-ways. Resource based industrial development plays predominantly a significant and prime role in accelerating the process of rural/industrial development in particular in developing countries of the world. Medium, small, micro and household level industries may play a significant role in economic development in the areas of trade/commerce/industry/health management/agricultural management, industrial organisation, spatial business activity and its interactive processes and the strategy of "never zeroing process of business operation/operations".

2. **Earlier Studies:** Bari, Raisaul and Munin Abdul, "Spatial Analysis of rural and urban linkage in Basti District (UP), 1. Bari Bipin (1970), Rural infrastructure in India, 2. Comprehensive District Agriculture plan (C-DAP)-Basti, UP, 3. Das, Abhiman, Socio-Economic Development in India, A Regional Analysis, 4. Derek Byerlee, Alaina de Janvry and Elisabeth Sadoulet, Agriculture for

# 17

# Conclusions

1. It is concluded that the impact of Covid-19 on Indian Economy – a study on new business opportunities with carona virus in India has its impact such as nation-wide lockdown, the economy has taken a very bad hit and inflicted untold miseries especially to the poor people of the country. The author's have concluded further, that the travel and hospitality sector has suffered the harshest blows and airline companies are on the verge of facing bankruptcy.
2. L.I.C. of India and the New India Assurance Co. Ltd., are the two important organisations which have been extending their services to the rural population, where as NIAC is the one and only one organisation relating to services especially goods influence. Now, L.I.C.'s funds have been diversified to the maximum possible extent to maintain that "people's money for people's welfare" and equally it has been serving to the cause of education for the people (9$^{th}$ to 12$^{th}$ class) by providing scholarship based on merit cum means.

   The NIA has been changing its strategy and to a tune to serve people to meet their medical claims (Medi-claim policy). Now (it) N.I.A. has become both life and non-life insurance unit in India. It has been identified that the changing business environment is visible over a period of time (changing patterns of business and its practices).
3. It is concluded that Indian Bank has been identified the needs of small and medium enterprises, under the scheme of Ind SME Secure, the purpose being, to extend the help by financing the SME based collateral security, cover and has fixed the minimum collateral requirement – 75 percent of the limits and there is every need to design such schemes by other banks also. It helps for the furtherance of individuals to gain from this scheme and services.

4. It is further concluded that E. Commerce and its activity is very intensive. Nowadays, the physical process of business has been switched over to and shifted towards new pattern of business i.e. E-commerce. Because of the changing business environment of the business, every business house is almost inactive. As a result, people must prone to e-commerce operations. Consumer's attitude has been changed totally and they are pro to E-commerce activity.
5. In the field of International Trade, it is observed that the changing patterns (spatial structural changes) are quite important and recorded to the maximum possible extent the basic structure of International trade assumes so many sweeping changes in the areas of total exports, total imports and the balance of payments etc.
6. The scope of SME, Small and medium scale enterprises should have to be changed and it is concluded that there is an urgent need to undertake such studies in Andhra Pradesh for a comparative study resource base and its changes have to be examined both for the past as well for the present period in order to identify and recognize the changes and also help to plan new strategies for development/new paradigms.
7. It is concluded that with the help of Remote Sensing and GIS technology and also with the satellite imageries more information could be able to secure to identify watershed as well as ground realities such as Hydrogeomorphology and river basin studies. Science and technology have been playing an important role in identifying the business and also help for designing strategies. It is further concluded that GIS & RS (GOI and State Govt.) should have to be developed on a large scale for its operation for achieving development.
8. It is concluded that there is every need to study the aspects such as HRD at the micro level/at macro level in order to identify the structural changes in HRD and the demand for goods and also the supply of goods in the given contexts for each micro and macro level units. There is every need to conduct a comprehensive and integrated surveys covering the aspects such as –
    1. Physical resources
    2. Economic Resources – Agriculture/Industrial
    3. Mineral resources
    4. Demography urban/rural (population/Human resources and Infrastructure

5. Education, skilled and un-skilled labour
6. Cultural resources

9. It is further concluded that there is a need to identify the poverty pockets in the rural areas as well as in urban areas which prompts the planner to plan for the poverty alleviation programmes and also to plan the occupation and skill development programmes to help the growing population for their sustainable development over a period of time.

Further concluded that, to achieve sustainable development for the existing population, there is a need to develop social capital for development (society).

Keeping in view of the ever increasing population, there is a dire-need to plan for skill development programmes in order to facilitate the planner for the maximum utilisation of the human resources for human welfare, finally, it has been identified that the human resources are less used, even though there are sufficiently viable human resources. The enriched poverty should have toto be eradicated through the execution of development plans in to whether it is at the Nation/State/and the lower units of a district (even) administration such as mandal level and village level at the micro level too!

# Annexure-I

**71st All India**
Commerce Conference of ICA
20–22 December, 2018

**Conference theme:**
Innovations,
Entrepreneurship &
Sustainable Development

Organised by:
**Department of Commerce**, Osmania University
Hyderabad, Telangana State

**In Collaboration with:**
Telangana State Council of Higher Education
Institute of Public Enterprise

**Suman Kalyan Chaudhary**
Faculty Member, P.G. Department of
Business Administration, Berhampur
University, Berhampur, Odisha;
PN: 760007

**Corporate Social Responsibility: A Brief Study**
Authors
**Dr. Jyotindra Kumar Pathak**
Assistant Professor, Tapeshwar Singh
Teachers Training College, Kayamnagar

**Dr. S.P. Jain**
Assistant Professor, Deptt. of BBA &
B. Com., D.K. College, Dumraon

**Managing Talent Through Corporate Social Responsibility**

Author
**Prof. Dr. Suresh Ravjibhai Savani**
Head & Dean, Faculty of Commerce,
Department of Commerce, Maharaja
Krishna Kumar Sinhji Bhavnagar
University, Bhavnagar-364002 (Gujarat)

**Corporate Social Responsibility and Its Role in Community Development: An Indian Perspective**

Author
**Dr. Hetal Jyotkumar Mehta**
Principal, Swami Sahajanand College of
Commerce & Management, (Affiliated to
M.K. Bhavnagar University), ISCON
Mega City, Bhavnagar-364002 (Gujarat)

**Corporate Social Responsibility Initiatives By IOCI: A Case Study of Guwahati**

Authors
**Chandana Kashyap**
Research Scholar, Department of
Commerce, Gauhati University
Guwahati – 781014, Assam
**Dr. Amrit Pal Singh**
Professor, Department of Commerce,
Gauhati University, Guwahati-781014,
Assam.

**Dr. Ashima Sharma Borah**
Associate Professor, Department of
Management, KC Das Commerce
College, Guwahati-781008, Assam.

**Corporate Social Responsibility: Challenges And Opportunities**

Author

**Dr. Morage Prakash V.**
Associate Professor, Govt. Women's
First Grade College Jewargi
Colony, Gulbarga. (Karnataka-India)

**Implementing of CSR in India: Issues And Challenges**

Author
**Dr. Ambanna Malkappa**
Assistant Professor, Govt. First Grade
College Farahatabad, Tq. &
Dist. Kalaburagi-585308

**CSR Expenditure in Education Sector of Odisha: An Empirical Study**

Authors
**Dr. Kishore Kumar Das**
(Second Author) Head, Department of
Business Administration, Ravenshaw
University, Cuttack

**Ms Ananya Mitra** (First Author)
Research Scholar in Utkal University,
Bhubaneswar

**Dr. Shradhanjali Panda**
(Third Author) Assistant Professor
(Finance) in Department of Business
Administration. Ravenshaw University

**ROLE OF NGO'S IN CORPORATE SOCIAL RESPONSILITY (CSR)**

Author

**Dr. Md Imteyaz Hasan**
H.O.D. Department of Commerce,
College of Commerce, Arts & Science.
Patna

**Dr. Saad Bin Hamid**
Associate Professor, Department of Commerce, Soghra College, Biharsharif
**Dr. Tanvir Ahsan Nizami**
Assistant Professor, Department of Economics, Oriental College, Patna City

**INNOVATION ENTREPRENEURSHIP AND SUSTAINABLE DEVELOPMENT**

Author
**Dr. Anil V. Surkar**
Lok Maha Vidyalay, Wardha, Maharashtra

**CORPORATE SOCIAL RESPONSIBILITY: POLICY AND PRACTICES**

Authors
**Kundan Kumar Singh**
Research Scholar, B.R.A.B.U. Muzaffarpur (Bihar)
**Dr. Md. Firoj Alam**
Research Fellow in Commerce, B.R.A.B.U. Muzaffarpur (Bihar)

**Dr. Anish Chandra Mishra**
Research Fellow in Commerce, B.R.A.B.U. Muzaffarpur (Bihar)

**EVALUATING PRADHAN MANTRI GRAMIN DIGITAL SAKSHARTA ABHIYAN**
(PMGDISHA) FOR SUSTAINABLE EXPANSION

Authors

**Dr. Ravindra Gharpure**
Assistant Professor, Central Institute of Business Management, Research and Development, Nagpur.
**Dr. Rahul Mohare**
Assistant Professor, Shri Ramdeobab College of Engineering and Management, Nagpur.
**Prof. Tanmary Gupta**
Assistant Professor, Shri Ramdeobab College of Engineering and Management, Nagpur.

**CORPORATE SOCIAL RESPONSIBILITY : POLICIES AND PRACTICES**

Authors
**Bharat Bhushan**
Research Scholar, Management
B.R.A.B.U., Muzaffarpur, Bihar
**Amrendra Kumar**
Research Scholar, Commerce
B.R.A.B.U., Muzaffarpur, Bihar

# Annexure-II

**Other Publications of Dr. K.L. Narasimha Murthy**

1. **Survey of Research Series**

    1. Research in Economics: A Survey (2021), Published by R. K. Books, Delhi.
    2. International Research in Social Sciences, 2020, Published by R.K. Books, Delhi.
    3. International Research in Geography, 2018, Published by Gyan Publishing, House Delhi.
    4. Research in Social Sciences, 2020, Published by Gyan Publishers House, Delhi.
    5. Indian Geographical Research: A Survey, 2017, Published by R. K. Books, Delhi.
    6. Research Methodology in Geography, 2014, Published by Concept Publishers, Delhi.
    7. Indian Social Science Research, 2012, Published by Teja Publishers, Hyderabad.
    8. Geographical Research, 1992, Published by Concept Publishers, Delhi.
    9. Research in Geography: A Survey, 1992, Published by Ashish Publishing House, Delhi.

2. **Conference Edited Volumes**

    10. Applied Geo-Environmental Studies, Vol. 1, 2009, Mangal Deep Publishers, Jaipur (India)
    11. Applied Geo-Environmental Studies, Vol. 2, 2008, Mangal Deep Publishers, Jaipur (India).

3. **UGC Minor Research Projects (Reports)**

    12. Applied Geo-Informatices, Mangal Deep Publications, 2007 Jaipur.
    13. Ecology, Environment & Development, Mangal Deep Publication, 2003. Jaipur

4. **Research Paper**

    14. Readings in Development Studies, 1995, Print Well Publications, Jaipur.

5. **Ph.D Thesis**

    15. Planning for Integrated Area Development, 1986, Published by BRPC, Delhi.

6. **Telugu Academy Publications**

    16. World Geography, 2003, Text Book, Published by Telugu Academy, Hyderabad, AP.

7. **Practical Geography Volume**

    17. IBA/B.Sc. Practical Geography, 2010, Published by Telugu Academy, Hyderabad, AP.

8. **Current Research Trend Series**

    18. Current Research Trends in Commerce & Management: A Survey, 2021.

        A: Commerce

        Tremds om Commerce & Management: A Servey, 2021

        B. Management

9. **Current Research**

    19. Quantitative & Qualitative Research: A Report on Interdisciplinary and Multi-disciplinary Approach and Appraisal)